89

9.7,   18222   ve No.

STRATEGY OF SURVIVAL

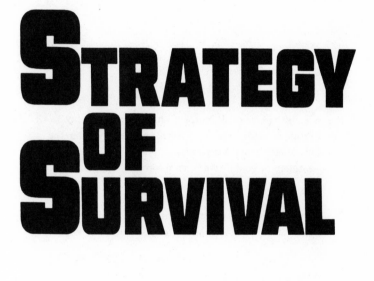

STRATEGY OF SURVIVAL

BRIAN CROZIER

ARLINGTON HOUSE·PUBLISHERS
NEW ROCHELLE, NEW YORK

First published in Great Britain 1978
by Maurice Temple Smith Ltd., London

P 10 9 8 7 6 5 4 3 2 1

Manufactured in the United States of America

Library of Congress Cataloging in Publication Data

Crozier, Brian.
    Strategy of survival.

    Includes index.
    1. Russia—History—1917-   2. World politics—
1945-   I. Title.
DK266.C76   947.08   78-8933
ISBN 0-87000-421-2

Contents

Maps

Chart

Author's Note

This is a tract for the times. The main ideas and arguments may be found in *Security and the Myth of 'Peace': Surviving the Third World War* (No. 76 in the Conflict Studies series of the Institute for the Study of Conflict, London). This pamphlet, which attracted international attention at the time, was addressed mainly to a specialised audience of people professionally interested in problems of strategy and security. It had been submitted to the distinguished Council of the Institute and, in its final form, represented something like a consensus.

The present work, written with a general world audience in mind, was conceived and written entirely afresh, although it incorporates some material from the earlier study. The author alone is responsible for the contents, which should be neither blamed on nor attributed to the Institute for the Study of Conflict.

BC

Spread of Soviet empire, 1939-49

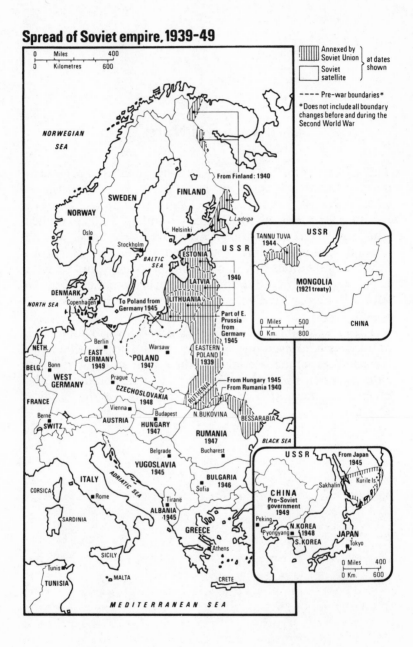

Annexed by Soviet Union — Soviet satellite — at dates shown

- - - - Pre-war boundaries*

*Does not include all boundary changes before and during the Second World War

Map labels:

NORWEGIAN SEA

SWEDEN

FINLAND

NORWAY

Oslo

From Finland: 1940

Stockholm

Helsinki

L. Ladoga

BALTIC SEA

USSR

ESTONIA

LATVIA — 1940

LITHUANIA

DENMARK

NORTH SEA

Copenhagen

To Poland from Germany 1945

Part of E. Prussia from Germany 1945

Berlin

Warsaw

EASTERN POLAND 1939

NETH.

EAST GERMANY 1949

POLAND 1947

BELG.

Bonn

WEST GERMANY

Prague

RUTHENIA

From Hungary 1945
From Rumania 1940

CZECHOSLOVAKIA 1948

FRANCE

Berne

Vienna

Budapest

N. BUKOVINA

BESSARABIA

SWITZ.

AUSTRIA

HUNGARY 1947

RUMANIA 1947

BLACK SEA

Belgrade

Bucharest

ITALY

CORSICA

Rome

ADRIATIC SEA

YUGOSLAVIA 1945

BULGARIA 1946

Sofia

SARDINIA

Tirane

ALBANIA 1945

GREECE

Athens

SICILY

Tunis

MALTA

CRETE

TUNISIA

MEDITERRANEAN SEA

Inset (top right):

TANNU TUVA 1944

USSR

MONGOLIA (1921 treaty)

CHINA

0 Miles 500
0 Km. 800

Inset (bottom right):

USSR

From Japan 1945

Sakhalin

Kurile Is.

CHINA Pro-Soviet government 1949

Peking

N. KOREA 1948

Pyongyang

S. KOREA

JAPAN

Tokyo

0 Miles 400
0 Km. 600

Scale (top left):

0 Miles 400
0 Kilometres 600

1

'The War Called Peace'

The time for compromise and evasion is over. There is no time
left. For more than twenty-five years the countries of the
Western Alliance have been preparing themselves against the
dread possibility of a nuclear war with the Soviet Union. This
war, which the strategists have called – quite wrongly, as I
shall show – the Third World War – has never come, and may
never come. Meanwhile, the real Third World War has been
fought and is being fought under our noses, and few people
have noticed what was going on.

Of course there was a ripple of interest when that great
Russian writer and political exile Solzhenitsyn, in his
celebrated public appearances in 1975 and 1976, told us that
the Third World War had been in progress for some time and
that the West was losing it. But the impact of his broadcasts,
tremendous though it was, was concentrated more upon the
nobility and courage of the man, in his solitary defiance of
an inhumanly repressive system, than upon the precise intellectual content of his warning.

At this point, let me make my objectives absolutely clear. In
writing this book I am going to spell out with as much precision as possible just what the Third World War is, how it has
been fought hitherto and why we have been losing it. I shall go
on to propose, again with as much precision as possible, the
fundamental changes in thinking that will be necessary if we
are to face up to the challenge, change course and end on the
winning side. This is what I mean by 'the strategy of survival'.

Although I am happy to pay my tribute to Solzhenitsyn, he
is not the only writer to have noticed that we are involved in a
war, against our will and whether we like it or not. Three
decades ago, a great and original American thinker, James
Burnham, pointed out in his prophetic book – *The Struggle for*

the World (1947) – that the Third World War had begun, and
even gave it a precise dating in April 1944, the date of a
Communist-led mutiny in the Greek Navy in Alexandria harbour. He suffered the usual fate of prophets in their own country, especially if they are right inconveniently ahead of official
thinking. The point, however, is this: three decades have
passed since Burnham's warning – decades of retreat and
defeat for the West and all it stands for. And now time has run
out. Unless the West reacts *now*, meaning before 1980, the
chances are that the tide of retreat will be irreversible. And yet
the point of no return has not yet been reached. If we act now, in the
short time span we have left, we can turn the tide back and
win.

First, what *is* World War III? The quickest way to understand what has been happening is to turn to the various maps.
The first point to grasp is that those who think of war ex-
clusively in terms of the involvement of vast armies, or (in contemporary terms) of the use of weapons of mass annihilation,
entirely miss the point. If the nuclear holocaust ever comes, it
will be World War IV. The war we are in is nothing like that.
Indeed, World War III differs from all previous great conflicts
in history. So far, it has not involved massive armed hostilities
between super-powers or rival military alliances. There has
been fighting, of course, but only in peripheral areas, far from
the great industrial and military centres of the developed
world. The Soviet armed forces were not involved in the
Chinese Civil War, nor in the Korean War, nor in Vietnam.
There were Soviet missiles in Cuba at the time of the Caribbean confrontation in 1962, but no Soviet ground forces.

In fact, the only times the Soviet forces have been involved
in actual fighting – though of a very one-sided kind and on
purely repressive duties – has been within the satellite countries in Eastern Europe: in Berlin in 1953, in Hungary in 1956
and Czechoslovakia in 1968. True, Soviet 'advisers' were present at all levels of the Egyptian armed forces in 1970-2, when
Soviet personnel operated the SAM missile system and even
flew interceptor planes over Cairo. Indeed, they offered 'advisers' to Vietnamese Communists, who wisely declined. But
at no stage in the 30-year World War III have Soviet forces
directly clashed with those of the United States; or the forces
of the Warsaw Pact with those of NATO.

In other respects, too, this has been a different kind of war, 'fought' for the greater part with non-military techniques, such as subversion, disinformation, terrorism, psychological war and diplomatic negotiations, including conferences. More strikingly still, and unlike previous wars, the Third World War has been almost entirely a *unilateral* war of expansion from the Soviet land mass: a war of aggression, with the rest of the world at the receiving end. The Western powers have occasionally reacted, when their individual special interests appeared to be threatened. This was true, for instance, in Malaya during the Emergency from 1948 to 1960, and in the two Indochina wars, involving the French from 1946 to 1954 and the Americans from 1962 to 1974. But there has been no concerted response on the Western side.

Look at the maps again. What is their message? It is surely quite plain for those who take the trouble to see facts as they are – that the aims of the Soviet Union can be defined in strategic terms only as world domination. This, of course, is not the way Soviet spokesmen or commentators put it. On their side, they refer to the need to defeat 'capitalism', and to 'the struggle between the two social systems'. But let us beware of semantic pitfalls: when Soviet or Marxist ideologists refer to 'capitalism' or to 'the capitalist system', what they really mean is the pluralist and representative systems of the West, which happen to function properly only in liberal, free market and free enterprise environments. In any case, the maps show at a glance that many of the most spectacular victories by proxy in Moscow's world imperialist drive have taken place in countries such as Vietnam or Angola, which in no senses could be regarded as citadels of 'capitalism'. When *Pravda* declared on 22 August 1973 that the struggle between the two world social systems would continue 'until the complete and final victory of Communism on a world scale', it made the point clear beyond doubt to all but those who refuse to face political realities: the target of Soviet imperialism is indeed the whole world.

The 'Target Area'
'The Target Area' is roughly what has always been understood by 'the free world'. Frankly, I have never liked that expression 'the free world'. The emotional overtones and the

intellectual woolliness of it have always bothered me, even
when it was most fashionable in the late 1950s and early
1960s. I searched for alternatives, but could come up only with
cumbrous and negative phrases, such as the 'non-Communist
countries' or 'non-Marxist' or 'non-collectivist' or 'non-
revolutionary' world. I discarded them all. The advantage of
the term 'the Target Area', which eventually I settled for, is
that it describes accurately the sweeping character of Soviet
strategy. Moreover, it is ideologically neutral. Not least, it
reflects the fact that countries at the receiving end of the
'World Communist Enterprise' (as James Burnham called it)
are essentially *passive*.

But I don't want to leave 'the free world' without explaining
precisely why I found the term unsatisfactory. For a start, it
embraced a wide range of regimes, some of which were a good
deal less free than, say, the United States. Was Franco's Spain
'free' in that sense? What about Portugal under Dr Salazar?
And South Korea? South Africa, Taiwan or Greece under the
colonels? Yet the statesmen and commentators who were ad-
dicted to 'the free world' lumped them all together.

There are, of course, degrees of freedom, and Franco's
Spain, certainly during the last fifteen years or so of the long
dictatorship, was a good deal freer than, say, the Soviet Union, China or any other totalitarian country. As I have pointed
out from time to time, a Spaniard could marry whomever he
or she wished, could buy a house, could change his or her
place of employment, could travel freely inside or outside the
country. Indeed, Spaniards could do many other 'free' things
not open to the citizens of Communist countries, or available
only in some of them (such as Poland or Hungary). They
could do all these things so long as they kept out of politics. In
the USSR, it was just the reverse, and the same was true of
China: you could do none of the things just mentioned, and
you could not opt out of politics. This led me to point out that
the *authoritarian* and *totalitarian* forms of government stood in
absolute contrast to each other.

What is more relevant to this book, however, is that the
authoritarian regimes have shown that they do not last
forever. During the past two years, for instance, the regimes of
General Franco, Caetano (Salazar's successor) and the Greek
colonels have all collapsed. But the totalitarian governments

appear to go on for ever. Since the first of these repressive regimes seized power in Russia in 1917, no single Communist government anywhere in the world has made way for a democratic one. (Some readers may think that the overthrow of the Allende regime in Chile was a contrary example, but the Chilean Communist Party was only one element in a left wing coalition and Chile was not yet fully in Communist hands at the time.)

Speaking for myself, I am in favour of pluralist and representative systems. How pleasant it would be if such systems prevailed in the greater part of the world! But not only do they not prevail, they are actually shrinking year by year. Make no mistake about it: when a democratic regime is replaced by a military one, as in Brazil or Uruguay for instance, the change is not necessarily permanent; and many of the liberties we associate with pluralist and representative systems will probably be restored in time. But this is not true of the advent of Marxist regimes. Whenever this happens, whether in North Vietnam or North Korea, in Czechoslovakia or Cuba, the change appears to be irreversible.

Because this is far from just an academic argument, it will be followed through to the end. Many liberals as well as leftists look back on the 'Prague Spring' of 1968 with some nostalgia. Surely, they argue, those exhilarating events showed that Communism, *left to itself*, can acquire a human face. And isn't Yugoslavia another example? Well, nobody knows what would have happened in Czechoslovakia if the hapless Mr Dubcek had been allowed to continue with his experiment in relative freedom. I suspect that before very long the Communist Party would have been sharing power with non-Communists, and that in time the Communist experiment itself would have collapsed. Sitting in Moscow, and anxiously following these events, Mr Brezhnev and the other Soviet leaders evidently saw this as the likely course of events. That is why they decided to invade Czechoslovakia. In Romania, Mr Ceausescu could get away with defying Moscow in foreign affairs, because he maintained a tight, repressive Stalinist regime at home. Mr Dubcek had reaffirmed his government's allegiance to the Warsaw Pact, but he was about to yield the Communist monopoly of power at home. This was what the Soviet leaders could not tolerate.

The operative words, therefore, are those I have italicised above.

In general terms, Marxism is a common enemy of all mankind and this is truer still of Leninism, which carries the permanent *duty* to spread Marxism all over the world. But Marxism-Leninism would be a containable problem were it not for the fact of Soviet power. True, Marshal Tito got away with defying Stalin in 1948 and was still in power in his 80s. But we may be sure that the Soviet regime will attempt to re-impose its hold on Yugoslavia once the old warrior has gone. Indeed, this may have happened by the time this book is published.

When Burnham coined the phrase 'the World Communist Enterprise' in the late 1940s, it was indeed a world enterprise centrally directed from Moscow. This enterprise still exists, and both in relative and absolute terms, Soviet power today is far greater than it was in Stalin's time. Of course it is less monolithic than it used to be. In February 1956, not quite three years after the death of the terrible Soviet dictator, Khrushchev denounced some of Stalin's crimes, and threw the whole international Communist movement into disarray. Some years later, Mao Tse-tung in Peking asserted his own independence. These were great and important changes, but they did not greatly alter the central fact of Soviet power. It was Soviet heavy and modern weaponry that enabled the Vietnamese Communists to seize South Vietnam. It was Soviet power and determination that brought fifteen thousand Cuban troops, armed and equipped by the USSR, from their small island home in the Caribbean to Angola in distant Africa, to set up a new Soviet satellite far from the Soviet land mass.

Perhaps the easiest way to grasp the fact of Soviet power is to imagine what the world would be like without it. Suppose for the sake of argument that the Soviet regime – which from 1917 has been a self-perpetuating autocracy – were overthrown and replaced by a regime, whether authoritarian or democratic, with a non-ideological basis. The World Communist Enterprise would immediately become a manageable problem. In fact, the whole strategic outlook would change dramatically for the better. All Communist Parties everywhere – including the mass parties of France and Italy which claim on dubious grounds to be independent of Moscow – would suddenly find the means at their disposal drastically curtailed. The international Communist movement would be deprived of the continuous backing of the enormous Soviet military machine, and of the equally enormous apparatus of subversion, espionage, disinformation and propaganda of the system. If such a dramatic event ever occurred, it is quite possible that the Chinese leadership would decide to take over the ideological world objectives of the USSR. But the Chinese People's Republic, even though it has a nuclear weapon, is not a super-power on the Soviet scale. Lacking strategic military power and the other non-military resources of the Soviet Union, it could not present a comparable problem to the countries of the Target Area.

In a very real sense, therefore, the main enemy of the whole world outside the Marxist bloc is the Soviet Union. Whether we like it or not, we are in the same unhappy boat in this respect as Rhodesia and South Africa, Chile and Uruguay, or Brazil and South Korea. We are all parts of the Target Area, and all of us are involved – again, whether we like it or not – in the struggle against the spread of irreversible totalitarianism.

In another sense, too, the Target Area is a useful concept, for if you look at the maps you will notice how the Target Area has been shrinking as the growth of Marxist-Leninist or otherwise hostile areas has continued. Almost every year the Target Area is smaller than it was in terms of territory and population. More vital still, in terms of our survival, is the dwindling access of the countries of the Western Alliance – especially those of Western Europe – to *safe sources of energy and strategic minerals*. By a 'safe' source I mean one located in a friendly country, or in one that normally trades freely within the Western exchange and credit system and is not in danger, actually or potentially, of action by the Soviet Union or one of its satellites which would interdict the free export and delivery of such materials to countries of the Alliance.

The Arab oil embargo of October 1973 showed how vulnerable the West was in this respect. The rôle of the Soviet Union in this affair is sometimes overlooked. For months, the Soviet propaganda radio services in Arabic had been inciting the oil-rich Arab countries to use what came to be known as 'the oil weapon', to force Western countries to desist from supporting Israel. In the event, Saudi Arabia initiated the oil embargo, which was particularly directed against America and Holland. Not that the Saudis acted merely because the Russians had put the idea into their heads, but the prolonged Soviet propaganda campaign – buttressed no doubt by diplomatic activity in the Arab world (though not in Saudi Arabia itself, which did not have diplomatic relations with Moscow) – must have played its part. The irony was that Saudi Arabia was, and indeed remained in general terms, friendly towards the West. Again, Iran, although it did not join the embargo as such, took the lead in subsequent pressures by OPEC (the Organisation of Petroleum Exporting Countries) to push oil prices up as far as possible. Iran was nevertheless a member of one of the Western alliances – CENTO (the Central Treaty Organisation).

The oil embargo, followed by the quadrupling of oil prices, severely affected the balance of payments of certain Western countries, especially the United Kingdom. In any case, Britain's economy was not exactly in a brilliant state in the autumn of 1973, but the oil crisis made things much worse, contributing to the defeat of Mr Heath's Conservative government the following February and landing the Labour government that followed in a vicious spiral of mounting foreign debts and new loans that further increased the total indebtedness.

The oil crisis brutally demonstrated what can happen to the advanced economies of the West when a vital commodity is suddenly made scarce and expensive. But oil is only one of a number of vital mineral resources, the loss of which would affect the survival of Western Europe. Both Western Europe and the United States are heavily reliant on imports of strategic minerals from South Africa. Nearly 11 per cent of the current production of uranium in the Target Area comes from that country. Southern Africa as a whole has the world's largest deposits of chrome, vanadium and platinum, and is rich in diamonds, gold and manganese. Now look at the maps again: there are Marxist and Soviet-protected regimes in South Yemen, Ethiopia, Angola and Mozambique, and powerful Soviet fleets patrol the Indian and Atlantic Oceans. These two circumstances – the advent of Soviet-protected regimes and the powerful Soviet naval presence in surrounding waters –

together represent a major potential threat to shipping lanes vital to the survival of Western Europe.

These lines were written at a time of intensified guerrilla and terrorist pressure on Rhodesia and of deepening isolation in South Africa. To guide Rhodesia in particular towards a regime of partnership between whites and non-Marxist blacks would have been a worthy objective for Western diplomacy, but it was by no means clear that either the British or the Americans had grasped the importance of keeping the Marxists out. Bearing in mind the experience of Cuba, Angola and elsewhere, it did not seem too fanciful to imagine a black regime not only in Rhodesia but in all or part of South Africa, set up by Soviet power and controlled through the repressive apparatus of the KGB. If this happened, such regimes would probably incur enormous debts to the USSR (as happened with Cuba) and be forced in consequence to pay their way – for instance in gold and diamonds at artificially low prices.

In South Africa itself, the pace of change was quickening. But given the efficiency of the repressive apparatus and the obvious determination of the white population, any fundamental change of course seemed likely to result only from internal revolutionary violence assisted from the outside. The so-called Bantustans, with their long frontiers within the Republic, were so many additional security risks, or opportunities for revolutionaries. There, too, there was an ultimate risk of yet another Soviet-protected Marxist regime. Should South Africa ever fall under Soviet control the USSR would have completed its stranglehold on Western Europe's economic future. And in that event, the past attitudes of West European governments and public opinions about Apartheid would be beside the point. In 'the war called peace', the countries of the Western Alliance are under the same threat as white Rhodesia and South Africa – all of us, whether we like it or not, are parts of the Target Area and at the receiving end of the Soviet war of expansion.

2

Phases of World War III
(1944–49)

In the late spring of 1945, Stalin was flushed with victory. Hitler's invasion of Russia had foundered, as Napoleon's had before him. At the Yalta summit earlier in the year, Roosevelt and Churchill had agreed with Stalin on occupation zones in Germany and zones of influence elsewhere in central and eastern Europe, although some areas – most notably Czechoslovakia – were left in vagueness. Accordingly, General Montgomery's forces stood by to allow Marshal Zhukov to 'liberate' Berlin. To the south, General Patton's 3rd Army, having been carried too far by his enthusiasm and *élan*, pulled back and waited until the Red Army 'liberated' Prague. In his war memoirs, Churchill makes it clear that Prague was supposed to be one of the cities that could be liberated by whichever forces got there first, and that the decision to allow the Russians to do so was an American one, taken against his explicit advice and warnings. As Chester Wilmot put it on p. 710 of his masterly work *The Struggle for Europe* (1952), '. . . the triumph of the Czech Communists in the *coup* of February 1948 had its origin in the fact that Prague was liberated by the Russians, not the Americans.'

Indeed the Soviet dictator was now in a position to impose Communism on Eastern Europe. By 'imposing Communism' I simply mean putting Communist governments in power. It took him about four years altogether. The Communist take-over techniques worked out at that time have come to be known as 'the Prague model', because they worked so spectacularly well in the capital of Czechoslovakia. But similar methods were equally successful in other capitals. By relentless infiltration, the Communists gained control of the police and trade unions, and set up factory militias. On 25 February 1948, with the reassuring presence of the Soviet army in the background, they threatened a *coup d'état* and forced President Beneš to approve a predominantly Communist government under Clement Gottwald. In the months that followed, a drastic purge transformed the Western-style democratic State of Czechoslovakia into a Marxist-Leninist Soviet satellite.

In Poland, in August 1944, the Soviet forces camped outside Warsaw while the Nazi occupation army slaughtered the Polish underground forces under General Bor. Later, with Allied approval, Stalin imposed a pro-Soviet 'government of national unity' on the Poles. In Poland, as in Hungary and East Germany, the local Socialists paved the way for a Marxist-Leninist victory by merging with the initially weak Communist Party. In Bulgaria, Romania and Albania, purges and executions marked the passage to the imposition of Soviet-model constitutions. Yugoslavia was a special case, because of the major part played by Tito's partisans in the defeat of the Nazi occupation forces. His Communist-dominated National Front was confirmed in power as early as November 1945.

All these changes, it should be remembered, took place under the protection of the Soviet Army. But further afield, beyond that protection, local Communist Parties tried hard to take power. In Greece, several thousand Communist guerrillas went into rebellion in 1946, and on Christmas Eve the following year, their leader – 'General Marcos' – proclaimed the 'First Provisional Democratic Government of Free Greece'. In Iran, Stalin tried different tactics. In May 1945, the Americans and British withdrew their forces, but Stalin ordered his to stay where they were. Later that year, a Communist party in all but name – the Tudeh ('Masses') Party – rose against the government in the province of Azerbaijan. Under intense diplomatic pressure from the Western allies, Stalin did withdraw his troops, but not until the following May. Even then, it was some time before the Shah could restore order. In France, too, in August 1944, the Communists challenged General de Gaulle as he returned and tried to assert his central authority. The Communists had played no part in the first phase of World War II (when Stalin, in league with Hitler, kept the Soviet Union out of the fighting), but had

The course of World War III. Shrinkage of the Target area. Phase 1: 1944–49

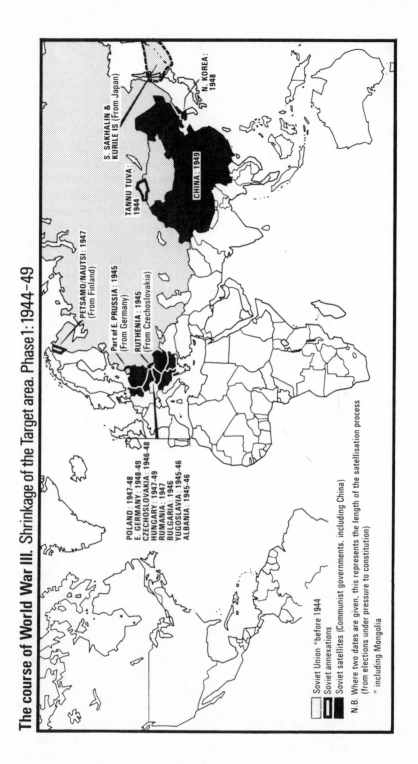

PETSAMO/NAUTSI : 1947
(From Finland)

Part of E. PRUSSIA : 1945
(From Germany)

RUTHENIA : 1945
(From Czechoslovakia)

S. SAKHALIN &
KURILE IS (From Japan)

TANNU TUVA :
1944

CHINA : 1949

N. KOREA :
1948

POLAND : 1947-48
E. GERMANY : 1948-49
CZECHOSLOVAKIA : 1946-48
HUNGARY : 1947-49
RUMANIA : 1947
BULGARIA : 1946
YUGOSLAVIA : 1945-46
ALBANIA : 1945-46

☐ Soviet Union *before 1944

☐ Soviet annexations

■ Soviet satellites (Communist governments, including China)

N.B. Where two dates are given, this represents the length of the satellisation process
(from elections under pressure to constitution)

* including Mongolia

dominated the Resistance after the German armies invaded Russia in 1941. Their armed partisans emerged from the shadows and exerted local power in many areas, torturing and executing 'collaborators', who in many cases were simply their class or political enemies. De Gaulle defeated them, but it was a near thing.

In the Far East, too, the Russians could claim spectacular victories. In China, the Communist leader Mao Tse-tung had embarked on armed peasant warfare, in defiance of Marxist-Leninist precepts and of Stalin's orders. Nevertheless, it was Stalin who made his final victory inevitable, by invading China in the last ten days or so of World War II and turning over to Mao vast quantities of captured Japanese arms and equipment. In North Korea, with Soviet occupation forces refusing to budge, Kim Il Sung's Communists proclaimed a 'People's Democratic Republic' on 9 September 1948. In North Vietnam, almost exactly three years earlier, the Communist leader Ho Chi Minh – a Comintern agent for many years, under Lenin's orders, then Stalin's – had proclaimed a 'Democratic Republic of Vietnam', though many years of hard fighting lay ahead before Communist rule could be extended to the whole of the country.

The first turbulent phase of World War III, then, had lasted just over five years, from the Greek naval mutiny in Alexandria in April 1944 until the proclamation of the Chinese People's Republic on 10 October 1949. For convenience sake, I shall call it 'Operation Satellite 1'.

And now, a brief glance back into history is necessary, to deal with an old and sterile controversy. Is 'Communism' to blame for the Soviet Union's expansionist policies? Or is the growth of Soviet power far from the boundaries of 1939 merely the continuation of Tsarist imperialism under another guise? As I stated, the controversy is essentially sterile, because the answer to both questions is Yes. Under the Tsars, the Russians had Messianic views and imperialist ambitions. They still have under the current Communist Party boss, Leonid Brezhnev, as under Khrushchev and Stalin. But Lenin's Bolshevik revolution in 1917 was a momentous event, which changed radically the pattern of Russian imperialism and vastly extended its potential. The Tsarist autocracy had little appeal for captive peoples. But Marxism-Leninism – the State ideology of the totalitarian regime in the Soviet Union – has an appeal that far transcends existing Soviet boundaries at any time. It was never easy for the Tsarist autocracy to recruit non-Russians in the service of Russian imperialism. It is far easier for the Soviet autocracy to recruit, use, manipulate or control non-Soviet citizens all over the world. Ideology is the efficient instrument of Soviet imperialism abroad; and at home the efficient instrument of total repression.

But the imperial tradition is there too. Lenin and Stalin are not the only ancestors of Khrushchev and Brezhnev. There is Ivan I of Russia, the notoriously tight-fisted 'Money Bags', who carried the hegemony of Muscovy into surrounding areas in the fourteenth century. Another imperial ancestor of Brezhnev was Ivan the Terrible, who conquered Astrakhan after destroying the Khanate of Kazan. Alexander I carried on the imperial tradition. Not only did he successfully defend Russia against Napoleon's *Grande Armée*, he also inspired the Holy Alliance and grabbed Finland, Bessarabia and much of the Caucasus. The last of the Tsars, Nicholas II, drove Russia's imperialist power to the furthest confines of the Euro-Asian land mass, occupying Port Arthur and Manchuria. The Bolsheviks murdered him, but kept what he had grabbed. On 15 November 1917, a few days after seizing power, Lenin proclaimed the right of the dependent peoples to secede and set up independent States. Several local leaders took him at his word, and independent republics were established in Azerbaijan and Georgia, and in Khiva and Bokhara. This is where the new ideology came into play. 'Independent' in Lenin's dictionary meant Marxist-Leninist regimes under Moscow's control. The new republics were declared 'bourgeois nationalist'. Lenin smashed them and by 1921 had replaced them all with administrations controlled by his Communist Party.

Stalin carried on in the imperial tradition. Long before Operation Satellite I had begun, he had taken advantage of the outbreak of World War II and of the Nazi-Soviet Pact to grab Eastern Poland and the Baltic States, to seize Bessarabia and northern Bukhovina, to wrest Ruthenia from Czechoslovakia, and to add large areas of Finland and East Prussia to his imperial dominions. In the Far East, he secured special rights in Dairen, and Port Arthur, and he took over

South Sakhalin and the Kuriles from Japan when the opportunity came his way.

Historians of the future may well decide that the struggle I have termed World War III really began with the Bolshevik seizure of power in 1917. But the intellectual origins of the great struggle went back to the Communist Manifesto of 1848, in which Marx and Engels declared that: 'Communists everywhere support every revolutionary movement against the existing social and political order . . .'; the German Communist leader Rosa Luxemburg put it in other words in December 1918: 'The struggle for socialism is the most gigantic civil war world history has ever known . . .' But it is more convenient perhaps to regard the period from 1848 to 1917 as the pre-history of World War III; and the twenty-two years from 1917 to 1939 as the preparatory phase of 'the struggle for the world', which did not really get under way until World War III had brought Stalin the opportunity he was waiting for.

Since this is an urgent book, I have set myself tight space limits. I shall therefore not attempt to cover the course of the Third World War in detail. Instead, I propose to outline and explain its principal phases. But before doing so let us dispose of a widespread source of confusion. The confusion arises from the ill-informed use of the terms 'Cold War' and 'peaceful coexistence'. Here, we are in the prickly realm of political semantics, which may seem arid but is crucially important. The confusion arises out of the fact that these terms are used in quite different senses on either side of the great ideological divide.

The term 'Cold War' is a Western coinage. It was first used by the American financier and presidential adviser Bernard Baruch during a congressional debate in 1947. The 1975 *Encyclopaedia Britannica* correctly defines it as 'denoting the open yet restricted rivalry that developed after World War II between the United States and Soviet Union and their respective allies, a war fought on political, economic, and propaganda fronts, with limited recourse to weapons, largely because of fear of a nuclear holocaust'. It was a useful concept in that it described accurately the sum total of hostile words and deeds on either side of the Iron Curtain, which began with the emergence of an expanded Soviet empire at the end of

World War II at a time of rapid Western demobilisation, forcing the West to react in various appropriate ways. In other
words, in Western eyes the Cold War is, or was, a two-way
traffic.

That's where the semantic problems begin. For in Soviet
eyes the Cold War is a one-way process: hostile words and
deeds against the Soviet Union and its allies, and coming entirely from the Western side. After two decades or so, the
Western allies began to tire of the Cold War, and gradually
stopped or greatly reduced their Cold War programmes, especially in the propaganda field. The Russians were left with
the field to themselves, and on both sides of the Iron Curtain it
became fashionable to refer to the Cold War in the past tense.
Thus the distinguished American historian and former State
Department official, Louis J. Halle, published in 1967 an
elegant but rather misleading treatise, *The Cold War as History*,
in which his basic premise was that the Cold War had begun
in 1945 and had ended 'roughly speaking, the other day'. Such
unconscious readiness to accept the Soviet definition of the
Cold War played right into the hands of those who continued
to wage it on the other side. For it was only on the Western
side that the Cold War had ended or was ending; on the other
side it continued unabated. But on the other side it was not
called 'the Cold War': it was called 'peaceful co-existence'.

This brings me to the other source of confusion. Unlike the
'Cold War', 'peaceful co-existence' is a Soviet coinage. It was
first used in the 1920s by Lenin's Foreign Commissar,
Chicherin, to describe the 1917 Revolution and the world
revolution that was bound to follow some time or other. It is
still used in this sense on the Soviet or Marxist-Leninist side,
but under Khrushchev, 'peaceful co-existence' was given a
new twist. When Communist parties from all over the world
met in Moscow at the end of 1960 – the last time the Chinese
and Russian Communists jointly took part in such an occasion – everybody agreed that peaceful co-existence implied
'the intensification of the international class struggle' – which,
when you look at it in practice, means almost exactly what we
understand by 'the Cold War'.

Because of these confusions, I decided to drop the term
'Cold War', which we have in effect surrendered to the enemy.
Since some Western and all Soviet commentators agree that

the Cold War is over, or that it should be, it follows that anybody who points out that it is still going on on the Soviet side must be a 'cold warrior', or is charged with 'seeking a return to the Cold War'. Moreover, 'peaceful co-existence' on the Western side continues to mean primarily that the two power blocs (or NATO and the Warsaw Pact, or what Soviet commentators call 'the two great social systems') can continue to live peacefully side by side, neither intervening with the other. In practice, this has usually meant that the Western powers do not interfere with the Soviet bloc, leaving the Soviet Union free to intervene wherever and however they like.

For all these reasons, I decided that the term the 'Third World War' or 'World War III' more accurately describes what has been going on for more than three decades: a unilateral war of aggression, expansion and attrition waged solely on the Soviet and Communist side.

Having dispelled, I hope, a myth or two, I continue with a summary description of the subsequent phases of World War III, bearing in mind that there is inevitably some overlapping and simplification.

3

Phases of World War III
(1945–64)

Operation Insurgency 1

In February 1945, Stalin announced that the doctrine of world revolution was still valid, confounding those who thought that he had settled for 'revolution in one country' when he had rid himself of the arch-advocate of world revolution, Trotsky. It became clear that 'revolution in one country' merely meant converting the USSR into the impregnable base for the world revolution.

Two years later, Operation Satellite 1 was in full swing, and the prospects for world revolution looked distinctly encouraging. Winston Churchill had said he would not preside over the dissolution of the British Empire; but he was no longer in power, and the dissolution was impending. It was clear that before long the old Indian Empire would split up into the independent States of India and Pakistan. Burma and Ceylon, too, were going to obtain their independence, and although emancipation was not on the agenda for Malaya and Singapore, it seemed unlikely that the British could maintain their hold there if it weakened elsewhere.

As for the Dutch, they were in grave difficulties in the rich East Indies, emerging from Japanese occupation. The French had shown themselves determined to keep their grip on Indochina, but were already deeply involved in war with the Communist terrorists and guerrillas, led by Ho Chi Minh. The only other colonial power in the area, after the collapse of Japan, was the United States; but the Americans, honouring a pre-war pledge, gave independence to the Philippines as early as July 1946.

The Western empires in South-East Asia were thus ending, and the question that exercised Stalin and his advisers was:

Who takes over? 'Bourgeois nationalism' was of no interest to
the Communists; Lenin had showed that on seizing power,
and Stalin was the heir to Lenin. Independence was only a
stage. The next thing was to make sure that the heirs to the
colonial empires made way for local Communists obedient to
Moscow. There were two reasons for this: if Communists took
over they would be forwarding the process of world revolution
and therefore (although this was never spelt out) of world
domination; moreover, the main target was still 'capitalism',
and the surest way of weakening capitalism and making it
collapse was to deprive it of its sources of raw materials. At
least, this was what Leninist doctrine said, and until now the
doctrine had served Stalin's ambitions well.

Those were the aims, and the machinery already existed in
the Asian Communist parties set up by the Comintern
(Lenin's Third International) many years before: in Indonesia
in 1920, in China in 1921, in India in 1925 and in Indochina in
1930. The Malayan Communist party, created in 1930, had
the great advantage of having spearheaded the resistance to
the Japanese during World War II; as indeed had the Bur-
mese party. In China, the Communists were set on their way
to eventual victory and would help in various ways.

In 1947, Stalin launched the Communist Information
Bureau or Cominform, which most observers took to be a
revival of the Comintern, dissolved by the dictator in 1943 to
reassure Russia's wartime allies. In this they were mistaken,
as we shall see later. However, it provided machinery to
transmit the Moscow line to Communist parties, and Stalin's
right-hand man, Zhdanov, used it in September 1947 for a
major announcement. The world, he said, was now split into
two hostile blocs, and the time had come for colonial peoples
to 'expel their oppressors'.

This was the signal for which the Asian Communist parties
had been waiting. But Zhdanov had to make sure Moscow's
precise instructions reached the right people, and to do this he
used two of the international front organisations which the
Soviet Communist Party had set up through intermediaries
over the previous two years. As the name indicates, a 'front'
organisation is one that conceals its true purpose and its ultimate control. The two front organisations involved in Operation Insurgency 1 were the World Federation of Democratic

Operation insurgency 1 (1948-60)

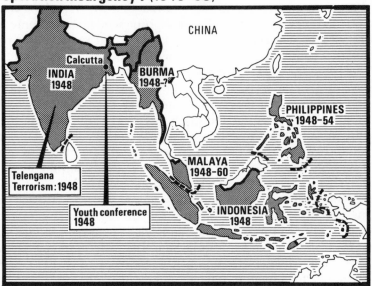

Youth (WFDY) and the International Union of Students (IUS), set up in London and Prague in 1945 and 1946 respectively.

As joint sponsors, the WFDY and the IUS convened an Asian Youth Congress in Calcutta in February 1948, and there the Asian Communist parties received their marching orders. To be sure, their preparations were already fairly far advanced when the Calcutta congress met, but that was where the necessary co-ordination took place. Within a few weeks or months, insurgencies broke out or took a fresh spurt in India, Burma, Malaya, Indonesia and the Philippines. With the exception of Malaya, these countries were either independent or about to get their independence; and in Malaya itself the delayed effect of the terrorist campaign that broke out in 1949 was an accelerated timetable for independence. Broadly speaking, the Communist-led insurgencies were seen to be irrelevant to popular aspirations, and all were defeated or contained. Much unnecessary suffering and loss of life were caused, however, and it is worth recalling that the orders for these bloody incidents came from Moscow. In retrospect,

Operation Insurgency 1 can be seen, from the Soviet standpoint, as an unsuccessful campaign in Moscow's unilateral war against the rest of the world – the Target Area.

Operation Indochina 1 (1946–54)

There were two Indochina wars. The first involved the French as the colonial power and lasted from the end of 1946 till the summer of 1954. The second involved the Americans as a protecting power: it started about three years after the first had been halted, and ended in the spring of 1975. The aggressor in each case was the Communist Party of Indochina (under various names). The first war gave that party undisputed control over North Vietnam, and the second extended that control over South Vietnam and Laos, leaving the ultimate control of Cambodia – where massacres on a sickening scale took place – still uncertain.

In this short section, we will look only at the first Indochina war, and only at the facts that illustrated Moscow's determining and in the end decisive rôle.

The key figure in both Indochina wars was Ho Chi Minh, although he died before the second one had ended in victory for his side. This extraordinary Vietnamese lived a life of revolutionary adventure. He was a founder-member of the French Communist Party, when it was set up in 1920. He studied Marxism-Leninism and revolutionary techniques in Moscow in the early 1920s, then went to South China as a Comintern agent in 1925. He was active there, and in Siam and his own Vietnam for several years, then in 1930 created the Communist Party of Indochina. The name was deliberate and indicated his determination to 'liberate' the whole of the French empire in that peninsula – that is, Laos and Cambodia as well as his own country.

Throughout his life, Ho reflected the thoroughness of his Moscow training. He set up front organisations, such as the notorious Vietminh (short for 'League for the Independence of Vietnam') and the Lien Viet (Vietnam People's United Front); and he created and controlled Communist parties in Cambodia (People's Revolutionary Party) and Laos (Laotian People's Party). Taking a leaf out of Stalin's book, he ostentatiously dissolved the Communist Party of Indochina in 1945 (as Stalin had 'dissolved' the Comintern two years earlier);

but it re-emerged in 1951 as the Vietnamese Workers' Party.

Admittedly, the peasant warfare methods of the Vietnamese Communists owed more to Mao Tse-tung's example than to Stalin's. But it should be remembered that throughout the first Indochina war, from the time of Mao's victory in October 1949, the huge Chinese People's Republic was a voluntary satellite of the USSR. The arrival of Mao's forces on the borders of Vietnam and Laos greatly eased Ho's supply problems and in the latter stages of the first Indochina war vast quantities of heavy Soviet arms, especially artillery, reached his gifted Commander-in-Chief, General Giap.

As the world knows, the French expeditionary corps was shatteringly defeated in a small fortified place called Dien Bien Phu on 6 May 1954 – one of the decisive battles of contemporary history. The war ended a few weeks later when the French conceded defeat in a famous conference at Geneva.

The events of 1946–54 are well documented and I draw attention only to the following points:

1   Ho Chi Minh set up the Communist Party of Indochina as an agent of the Comintern, that is of Soviet imperialism.
2   Throughout the struggle, he applied the lessons and techniques he had learnt in Moscow.
3   The French would probably not have been defeated at Dien Bien Phu if Giap, in defiance of logistic odds, had not brought Soviet artillery to bear on the beleaguered fortress.
4   Strictly speaking, the defeat at Dien Bien Phu was not decisive in military terms. The French *could* have fought on if they had so wished. But their morale and will were shattered, and in this collapse the huge propaganda machine of international communism, and especially of the French Communist Party itself, played the decisive part.

These facts must be remembered if the first Indochina war is to be seen in its right perspective as a campaign in the Third World War.

The Time of Flux and Doubt
With the death of Stalin in 1953, the Soviet leadership entered a crisis, which was resolved, but unsatisfactorily, by the emergence of Nikita Khrushchev as party boss. Khrushchev

was no Stalin. Although in common with all who had survived Stalin's Great Terror he had done the dictator's bidding, he had neither the single-minded will nor the authority to carry on as before. The terror had consumed too many of the top Soviet citizens and had to end: everybody agreed on that. At the same time, the autocracy had to perpetuate itself, so there was never any question of dismantling the 'top secret' police State.

Looking back on the Khrushchev period – so recent in historical terms – it can be seen as a time of flux and doubt, during which the USSR probably lost more than it gained in World War III. Khrushchev took over as party boss in 1953, but did not achieve full power until 1955, when his chief rival, Malenkov, was ousted from the premiership; and he was overthrown in October 1964. So we are talking about a period of nine years. Moreover, Khrushchev's authority was seriously challenged by some of his colleagues in 1957, and although he came out on top it could never be said that he was the unquestioned dictator Stalin was.

From the first, Khrushchev faced a dilemma that would have faced anyone who took over after a monstrous personality like Stalin. During Stalin's period the international Communist movement was an obedient monolith that swallowed all atrocities and enormities virtually without question (although there were rebellious murmurs in various places when the Nazis and Soviets signed a pact in August 1939, and when the Red Army invaded Finland later in the year). Tales of Stalin's crimes were either rejected as bourgeois propaganda (and kept out of Communist newspapers everywhere) or justified as necessary steps in the Revolution.

But Khrushchev could not keep up the pretence for ever, and in February 1956, during the 20th congress of the Soviet Communist Party (CPSU), he gave the game away with an extraordinary speech, initially intended to be 'secret', in which he provided selective details of Stalin's crimes. Since Communism is, as I argue, a counter-church, it was as if a Pope should denounce the sins of his predecessor.

The Communist world was shaken to its foundations, and has never been quite the same again. For, not content with toppling Stalin's idol as the god who could do no wrong,

Khrushchev also called in question two of the sacred dogmas of Marxism-Leninism. One of these was the doctrine that wars were inevitable so long as 'imperialism' (that is, powerful Western powers) existed. The other was that 'socialism' could come about only as the result of violent revolution. War, said Khrushchev (conscious of the horrifying destructive power of nuclear weapons), was no longer fatally inevitable. As for the transition to socialism, it might in certain circumstances be achieved by parliamentary means.

In Italy the Communist leader, Palmiro Togliatti, who had served Stalin as blindly as Khrushchev, coined the word 'polycentric' to mean that different Communist parties need no longer look to the Soviet model as a guide to action. The counter-church had lost its Holy See. Soon the ripples were spreading outwards to parts of the enlarged Soviet empire. The Polish Communists asserted themselves and gained a measure of independence from their imperial masters in the autumn of 1956, the year of Khrushchev's secret speech. The Hungarians tried to assert themselves but a great wave of popular feeling took the experiment too far, so that it got out of hand. At Mao Tse-tung's urging (a point often overlooked), Khrushchev twice sent tanks into the streets of Budapest to crush the Hungarian workers. All over the world, hitherto faithful Communists quit their national parties in droves.

Not long after, it was China's turn to get restless. Why had Mao urged Khrushchev to be firm in Poland and Hungary? It was a complex case. The Chinese leader had persistently and successfully defied Stalin's directives during his struggle for the control of the most populous country in the world. But in the end, Stalin's military intervention had been decisive for his victory over the Nationalist leader Chiang Kai-shek. In return, Mao publicly kow-towed to the Soviet dictator and accepted satellite status in February 1950 when he signed a 30-year treaty with the USSR.

Because of China's size and importance, however, and especially because of two signal services to the Soviet leadership, Mao Tse-tung undoubtedly expected special treatment from the CPSU. In this he was bitterly disappointed.

The first service was during the Korean War (1950–53). Stalin probably incited the North Koreans to attack, but he failed to consult Mao. When General MacArthur's United

Nations forces started sweeping northward, Mao sent 'people's volunteers' into North Korea and turned the tables on the defenders of South Korea. Obligingly, Stalin gave Mao the weapons he needed and promised to defend China if Mao's Republic were itself attacked. He also promised greatly increased economic aid, but forgot about his side of the bargain; then died. In a sulk of hurt pride, Mao stayed away from his funeral.

Stalin's successor did make up for this neglect, and within months of his death, a fresh army of Soviet 'advisers' swarmed around China building factories and power stations. At the end of February 1956, however, Mao was again deeply offended with the Russians. For a Soviet leader to make a speech denouncing Stalin's crimes and abandoning articles of the faith was a momentous decision to take. And Khrushchev had taken it without consulting Mao Tse-tung. Later that year, when the Russians were predictably in trouble over Poland and Hungary, Mao had stepped in to bolster Khrushchev's flagging will. Clearly he expected something in return for this great favour (as he saw it: and indeed, if the Russians had not intervened in Hungary, it might have been the end of the Soviet empire). Specifically, Mao expected the Soviet leaders to give top priority to China's daunting economic needs, and to hand over the secrets of nuclear know-how to China's scientists.

Khrushchev did neither of these things. Instead, Mao watched in growing rage as he embarked on a programme of massive economic aid to Egypt, India and other countries – to China's detriment as Mao reasoned. And the Soviet leaders made it quite clear that nuclear secrets were not for the likes of the Chinese. To make matters worse, Khrushchev rejected Mao's advocacy of total hostility towards the United States and the rest of the capitalist world, and sought some kind of understanding with America. Insultingly, he even adopted a neutral attitude in China's dispute with India over the Himalayan boundary.

All this added up to a decision on Mao's part to reject Moscow's leadership utterly. The break came in 1960, when the Soviet technicians who had been helping in China's economic projects were all withdrawn. Nevertheless, the Chinese did send a delegation to Moscow at the end of the year, to attend a great gathering of the world's Communist parties. And the Final Declaration (an important document, to which we shall return) was signed by the Chinese delegation. It was the last time, however, that the Chinese and Soviet parties would take part in this kind of meeting. Two years later, when a Chinese army crossed over into territory which the Indians claimed as theirs, the Russians sided with the Indians, giving them arms as well as comfort.

By that time, Khrushchev had many other international problems to worry about. At home he had made extravagant promises about overtaking the Americans in industrial output, which were clearly not going to be fulfilled in the lifetime of anybody reading the claims, if ever. In November 1958, he gave the Western Allies an ultimatum over West Berlin (still under formal occupation by the US, Britain and France since World War II). Either they agreed to give West Berlin the status of a 'free city' within six months or the Soviets would hand over their own responsibilities in East Berlin to their East German satellite.

The Allies stood firm and in the end all this bluster fizzled out. Khrushchev would have been left looking rather foolish, but for the capture on Soviet soil of an American spy-plane, the U–2, with its pilot. Khrushchev used this as the excuse to wreck a proposed summit conference in Paris, and it was President Eisenhower who was left looking foolish.

Berlin, however, remained the great running sore of the Soviet empire. Every month, tens of thousands of East Germans 'voted with their feet', crossing the boundary between East and West Berlin, then claiming freedom in West Germany. At all costs, this continuing drain in human resources – such a bad example, moreover, to other captive peoples – must be stopped. Here, at least, Khrushchev scored an undeniable and lasting triumph. In mid-August 1961, he ordered the building of a concrete wall, topped by barbed wire, which cut the former German capital in two. President Kennedy and his European Allies did nothing. Power is what you can get away with: Khrushchev had won.

The Berlin Wall victory emboldened Khrushchev. Earlier in the year, President Kennedy, newly come to office, had suffered a humiliating reverse in the fiasco of the Bay of Pigs, when a CIA-backed expeditionary force consisting of Cuban exiles had foundered on Cuban soil. In June, between the Bay of Pigs affair and the building of the Berlin Wall, Kennedy and Khrushchev had met in Vienna, and Khrushchev had decided that the younger man was no match for him. When he got away with building the Wall unopposed by American power, he concluded he was right, and decided to test the President's will to the utmost.

That clash of wills is now known as the Cuban missile crisis of October 1962. The details are indeed well known. The Soviet Union stockpiled nuclear weapons on Cuban soil and pointed them at America. Kennedy blockaded the island to prevent further supplies of the deadly missiles from arriving, then forced Khrushchev to withdraw them. As I shall argue in a later chapter, the Russians didn't do too badly in the final deal, but it was a humiliating moment for Moscow, for which Khrushchev's colleagues blamed *him*. The Sino-Indian clash in the Himalayas, in which the Chinese inflicted a painful defeat on the Soviet-supported Indians, was almost exactly simultaneous with the Cuban missiles crisis. It too did nothing for Khrushchev's prestige.

In other areas as well, Khrushchev did rather badly for the USSR during this phase of the Third World War. Twice in three years (in 1960 and 1963), the entire Soviet and Czech embassies were expelled from the ex-Belgian Congo (later Zaïre); and the Soviet ambassador in Guinea, Daniel Solod, also had to pack his bags and leave. In South-East Asia, scene of the abortive Soviet-inspired insurgencies of the late 1940s, pro-Moscow leaders of the local Communist parties made way everywhere for pro-Peking ones. In Laos, one of Khrushchev's initiatives went sour when planes he had supplied to an initially anti-American leader called Kong Lae were later used against the local Communists. An exasperated Khrushchev told the visiting British Foreign Secretary, R. A. Butler, in the summer of 1964 that he had had enough of involvement in the Indochina war.

About this time, Khrushchev's colleagues decided they had had enough of *him*, and in October 1964 – almost exactly two years after the Cuban missiles crisis – they unceremoniously bundled him out of office. Communist regimes punish failure and Khrushchev had failed too often.

With Khrushchev's removal, the Soviet conduct of the

unilateral Third World War entered a dynamic new phase of expansionism.

4

Phases of World War III
(1964–77)

The lull that had set in during Khrushchev's last two years in power was quickly broken once he had been removed. Looking back, it is clear that the new collective leadership in Moscow had decided to open a fresh phase of all-out expansionism in the Soviet Union's unilateral war of aggression against the rest of the world – the Target Area.

The first sign that something new was in the air passed almost unnoticed at the time, except for the prying eyes of specialists – and even they couldn't be sure what it really meant. In November 1964, only a month or so after Khrushchev's removal, the political wing of the Viet Cong guerrillas in South Vietnam were invited to open an office in Moscow. The political wing called itself the National Front for the Liberation of South Vietnam or NFLSV. The point was that at that time the NFLSV already had offices in Peking, Pyongyang, Djakarta, Cairo, Havana and East Berlin; and the second Indochina war had already lasted seven years. During that lengthy period the Russians had hardly intervened at all. Now, however, the war was going badly for America's protégés in South Vietnam, and the Russians may have reasoned that they could get away with a more active intervention, and still not run the risk of a major confrontation with the United States. This at any rate was a possible interpretation at the time, and it was soon seen to be correct.

Another straw in the wind was the resumption of an airlift of Soviet weapons to left-wing guerrillas in the Congo. The arms came from Algeria and Egypt in Soviet-built AM12 transports. The airlift had been suspended for some time, because an anti-Communist government was in power in the Sudan, whose territory was necessary for a staging point. But

Shrinkage of the Target area. Phase 2: 1950-70

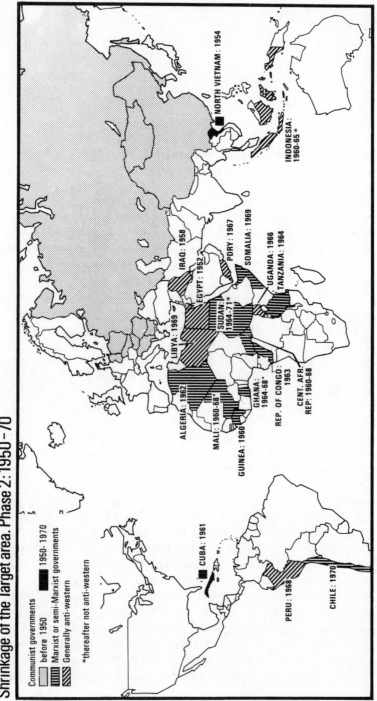

Communist governments

■ before 1950   ■ 1950-1970

▤ Marxist or semi-Marxist governments

▨ Generally anti-western

*thereafter not anti-western

NORTH VIETNAM : 1954

INDONESIA : 1960-65 *

IRAQ : 1958

PDRY : 1967

SOMALIA : 1969

EGYPT : 1952

UGANDA : 1966

TANZANIA : 1964

LIBYA : 1969

SUDAN : 1964-71 *

ALGERIA : 1962

GHANA : 1964-68 *

REP. OF CONGO : 1963

CENT. AFR. REP: 1960-68

MALI : 1960-68 *

GUINEA : 1960

CUBA : 1961

PERU : 1968

CHILE : 1970

in November 1964 – about a month after Khrushchev's overthrow – there was a pro-Communist coup d'état in the Sudan, and the airlift could be resumed. At the time, however, these events were not easy to interpret. Was the airlift resumed because a pro-Communist government was now in power in the Sudan? Or because Khrushchev's successors in Moscow were more aggressive than he had been in his last two years? It was impossible to say.

Today, the facts fall neatly into place. Moreover, we know that the new men of power in Moscow had decided to catch up with, and even overtake, the United States in strategic weapons systems; and to expand the Soviet Navy until it could make its presence felt in all seas and oceans of the world. These were momentous decisions in World War III, and within a decade the objectives had been substantially achieved.

Let us now look at the principal stages of the Third World War in the recent period.

The Military-Naval Programme

A couple of years or so before the Cuba confrontation of October 1962, American nuclear specialists believed that the Russians were ahead of them in weapons systems – both in numbers and in the power and thrust of the missiles with their nuclear warheads. This was known as 'the missile gap'. It was the conventional wisdom of the time, and it happened to be a fiction. When the time came for Kennedy to face up to Khrushchev, he knew not only that there was no missile gap in Russia's favour but that the USA was substantially ahead of the USSR. He knew this mainly because of a flow of extraordinarily detailed technical 'top secret' information provided during the previous year or so, and at agonising personal risk, by Colonel Oleg Penkovsky, a Western agent right in the higher reaches of the Soviet establishment.

The men who overthrew Khrushchev were determined they would never find themselves in a similar situation of strategic inferiority in relation to America. They therefore launched a massive new programme in the spring of 1965. There is no need to go into the technical details in this short book. It is enough to point out that during the ten years from 1965 to 1975, the number of Soviet Intercontinental Ballistic Missiles

(ICBMs) *doubled*. More worrying, even, was a new Soviet attitude towards the possibility of nuclear war. In Khrushchev's day, the Russians seemed to have come round to the Western consensus that nuclear war was just too destructive to contemplate, and that it had to be ruled out by mutual consent (although this view did not stop the nuclear build-up from continuing on both sides).

In the spring of 1965, the Soviet military strategists were saying that nuclear war was 'a risk that must be faced' – another way of saying that it had to be prepared for. Some years later, the Russians started building an Anti-Ballistic Missile system to protect Moscow and Leningrad against nuclear attack. Since then Soviet preparations for civil defence in the event of a nuclear war have been moving ahead very fast.

All this raised alarming possibilities – not so much of a potential decision to strike first (although this could never be ruled out) as of the Soviet leaders putting themselves in a position where they could threaten the United States and force concessions from the Americans in the knowledge that they – the Soviets – were the stronger and more resolute side.

As usual, the experts disagreed with each other over the relative strength of the US and USSR. In successive issues of the well-known American quarterly, *Foreign Affairs*, two of them expressed divergent views. Paul H. Nitze argued that the Soviet Union was well on the way to securing a 'throw-weight' advantage in nuclear capability. He referred to the advanced civil defence arrangements in the USSR and argued that the fact that there were no corresponding facilities in the US 'gives the Soviet Union an asymmetrical possibility of holding the US population as a hostage to deter retaliation following a Soviet attack on US forces'. The preceding paragraph is really a simpler paraphrase of Mr Nitze's views, which I share.

However, in the next issue, Jan M. Lodal said he didn't think throw-weight superiority was particularly relevant. There was little to choose between the two experts, whose credentials were equally formidable. Mr Nitze had been a senior member of the American delegation to the Strategic Arms Limitation Talks (SALT) with the Soviets. Mr Lodal had been Director of Programme Analysis in the National Security Council. On this crucial issue, the position of the

then Secretary of State, Dr Henry Kissinger, seemed to fluc-
tuate. But on 19 September 1974 in a statement to a Senate
Committee, Dr Kissinger acknowledged that 'the appearance
of inferiority – whatever its actual significance – can have
serious political consequences . . . the psychological impact
can be crucial.'

That is the real point. Everybody knows that Soviet rockets
are more powerful than America's and that they deliver a
greater tonnage of destruction. It can be argued that the
American side makes up for this 'throw-weight' inferiority by
the greater sophistication and accuracy of its missiles. But the
throw-weight superiority of the Soviets has an undeniable psychological impact. It was the knowledge that the American
side had throw-weight and other advantages that enabled
Kennedy to stand up to Khrushchev in October 1962.

One problem was that nobody knew for certain just how
much the Russians spent on 'defence'. Of course the Soviet
government, in common with other governments, publishes
defence budgets. But Western specialists are aware that the
published figures greatly understate the true position. Other
areas – including scientific research and even education –
probably conceal large defence expenditures in their separate
budgets. Some experts believe that the Russians devote between 18 and 25 per cent of their Gross National Product to
defence.

A more conservative estimate of 10 to 12 per cent of GNP
was given by Mr Roy Mason, at that time the British Defence
Secretary, in a statement to the House of Commons on 18
May 1976. He had just issued a memorandum on 'Military
Production in the USSR', the first paragraph of which is
worth quoting:

> During 1976, the Soviet Union will bring into service over
> 200 new generation intercontinental ballistic missiles
> (ICBM); a variety of other missiles; 1,000 combat aircraft,
> mostly swing-wing types; over 700 helicopters; over 3,000
> tanks; 4,000 armoured personnel carriers; up to ten nuclear
> submarines – of which six will each carry 12–16 ballistic
> missiles of 4,800 miles range; and major surface ships, in-
> cluding a 40,000-ton aircraft-carrier.

For comparison, the American proportion of GNP devoted to defence is only 5.9 per cent; the British, 5 per cent; and the French and German about $3\frac{1}{2}$ per cent. The reference to a '40,000-ton aircraft-carrier', in the above statement, however, caused ripples of interest among the well-informed. This 'aircraft-carrier', the *Kiev*, was almost an offensive system on its own, with eight SSM launchers (Surface-to-Surface Missiles) armed with nuclear warheads to give it devastating hitting power.

The *Kiev*, which sailed unchallenged through the Dardanelles on 18 July 1976, in clear breach of the Montreux Convention of 1936, was merely one, though at that time the most advanced and sophisticated, of the great range of vessels comprising the Soviet Navy. The *Moskva* and *Leningrad* helicopter cruisers, bristling with electronic devices; *Echo II* missile submarines and lesser varieties of the deadly breed; *Sverdlov* class cruisers (just under 20,000 tons); *Krivak* class destroyers (with quadruple launch tubes for SS N–10 missiles) and many other types of varying but constantly rising sophistication – all constituting the most formidable naval fighting force in the world, and in world history.

Why does the USSR – a largely land-locked or ice-bound continental land mass – need this gigantic fleet? Let its main architect – Admiral of the Fleet Sergei Gorshkov, Commander-in-Chief of the Soviet Navy since January 1956 – give his own answers. This is what he said in July 1967:

The Soviet Navy has been converted, in the full sense of the word, into an offensive type of long-range armed force . . . which could exert a decisive influence on the course of an armed struggle in theatres of military operations of vast extent . . . and which is able to support State interests at sea in peacetime.

That phrase 'State interests at sea in peacetime' makes one wonder. More recently, Admiral Gorshkov put it this way: 'The Soviet Navy is a powerful factor in the creation of favourable conditions for the building of Socialism and Communism, for the active defence of peace and for strengthening international security.' We are back to 'the war called peace'. For 'peacetime', read 'World War III'. For 'international

security', read 'Soviet hegemony'. And for 'the creation of
favourable conditions for the building of Socialism and Communism', a suitable paraphrase might be 'intervention, intimidation and wars by proxy'. We shall see below how true
this paraphrase is.

Meanwhile, let us bear in mind the weight, power and ubiquitous presence of this colossal war machine. With facilities
at Aden and Hodeida in the Yemen Arab Republic, and the
Russians control in other places the approaches to the Red
Sea and Indian Ocean. In Conakry, in Guinea, they have a
powerful presence in the Atlantic; and at the other end of
that ocean they have strategic submarine bases at Havana
and Cienfuegos. Britannia has long since ceased to 'rule the
waves', and America's great naval power has yielded top place
to Russia's.

The 'World Revolutionary Process'

As always with Communists and Communism, we have to dis-
entangle ourselves from the thick undergrowth of jargon
before we can see daylight ahead. Boris Ponomarev, who
heads the subversive apparatus of the Soviet Union, occasionally gives us the benefit of his thoughts on the setbacks
and successes of the mighty machine under his control. In October 1971 an article of his appeared in *Kommunist*, the
theoretical journal of the Soviet Communist Party. The title of
it was cumbrous but revealing: 'Topical Problems in the
Theory of the World Revolutionary Process'. Three years
later, he returned to his theme in an article published in June
1974 by the organ of the international Communist movement
(in a sense, Ponomarev's own 'house magazine'), *World Marxist Review*, which appears in Prague in several languages. This
time the title was 'The World Situation and the Revolutionary
Process'.

Well, what does 'the world revolutionary process' mean?
Essentially, it comprises all events and developments that
favour the Soviet Union's unilateral war of aggression against
the Target Area, and everything that weakens or reduces the
Target Area. More specifically, it refers to:

The financial and economic crisis in the Western countries,
which is described as the 'general crisis of capitalism'.

Any political and social problems in those countries,
such as strikes in Britain or Italy, anti-war demonstrations
in America (in 1971), campaigns for black equality in the
United States, disorders in Ulster. (Such movements or
events are not necessarily or even mainly Communist-
inspired, of course, even though Ponomarev actually names
them.)

The infiltration of social democratic parties in Western
Europe by the Marxist-Leninists.

From 1973 on, the energy crisis, unemployment and inflation ('stagflation').

Any conflicts between Third World countries and the
West.

The 'national liberation movement' – meaning the
Soviet-assisted terrorists and guerrillas in the ex-
Portuguese territories of Africa, in Rhodesia, South Africa,
Latin America and elsewhere.

The 1971 article contained interesting references to the
'New Left' – that is, the proliferating Trotskyist or Maoist
groups that sprang up in various countries in the wake of the
Soviet crushing of the Hungarian revolution in 1956 and again
after the occupation of Czechoslovakia in 1968. One would
not, of course, expect a defender of Soviet ideological
orthodoxy such as Boris Ponomarev to approve the New Left
unreservedly. Indeed, he described it (in 1971) as 'neither
ideologically nor organisationally homogeneous'; it included
'various types of adventuristic elements, including Maoists
and Trotskyists'. Its members were 'easily affected by
revolutionary phraseology'. They lacked 'the necessary en-
durance, the capability verbally to evaluate the circumstances'. Some of them, moreover, were 'clearly con-
taminated by anti-Communist prejudices'. But, he went on:
'. . . their overall anti-imperialist direction is obvious. To
neglect this segment of the mass movement would mean to
weaken the stress of anti-imperialist struggle and hinder the
creation of a united front against monopolistic capitalism.'

When Ponomarev wrote his article for *Kommunist* in 1971,
things appeared to be going well for the Soviet Union in World
War III in Latin America. In Chile, the Allende government,
in which the Communist Party played a major rôle, was in

power and moving fast towards the kind of revolution the Russians wanted. In Uruguay, the Tupamaros revolutionaries were still doing nicely. In Peru, what Ponomarev called a 'new phenomenon' had manifested itself in that the military regime had shown itself capable of revolutionary ideas – or to use Ponomarev's euphemism, they were 'patriotic'.

By the time the 1974 article appeared, things were no longer going so well. The Allende government had been overthrown in Chile; and in Uruguay the Tupamaros had been crushed. The Chilean reverse was a particularly stinging one. What had gone wrong? As Ponomarev saw it, the teachings of Lenin had been ignored. The revolutionaries had failed to consolidate their gains. And they had failed in preparations to meet any kind of challenge, including that of a military coup. He went on to draw lessons to be applied elsewhere in the event of a similar situation, calling on revolutionaries:

1 To gain control of the mass information and propaganda media.
2 To gain control of the army.

In the same article, Ponomarev called on Russia's allies within the social democratic parties to 'neutralise' the right-wing and anti-Communist leaders. Co-ordinated international strikes against the multinational companies ('joint, practical working-class action') was also advocated. Revolutionaries everywhere should remember that 'international détente means extending and carrying deeper the ideological struggle, and does not mean "peaceful coexistence" of the two opposed ideologies'. Last but not least, revolutionaries should remember that 'anti-Sovietism' played into the hands of the 'imperialists'.

Throughout both articles, and in many speeches and statements by Soviet leaders over the past few years, there has been a gloating tone over any misfortune in the Western countries. During the years of the Vietnam war, America's involvement was presented as 'the disease of the entire capitalist system' (the 1971 article). Britain's problems in Ireland have been consistently presented as an imperialist attempt to crush the Irish people.

There is nothing surprising in any of the things I have

quoted above: they are exactly what should be expected from
the man who heads the Soviet Union's subversive apparatus
all over the world. What *is* surprising, though, is that this
same man, Boris Ponomarev, was invited to the United States
by the American Congress in 1974, and to Britain as an
honoured guest of the ruling Labour Party in 1976. The point
of such invitations, other than appeasement of the enemy, is
elusive. The United States is big and powerful enough not to
need to appease the Soviet leadership. Britain is much weaker,
but has nothing to gain from the temporary presence of a man
like Ponomarev. We shall return to this point in another context.

The Soviet attitude to the New Left is particularly instructive and deserves a passage to itself. Each time the Soviet
leadership does something particularly outrageous – such as
Stalin's pact with Hitler just before the start of World War II,
the invasion of Finland, the brutality of the Hungarian occupation in 1956 and the invasion of Czechoslovakia in 1968 –
Communists leave the parties they have served faithfully, in
some cases for many years, in droves. Some of them turn
against the whole business of Marxism and Leninism. Others
become 'armchair Marxists, – dropping the Leninist commitment to action. But many more remain full-time Marxist-
Leninists; only they conclude that things have gone hopelessly
wrong in the Soviet Union, even though Russia was the
original home of the first 'workers' revolution'. These are the
most dangerous. Instead of acknowledging that Marxism, installed as a State ideology by Leninist action, inevitably
becomes a totalitarian tyranny, they want to start all over
again.

Trotsky provides a natural rallying point for such as these.
Conveniently forgetting Trotsky's own involvement in the
revolutionary excesses of the early years in Russia, they regard
his expulsion and murder by Stalin as proof that he was essentially different from the Georgian monster. They join
Trotskyist groups, or create new ones. Some of them become
wedded to Mao Tse-tung's theories of peasant revolutionary
war, and set up splinter Communist parties aligned on Peking
instead of Moscow. Still others get carried away by the
romantic revolutionary notions of the late Ernesto 'Che'

Guevara, and celebrate his death as a kind of martyrdom. And there were those, during the second Indochina war, who marched to 'battle' in their anti-war demonstrations to mindless shouts of 'Ho, Ho, Ho Chi Minh!'

All these groups collectively, including the armchair Marxists and the Trotskyists – some of them not exactly 'new' – constitute the 'New Left'. In the early 1960s, the Russians tended either to ignore or deride the New Left but they suddenly changed their tune when events in 1968 demonstrated to them and to the world the unexpected power and influence of the groups they had despised. One of these was President Johnson's decision in March 1968 not to run for the Presidency a second time. His reasons were complex, but dominant among them was the psychological shock of the Vietnamese Communists' Têt Offensive a few weeks earlier, which had been a military defeat for the Vietcong, but had had a tremendous impact on American public opinion, culminating in massive anti-war demonstrations, and a concerted campaign of anti-war advertisements in the international press, which the world Communist movement undoubtedly helped to foster. To say that the New Left had brought down an American President was not the whole truth but it was certainly an aspect of the truth.

Another significant development was the so-called 'Prague Spring' that same year. The hapless Mr Dubcek's attempt to give 'a human face' to Communism in Czechoslovakia could be interpreted as a victory for New Left propaganda. Another way of putting it was that the New Left was in power in Prague, for a few exhilarating weeks. Finally – still in the first half of 1968 – came the student riots in Paris and other French cities in May and June, which almost brought down the hitherto apparently stable government of General de Gaulle. Indeed, although de Gaulle reimposed his authority, he resigned within the ensuing year, so that the New Left could claim legitimately to have shaken his Fifth Republic to its foundations.

Clearly, the New Left had become a force to be reckoned with, and Boris Ponomarev's article reflected a decision to work with it wherever possible, while admonishing it on points of ideology and doctrine, and at all times to be prepared to pick up the pieces in any revolutionary opportunities created by the Trotskyists. After all, the Maoist and Trotskyist groups were all equally devoted to the cause of Marxism-Leninism. But most of them lacked a power base. Many of the so-called Maoist groups were not under Peking's control, and indeed would have been disowned by the Chinese Communist Party. Those that did owe allegiance to Peking – such as the tiny Communist Party of Great Britain (Marxist-Leninist) – were mostly small and ineffectual. As for the Trotskyists and other fundamentalists, their successes could, on occasion, yield them a power base of sorts, as in Uruguay, but events in that country and elsewhere would soon show how fragile the base was. In comparison, the Communist parties more or less loyal to Moscow had the most powerful base in the world, with the backing of the financial and military resources of a super-power. In time, the Soviet leadership could reasonably hope to bring the New Left entirely under its control.

To be sure, the emergence of the New Left created new and almost insoluble dilemmas for the Russians. It made 'competitive subversion' inevitable on the local scene. If a Trotskyist group of workers decided to strike in a British factory, for instance, it was difficult for the Communists in the same factory to preach industrial moderation. If they did, their revolutionary credentials would lose credibility. If they went too far in the revolutionary direction, on the other hand, the Communist parties – especially in Western Europe – would lose the reassuring and relatively respectable image they had been trying to cultivate as parties that had abandoned violence and were converted to the democratic process. Fortunately for the Russians, there were effective clandestine techniques for bringing the tiresome Trotskyists under their ultimate control. The KGB could hand over sums of money, or provide arms or training courses in terrorism and guerrilla war, thus placing the more violent revolutionary groups in a state of dependence on Moscow. Moreover, since the Trotskyists in particular derived their revolutionary appeal to young people from their ritual denunciation of the repressive party bureaucracy in the USSR, it would be impossible for them to disclose the extent of Soviet assistance to them. In such situations, the existence of satellites old and new was very useful to both sides. Somehow, it seemed less publicly reprehensible to receive arms – even Soviet arms – through

Czechoslovakia, or training from Cuba, than directly from the Soviet Union.

To grasp the full significance of the 'world revolutionary process', we have to take a close look at recent phases of World War III – 'Operation Satellite', 'Operation Indochina' and 'Operation Terrorism'.

Operation Satellite 2 (1965–)

At the end of Operation Satellite 1, the conventional wisdom was that the Soviet Union could set up satellites only when the Red Army was on the spot or within comfortable marching distance. This was 'the theory of contiguity', or as I preferred to call it, 'the theory of contiguous satellites'. The theory certainly seemed true in Stalin's day, and even in the early days of Khrushchev's leadership, when monolithic Communist power strode across the giant land mass from the Oder-Neisse Line in the West to Vladivostok in the East, with Peking and Pyongyang thrown in. And indeed the Russians did not gain any new satellites between 1949 (China) and the late 1960s (Cuba). Then within a few years a new string of client States or satellites reduced the Target Area still further – Egypt and Somalia (for a while), India, Iraq, Angola and Mozambique, while the status of Indochina was still in the balance as these lines were revised late in 1977.

The inclusion of India in this list may startle people who still think of that country in the 'non-aligned' terms of Pandit Nehru. But the fact remains that in August 1971 the Indian government signed a Treaty of Peace, Friendship and Co-operation with the Soviet Union, on lines remarkably similar to that signed in Cairo at the end of May that year. (Students of political semantics may care to note that the Soviet Egyptian pact was styled a 'Treaty of Friendship and Co-operation' – omitting the word 'Peace'.) And in December, when India and Pakistan were locked in a 14-day war, out of which emerged the new Republic of Bangladesh, the Central Committee of the Soviet Communist Party sent a representative to Delhi, with the express instruction of advising the prime minister, Mrs Gandhi, on just how far she could go and count on Soviet support. Although India did not become a Soviet satellite, its dependence on Soviet military supplies, and its deep involvement in 'cultural exchanges' with Moscow during

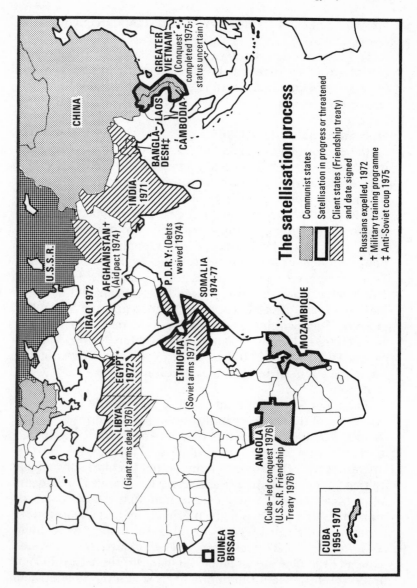

the years of Mrs Gandhi's rule, justified the designation of client-State.

To be fair, the advent of 'remote control' satellites did not entirely disprove the theory of contiguity. In distant Chile, for instance, the Allende regime was well on its way to becoming a remote control satellite when the armed forces intervened and forcibly stopped the headlong rush to 'socialism' Moscow-style. And the Soviet army was just too far away to do anything about it. Still, Cuba and elsewhere, the Russians have demonstrated that they now have the muscle to 'satellise' a country thousands of miles away and make it stick.

Two techniques brought Moscow the striking successes of Operation Satellite 2: the creation and control of local security and intelligence services; and massive military aid programmes. Neither was entirely new. One of the first things Stalin did in the East European satellites during Operation Satellite 1 was to bring the local security apparatus firmly under the control of the Soviet secret police. (The Russians were in no position to do this in China, and this is undoubtedly one of the fundamental reasons why it was possible for Mao Tse-tung to break with the USSR.) As for military aid programmes, the Soviets had stunned the world in 1955 with the so-called 'Czech arms deal' with Egypt, under which President Nasser mortgaged his country's economy for decades ahead. They later tried to repeat the experiment in Indonesia, but were frustrated when President Sukarno was overthrown by the military in 1965.

Watch out for Tass correspondents. This useful slogan for World War III was well illustrated during what might be called the pre-history of the satellisation process in Cuba, from 1959 to 1962. The 'father' of Cuban intelligence, a Soviet citizen named Aleksander Alekseyev, posing as a Tass correspondent, arrived in Cuba in 1959 – the year of Castro's victory. He was, in fact, a senior KGB officer, whose real job was to establish a Cuban intelligence service. He went on to be appointed Soviet Ambassador to Havana at Castro's personal request, and stayed in his post until 1967. The new Cuban intelligence service was named the Dirección-General de Inteligencia (DGI) and was initially designed to serve both Cuban and Soviet needs. The Russians needed an efficient intelligence service that would pass on information to them and operate in areas (principally Latin America) where it was easier for a Spanish-speaking organisation to function than a Russian-speaking one.

Castro's plans at that time were more ambitious: flushed
with his own revolutionary success, he wanted to export
revolution Castro-style all over Latin America. He certainly
tried hard - in Peru, Colombia, Brazil, Venezuela and other
countries. But apart from causing a certain amount of local
disruption, the Castroite efforts never did come to very much.
The Russians never encouraged Fidel Castro's foreign adven-
tures. This was not the way to make revolution, according to
the Marxist-Leninist holy texts. They saw it all as amateurish
bungling, left-wing romanticism and 'adventurism'.

In 1967, events seemed to prove the Russians right. The
most glamorous figure of the Cuban revolution, next to Fidel
himself, was the young Argentine revolutionary, Ernesto 'Che'
Guevara. He had gone to Bolivia to start a revolution, with a
small band of followers. None of them spoke the local Indian
dialect, Quechua, and the Andean peasants were indifferent
to their alleged exploitation by the regime. Moreover, the local
Communist leader, Mario Monje, under Moscow's orders,
refused the slightest co-operation. In the end, Guevara was
captured and killed by the Bolivian security forces.

The Russians had had enough of this nonsense, and
decided to bring Fidel Castro and the DGI to heel. The *Líder
Máximo*, however, with his charismatic personality, his energy
and mesmeric oratory, was a tough nut to crack. There was no
point in even attempting to overthrow him. On the other
hand, his younger brother Raúl, who had been a Communist
(whether or not in a formal sense hardly matters) for more
than a decade, was a more pliant instrument of Soviet policy.
The KGB decided to work through him to influence his elder
brother. But they soon found they were making no headway.

What happened next has been revealed by Cuban defectors.
Early in 1968, the Russians threatened to cut off all economic
aid unless Castro stopped criticising the Soviet Union and
launching world guerrilla plans without consulting Moscow.
The flow of imported oil slowed to a trickle, and a Soviet
blockade halted all supplies of industrial materials for several
weeks. Factories began to close down and the urban workers
were sent to the sugar cane fields. The older satellites were
mobilised on Moscow's behalf. Czechoslovakia, for instance,
sold $570,000-worth of arms to Uruguay for the police of
Montevideo in February 1968 – ironically, to help counter the

local Tupamaros insurgents, who were supported by Castro but were not Communists according to Moscow's definition. Castro's natural inclination was defiance, but he panicked and his resistance collapsed with unexpected suddenness. A new economic agreement with the USSR was negotiated, providing for oil, raw materials and agricultural machinery. Many of the Russians had been withdrawn during the crisis; now they came back in their thousands, and the Soviets began to re-equip the Cuban armed forces with advanced weapons, including surface-to-air guided missiles.

In July 1969, one of the top Soviet trouble-shooters, the then Defence Minister, Marshal Andrei A. Grechko, visited Havana. Now things were really going the Russian way. Under Soviet supervision, work began on the building of a base for Soviet nuclear submarines at Cienfuegos – giving the Soviet navy an operational centre for the Atlantic. In April and May 1970, Moscow's favourite Cuban, Raúl Castro, visited the Soviet Union. He came back with firm orders to slash the Cuban army and use the money saved to build up the DGI.

This time Fidel Castro stopped arguing. He had already given in publicly on 23 August 1968, when he stunned his followers abroad as well as in Cuba by publicly supporting the Soviet Union's right to invade and occupy Czechoslovakia. Now he bowed to Russia's demands. He summoned to his office the boss of the DGI – Manuel Piñeiro Losada, known as 'Red Beard' (Barbarossa) – and told him he would have to go. Technically, there was nothing wrong with the way Piñeiro had been running the DGI. Ideologically there was: he was anti-Soviet. With him, in a drastic purge, went all other anti-Soviet personnel. It was mid-1970, and the satellisation of Cuba was complete. From that time forward, the Russians could use the Cubans as proxies for operations of their own choosing.

Cuba, then, was Moscow's first remote-control satellite. It was not, incidentally, the first such attempt by the Soviet Union, but it was the first successful one; and it was not the last. In Africa in the 1960s, Kenya, Mali and Guinea were targets for Soviet subversion, with unsatisfactory outcomes from Moscow's standpoint. In Ghana under President Kwame Nkrumah, however, the Russians came tantalisingly near to

complete success. The East Germans had been training
Nkrumah's men in intelligence methods. The Russians knew
how to play on the black dictator's vanity and the cult of personality which he encouraged. On Soviet advice, the Kwame
Nkrumah Ideological Institute was used as the sole selecting
ground for members of the President's Personal Security Service. However, Nkrumah was swept out of power in 1966 and
with him went a promising satellite in the making.

Another ambitious leader the Russians knew how to flatter
was the late President Gamal Abdel Nasser. They showered
him with arms and taught him (not very successfully) how to
use them. They built a high dam at Aswan for him and
Khrushchev even made him a 'Hero of the Soviet Union'. The
Russians delicately averted their eyes at the sight of Nasser
persecuting Egyptian Communists – although in the end, under Soviet pressure, the Egyptian leader did allow local Communists to leave their gaols, on condition they behaved themselves and joined his Arab Socialist Union. So warm was the
Soviet-Egyptian friendship that 'fraternal links' were established between the Arab Socialist Union and the Soviet
Communist Party (CPSU). By the time Nasser died, on 28
September 1970, Egypt was in the fullest sense a client-State
of the Soviet Union, and well on the way to becoming a
satellite.

There is, of course, an important distinction between the
two terms. A client-State is one that is heavily dependent on a
major power, either economically, or militarily, or culturally
or any combination of the three. But it retains its ultimate
sovereignty and, in a number of spheres, a certain freedom of
action. Legally, a satellite also retains its sovereignty, but its
independence is purely nominal. In practice, it takes its orders
from the controlling major power. Nasser's successor – President Anwar Al-Sadat – was to demonstrate dramatically the
value of residual sovereignty in a client-State.

At first, Sadat had seemed docile enough. Soviet influence
was strong in the Arab Socialist Union and in the armed
forces. There were thousands of Soviet 'advisers' both in
government and in the armed forces, and at all levels.
Moreover, under the pretext of strengthening Egypt's defences
against Israel, Russian air units under Soviet command had
been introduced into the country. Then in April 1971, Sadat

began to demonstrate his taste for independence. He pounced on pro-Soviet officials and ministers, turned them out of office and gaoled some of them. The best known of these was Ali Sabry, a former vice-president of the United Arab Republic and Secretary of the Arab Socialist Union.

Disconcerted, the Russians sent President Podgorny to Cairo, along with the influential head of the International Department of the CPSU, Boris Ponomarev, in an attempt to bring the Egyptians back into line. Apparently docile again, Sadat signed the fifteen-year Treaty of Friendship and Co-Operation already mentioned with the USSR on 28 May 1971. 'Friendship Treaties' on the Egyptian model were to become an important formal stage in the satellisation process in other countries as well as Egypt. In the Egyptian treaty, one of the clauses could be interpreted as justifying a future Soviet decision to intervene in the internal affairs of the country.

But the Soviet victory was short-lived. On 18 July 1972, Sadat suddenly announced the expulsion of the 17,000 Soviet 'advisers' from Egypt. Although this was a clear and public blow to Soviet prestige, the Russians quickly decided they had no alternative but to comply, and by the end of the year the Soviet presence in Egypt, which had seemed so threatening, had been reduced to a few hundred servicemen. For the time being at least, the satellisation process was over in Egypt.

By the token of 'Friendship Treaties', client status came to India in 1971, to Iraq in 1972, to Somalia in 1974 and to Angola in 1976.

In Somalia, the Russians used both the Cuban model (control of security/intelligence) and the Egyptian model (military aid programme). The Somali strong man, General Siad Barre, turned to the Russians for help in setting up a security service, and in indoctrinating his people. Doubtless the Russians had hinted at how helpful they could be. He turned to them as early as 1969 (while Soviet pressure was yielding results in Cuba). The head of the KGB, Yuri Andropov, made an unpublicised visit to Somalia in 1972 to ensure that the new Somali National Security Service (NSS) was on the right lines. The head of Somalia's security and intelligence, Colonel Suleiman, enjoyed the unreserved support of the KGB. After Andropov's visit to Mogadishu, Suleiman turned up in Moscow to study KGB operations.

For political indoctrination, too, General Barre turned to the Russians, and his 'Victory Pioneers' (Gulwadayasha) were modelled on a Soviet auxiliary police organisation of young people called Druzhinniki, established in 1959. By mid-1974, about 90 per cent of all Somalis with higher education had attended Soviet schools; and hundreds more were required to attend ideological courses in their own country under Russian instructors. Soviet advisers supervised the political orientation course at the Halane Centre, which Somali civil servants had to attend for three months. National Guidance Centres, established under Soviet advice, sprang up throughout Somalia, under the control of 'public relations officers' trained in the Soviet Union and directly responsible to the President's office.

The Soviet military aid programme for Somalia was spectacular, bearing in mind the population of under three million, and the generally low state of public education. In 1964, Somalia's army totalled no more than 4,000 poorly equipped men, a tiny navy and no air force. Ten years later, the Somali army totalled 17,000 men, with 250 tanks, guns, 300 armoured personnel carriers, 200 coastal batteries and auxiliary armour; with more than 50 Soviet-made MiG fighter aircraft, the Somali air force was the largest in that area of the African continent. There was also an SA–2 ground-to-air missile complex. In return, the Somali government had given the Russians important naval facilities at Berbera on the Gulf of Aden, and full access to all Somali airfields. The climax to these developments came in July 1974, when President Podgorny visited Mogadishu with a high-powered retinue, and the Soviet-Somali Friendship Treaty was signed. Then suddenly on 13 November 1977, on generous promises of Saudi Arabian aid, the Somalis took a leaf out of Egypt's book, and announced the expulsion of their 6,000 Soviet 'advisers'. By that time Somalia was locked in battle with neighbouring Ethiopia, also in receipt of Soviet arms.

Operation Indochina 2 (1964–75)
The Soviet invitation to the Vietcong to open an office in Moscow in November 1964, mentioned earlier, was soon revealed as a major decision to intervene in the Vietnam war. On 26 November, the Russians pledged all necessary help to

North Vietnam. The following February the Soviet Premier, Mr Kosygin, led a high-powered delegation to Hanoi. Although the Russians went home without a specific public announcement, Mr Brezhnev announced in September that North Vietnam had already received 'a considerable amount of weapons and military equipment from the Soviet Union'. Aircraft and rockets, modern surface-to-air missiles, quick-firing self-tracking anti-aircraft guns and supersonic interceptor fighter planes also went to the Vietnamese Communists. By the spring of 1972, when the North Vietnamese Army launched a major offensive against South Vietnam, the Communist side had a technological edge over the American-equipped Southern forces. On that occasion, nevertheless, it was the Southerners who could claim victory.

Inexorably, however, it became clear that *final* victory would go to the Communist side. As in all 'people's revolutionary wars' (China and Algeria are other examples), the determining factor was morale. More important even than arms is the psychological war on the enemy's own front – the battle for public opinion in the open societies of the Target Area. Thus it was with the French in Indochina in 1954 and in Algeria in 1962. And the Americans lost the second Indochina war not on the battlefield but on the family television screens of the great American people. The Communist enemy lived in his closed society or in clandestinity in the ricefields and jungles. The Americans fought their war in the open, with their South Vietnamese protégés. Any brutality or 'atrocity' on the American and South Vietnamese side was widely reported and usually televised. Everybody heard about the My Lai massacre. But the Vietnamese Communists did not invite American television teams to watch them bayoneting pregnant women in the villages or decapitating headmen.

The indoctrinated peasants and workers of North Vietnam could not protest against conscription. In America, however, the draft was unpopular. The rising spiral of military expenditure took its toll. The Americans seemed to be spending more and more and achieving less and less. Essentially, the protest movement was genuine; but it was a bonus for the great propaganda machine of the international Communist movement, which provided aid – usually not recognised as such by the recipients – on a massive scale. Protesters turned

the tide of public opinion against the American involvement in
Vietnam. Morale was sapped, then brought to snapping
point. In South Vietnam itself, a well-organised traffic in
drugs (in which the Chinese Communists were involved, according to Chou En-lai) took a fearful toll among the
American soldiers, black and white. The war was already lost
when President Nixon and his Secretary of State, Dr Henry
Kissinger, decided to negotiate with the Vietnamese Communists.

The cease-fire agreement signed in Paris in January 1973
enabled the United States to withdraw. America's South Vietnamese allies were left in the lurch. This had not been the intention of the Nixon Administration, but in the wake of the
Watergate scandal the American Congress blocked ammuni-
tion supplies for South Vietnam. There, too, demoralisation
set in, and Saigon fell to the North Vietnamese forces on 30
April 1975. It was the Vietnamese Communists who had done
the fighting and brought victory to Hanoi. But it was Soviet
arms that had made the victory possible. Indeed, the final conquest of Vietnam in 1975, and the subsequent Communist
take-overs in Laos and Cambodia (marked in the latter country by frightful massacres of the civilian population), were the
delayed culmination of a protracted subversive process which
had begun decades earlier when the Comintern turned Ho
Chi Minh loose on the countries of East Asia.

Operation Terrorism (Permanent)
A passenger plane is hijacked and the hijackers extort a ran-
som of money or political concessions. Israeli athletes are
murdered at the Olympic Games. A Vietcong 'guerrilla' hacks
a woman to pieces. An IRA thug kneecaps a 'traitor'. An ambassador is kidnapped and held in a 'people's prison'. A
business man opens a letter-bomb and loses a hand in the ex-
plosion.

All these and many more, are acts of terrorism and happened during the past few years. It is still not generally known
that the Soviet Union is deeply involved in terrorism – by
training terrorists, giving them arms or money, or in other
ways.

This section could also be entitled 'Operation Insurgency
2', for terrorism and guerrilla war often overlap. They should

Operations Indo-China ❶ (1946-54) and ❷ (1964-75)

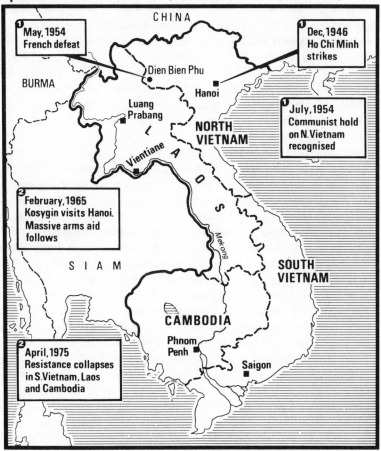

not be confused, however. An insurgency, especially of the kind known as 'people's revolutionary war', usually includes a phase of terrorism, either in the countryside or in the towns. But then again, terrorism can be almost a way of life in itself, apparently without any strategic objective more specific than the general disruption of life and society, and providing the terrorists with a life of risk and adventure (and high living).

I believe it is important to distinguish between the various kinds of terrorism. Obviously terrorism as a way of life requires one kind of response, while terrorism as a phase in a protracted war calls for another. The Russians did not invent 'people's revolutionary war': it was a Sino-Vietnamese invention. Mao Tse-tung practised it successfully against Chiang Kai-shek's government in China, and theorised about it as well in various works. But it was left to the Vietnamese Communists in both Indochina wars to bring revolutionary war to a kind of chilling perfection, in the process defeating a major power (France) and a super-power (the United States). We have already covered both Indochina wars, and noted the decisive nature of the Soviet involvement.

As Marxist-Leninists, the Russians feel slightly uncomfortable about revolutionary war, partly because they didn't think of it (nor did Marx or Lenin), partly because Mao and the Vietnamese put their faith in peasant warriors instead of the 'proletariat' as Marx and Lenin taught), and most of all because Mao was a Chinese and an ideological heretic who got away with his heresy. But as Marxist-Leninists, the Russians will take advantage of any revolutionary opportunity that comes along, even if they didn't create it in the first place.

When Fidel Castro and his follower 'Che' Guevara, came out with their notions of instant revolution (just start fighting and you'll create a revolutionary situation), the Russians hardly bothered to hide their contempt for such half-baked ideas. Their main quarrel with Castro, until the KGB brought his intelligence apparatus under Soviet control, was about his obsessive urge to start revolutions or insurgencies all over Latin America and further afield. Pretty well all these attempts came to nothing, as the Russians said they would. But they weren't above trying similar things themselves, for that was different: if the Russians themselves gave the orders, the situation, they felt, could be kept under control.

The Russians are capable of learning from their past mistakes and will change tactics accordingly; but the strategic aims never change. The Target Area, ever shrinking (apart from temporary setbacks), consists at any time of *whatever portions of the world still escape Soviet control.*

Indochina was one of the major pieces of Soviet strategic foresight. Another was the Portuguese territories in Africa. In the most advanced of three territories, Angola, Portuguese Communists had set up a clandestine Communist Party as long ago as 1955. About a year later, a cover organisation emerged: the Popular Movement for the Liberation of Angola (MPLA), from the initials in Portuguese. About 1959, a decision was taken to go into rebellion against Portuguese authority, and for the next two years the MPLA simply vanished inside Angola itself, although it was very active as a propaganda organisation outside the country. Years later, it was learned that from the start the Russians had provided training facilities for MPLA terrorists and guerrillas in vast camps in the Soviet Union.

The revolt started in 1961. Two years later, the present MPLA leader, a hard-liner called Agostinho Neto, took over. He was still around, twelve or thirteen years later, to collect the spoils of victory.

It was much the same in Mozambique, on the eastern coast of southern Africa. The Front for the Liberation of Mozambique (FRELIMO) was set up in 1962, and the revolt broke out two years later. The original FRELIMO leader, Eduardo Mondlane, was murdered at his headquarters in Dar-es-Salaam in February 1969, and Moscow's man, Samora Machel, took over the following year. A hard-line Communist, he had been trained in the USSR, and Algeria, which also ran a school for guerrillas. The Chinese competed with the Russians for ultimate control of FRELIMO, and for a while appeared to be succeeding. But in the end the greater resources and staying power of the USSR won the day. When victory over the Portuguese came in 1975, Moscow's man, Machel, was there to present the Russians with their strategic prize.

In Portuguese Guinea, the PAIGC (African Party for the Independence of Guinea and Cape Verde Islands) began as a town-based clandestine organisation under the leadership of Amilcar Lopes Cabral, who later became one of the most successful guerrilla leaders in Africa. Cabral drew heavily on Ho Chi Minh's tactics in Vietnam. He was the undisputed leader until death robbed him of the taste of victory in January 1973. Did the Russians control Cabral? He attended the 24th Congress of the Soviet Communist Party in Moscow in 1971, and had this to say: '. . . it is precisely from the Soviet Union that we are receiving the greatest aid in our struggle.' He ought to have known. The quotation appears in the important article by Boris Ponomarev published in October 1971 and analysed earlier in this chapter.

From the experiences of the French in Indochina and Algeria, and of the Americans in Vietnam, the Russians had grasped the central fact of 'revolutionary war' – that it is won or lost on the home front. During the long years of the three wars of attrition in Africa, the Portuguese armed forces were never in serious danger of defeat in the field. But Portugal is a poor country, and its very conservative dictator, Dr Salazar, was more interested in balancing the budget than in economic growth. He went on balancing his budgets to the end, but increasingly at the expense of other things he might have done, such as building houses or providing better medical services and schools. Towards the end, the Portuguese were spending 40 per cent of their budget on the African wars.

While the iron-willed dictator was around, the mounting expenditure and the frustrating sacrifices of the officer corps were borne stoically. But Salazar's successor, Marcello Caetano, although an able and intelligent man, lacked the will and aura of his austere predecessor. Moreover, pressures were building up below the surface in the armed forces that were bound to explode sooner or later. There was indignation among junior officers, some of them ex-students whose studies had been interrupted for wars that never seemed to end. There was indignation of another kind among regular Army officers, when a law passed in July 1973 allowed national service officers to join the regular Army and keep whatever rank they had reached. In the end, these varied resentments merged into general opposition to the wars and to the regime. Protest groups emerged, which collectively took the name of 'Armed Forces Movement'.

The rôle of the Portuguese Communist Party in these events is of special interest. One thing should be remembered: whatever other European Communist Parties may claim from time to time, the Portuguese party was an unregenerate 'Stalinist' one, a pure instrument of Moscow's will. Not for the PCP the tortured doubts of other West European parties over the Hitler-Stalin pact, over the invasion of Finland, the crushing of the Hungarian revolution and the occupation of Czechoslovakia. At every twist and turn, the party boss, Alvaro Cunhal, would obediently echo the Moscow line.

We may therefore safely assume two things: that when the PCP changed its tactics, Moscow approved; and that just as soon as the PCP learned about the Armed Forces Movement, so did Moscow. Well, the PCP changed its line twice – in October 1970, and again in May 1973. On the earlier occasion, the party decided on violence, and launched its own terrorist organisation, Acção Revolucionaria Armada (ARA). For two and a half years the ARA did the usual terrorist things: bombings and shootings. Then in May 1973, the ARA suspended violent action, and the PCP switched to 'political action'.

Looking back, this was a remarkable piece of political foresight on the part of the PCP. So remarkable that it may have been due to inside information. At all events, the first meeting of the AFM took place (on Sunday, 9 September 1973) in a farm outside Lisbon, owned by a party member. So although the PCP probably didn't *initiate* the AFM or the conspiracy to topple the regime, it was undoubtedly 'in' on it from the start. And Moscow therefore had advance knowledge of what was about to happen.

On 22 February 1974, Cunhal, who had spent years in exile in Moscow and Prague, was sixty. To mark the occasion (and no doubt to show how important Cunhal was in their eyes) the Soviet leaders celebrated with a special ceremony in Moscow. The Soviet party boss, Leonid Brezhnev, personally pinned the Order of the October Revolution on Cunhal's breast. Also present were the two Soviet leaders who (with Andropov of the KGB) are most closely associated with world-wide subversion: M. A. Suslov and Boris Ponomarev. (Being a full member of the ruling Politburo, Suslov is senior to Ponomarev, who is only a candidate member. Broadly speaking, Suslov lays down the general line, and Ponomarev gives the orders for subversion throughout the world.)

There were speeches, of course, and the most significant was made by Suslov, who recalled something Cunhal had said, to the effect that 'permanent and indestructible solidarity with the Soviet Union and the CPSU are the unconditional duty of Communists and working people in all countries.'

The dissident officers overthrew the Caetano regime in a bloodless coup on 25 April 1974. Cunhal went straight home from his long exile to a cabinet job as Minister without Portfolio in the revolutionary government. Quite literally, Moscow had its own man in office in Lisbon.

I am not going to trace the zigzag course of the Portuguese revolution in this book (although we shall come back to the subject). At this stage, I just want to make the point that the left-wing military revolt in Portugal served Moscow's wider strategic purposes in the Third World War by hastening the end of the wars in Africa. At any rate one set of wars ended: the wars of the African guerrilla groups against the Portuguese forces, which had opted out of the fighting. Another kind of struggle could now begin – the struggle for the succession.

The Russians had long been preparing for this moment. In Mozambique and Portuguese Guinea, the Marxist FRELIMO and PAIGC respectively had little or no trouble in seizing power from the departing Portuguese. In Mozambique, the only question was whether FRELIMO was going to lean to the Chinese side or the Russian. But this question was soon resolved in Russia's favour, by the sheer weight of Soviet power and of the thousands of personnel trained in the USSR. Soon it was clear that Machel was Moscow's man. In Guinea, the issue had never been in serious doubt.

It was only in Angola that a real struggle for power loomed ahead. For the MPLA did not by any means have the monopoly of resistance to the Portuguese. There were two other groups in the field: Jonas Savimbi's UNITA (National Union for the Total Independence of Angola), which was anti-Communist; and Holden Roberto's FNLA (National Liberation Front for Angola), which was not so much anti-Communist as anti-Soviet, and indeed was getting arms from China.

The men in Moscow dealt with these challenges in the usual way: by a display of 'muscle'. First, they stepped up arms deliveries to the MPLA. The build-up was in full swing by November 1974, but the tempo was greatly increased in the ensuing months. In financial terms it was a massive effort. Between 1960 (when the Russians first began aiding the MPLA) and November 1974, the Soviets had spent about £27 million in arms for the MPLA. But between November 1974 and October 1975, the expenditure totalled some £55 million. In 1975 alone, the Russian training for Angolan terrorists and guerrilla fighters cost the USSR about £730,000

Then came a new and dramatic development. At the begin-

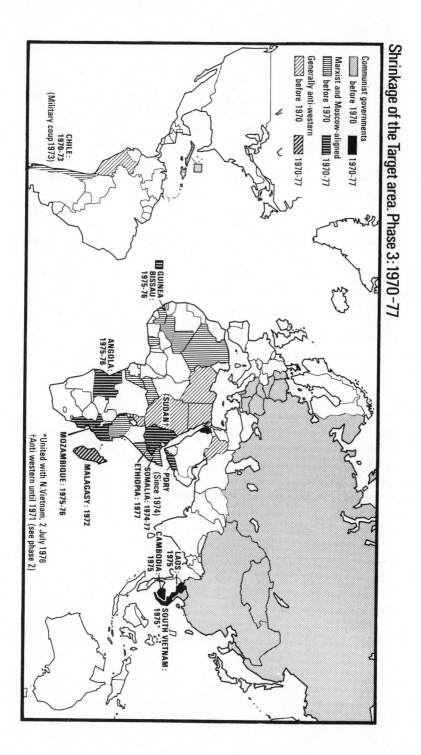

Shrinkage of the Target area. Phase 3: 1970-77

Communist governments
before 1970
1970-77

Marxist and Moscow-aligned
before 1970
1970-77

Generally anti-western
before 1970
1970-77

CHILE:
1970-73
(Military coup 1973)

GUINEA
BISSAU:
1975-76

ANGOLA:
1975-76

SUDAN

MOZAMBIQUE: 1975-76

MALAGASY: 1972

ETHIOPIA: 1977

SOMALIA: 1974-77

PDRY
(Since 1974)

CAMBODIA:
1975

LAOS:
1975

SOUTH VIETNAM:
1975*

*United with N.Vietnam, 2 July 1976
†Anti western until 1971 (see phase 2)

ning of 1976 intelligence reports revealed the presence of thousands of Cuban troops in Angola. Within weeks, some 15,000 of them had been transported in Soviet ships and planes, and with Soviet weapons and equipment to match. Some of them came from unexpected places in Africa and the Middle East, for instance from Syria, from which 400 Cuban tank crewmen, plus their Soviet tanks, were flown to Angola for immediate action.

For the Russians, this was the handsome payoff for the satellisation of Cuba some years earlier. Fidel Castro made vainglorious speeches about 'aiding our African brothers', but the world was not fooled. The Cuban forces were there at Moscow's orders to carry out Soviet policy. And soon enough they brought victory – at least in the main centres of the country – to the Soviet-protected MPLA.

Let us see things as they are. This was not just a victory for the MPLA, or even for the Cubans. It was a victory for the Soviet Union in its unilateral war of aggression against the rest of the world. And as a result, the Target Area shrank yet again.

Miscellaneous involvements
The Soviet use of Cuban proxies was not the only case of its kind in recent years. A more curious and less well-known one was that of the Mexican terrorists in 1971. A young man called Fabricio Gómez Souza had been recruited by the KGB, along with other young people, for training at the Patrice Lumumba Friendship University in Moscow. They got their training all right, but not in Russia. One day an Aeroflot plane flew them to North Korea, where the reigning Communist leader, Kim Il Sung, had developed ideas of world influence through terror.

Having got their training in the usual techniques of terrorism, they were brought back to Moscow for their final briefing, then sent back to Mexico to launch a campaign of terrorism and insurgency. There were about fifty of them, and they called themselves the Movement of Revolutionary Action, or MAR. Soon they were using their weapons – American-built ones for reasons of availability and security, in whose use indeed they had been trained north of Pyongyang – in Mexico. Unfortunately for them, a policeman stumbled

across one of the MAR cells near Jalapa, and soon the whole
organisation was broken up. As soon as the Mexican
authorities had discovered Moscow's involvement they expelled the Soviet ambassador in Mexico City and four of his
staff, unmasked as KGB personnel operating under
diplomatic cover.

The Soviet taste for clandestine operations sometimes leads
the Russians into bizarre situations. None was odder than
that in Chile during the period of the flamboyant Socialist
leader, Salvador Allende, when Santiago became the centre
for Cuban and Soviet subversive operations throughout Latin
America. Into the new Cuban embassy moved a new breed of
'diplomats', members either of the Soviet-controlled General
Directorate of Intelligence (DGI) or of Fidel Castro's very own
Directorate of National Liberation (DLN), staffed – as
Castro's way of showing he was still 'independent' – by the
anti-Soviet personnel who had been sacked from the DGI
when the Russians completed their satellisation of Cuba. Also
at hand were a strong contingent from the KGB, and a team of
North Korean specialists in violence.

In the politics of 'competitive subversion', treachery is the
order of the day. Soon the Soviet KGB was providing training
courses in terrorism, not for the Chilean Communist Party but
for its rivals of the extreme Left, the Miristas, so styled
because their 'party' was named the Movement of the
Revolutionary Left (in Spanish, Movimiento de la Izquierda
Revolucionaria, and hence known as the MIR). In other
camps, the North Koreans meanwhile were training young
terrorists from the most extreme faction in Allende's own
Socialist Party. These particular extremists took their orders
from the fiery Senator Altamirano, who had gone to
Pyongyang (from Cuba) some time before in a Presidential
plane thoughtfully provided by Kim Il Sung.

All this may have been bizarre, but from a Leninist
standpoint it was consistent. The Russians had their own plan
for taking over the Allende regime and the main threat to that
plan came from the Miristas who (again from a Leninist
standpoint) were revolutionary adventurists, liable to spoil
everything by land seizures and trigger-happy incidents in the
cities. By training the Miristas they probably reckoned they
would in time bring them under Soviet control – which after

all was what had happened in Cuba. They were not, in fact, given enough time, for on 11 September 1973 the armed forces overthrew Allende, who took his own life.

The Communist plan for Chile is worth recalling. The well-disciplined Chilean Communist Party, a Moscow-line party and the biggest in Latin America, had never polled more than 16 per cent of the national vote in general elections. For that matter, Allende himself only attracted 36 per cent in the Presidential elections of 1970, but came to power in a three-cornered contest because his opponents would not work together. I call the Communist plan the Santiago Model, and it very nearly worked. Sharing power with Allende's own Socialists, and the Miristas, the Communist Party was given the ministries of Labour and Finance, while the Economics ministry went to an 'independent' Marxist who worked closely with the Communists.

There was no Red Army at hand to intimidate the people (most of the intimidation came from the violent MIR), nor did the Communists control the Ministry of the Interior (as in the Prague Model of 1948). However, the Chilean economy was pretty firmly in Communist hands, and this could have been enough. The government set about harassing private firms, driving them out of business by compulsory wage increases and price freezes or strikes (through the Communist-controlled trade unions), then sending officials to take over. By the time of the military coup, what was left of private enterprise was badly shaken and demoralised. And the Santiago Model would almost certainly have yielded another Soviet remote-control satellite, if only Allende and the Miristas had left well alone. Instead, the irresponsibility of the President and the violent impatience of the revolutionary Left, made a military intervention inevitable. The collapse of the Allende regime was a serious blow to the Soviet strategic planners in the Third World War. Soon it was to be the object of countless seminars and self-questioning sessions by Communist Parties the world over. Hence Ponomarev's insistence (in his 1974 article analysed earlier in this chapter) on infiltration of the armed forces wherever revolutionary action is contemplated.

Before leaving Latin America, let us look at one of the most extraordinary of the Soviet Union's terrorist involvements, which happened to begin in that area. A young man called Ramírez Sánchez, whose Communist father named him Ilich after Lenin (Vladimir Ilich Ulyanov), was recruited by the KGB in his native Venezuela. In the late 1960s, he was sent to Cuba, where he was trained in terrorism and guerrilla warfare in the large camp of Matanzas outside Havana. His tutor was the KGB Colonel Victor Simonov. In 1968 he went to Russia for further training, after attending the Patrice Lumumba University. At that time he was 22 or 23 years old. He was a promising pupil, who combined a ruthless delight in killing with special aptitude in target practice. He was singled out for the full treatment: political indoctrination, sabotage, the use of weapons and killer karate.

In 1969, the promising young terrorist was expelled from Moscow's institutions of violent 'learning'. Expelled? That, at least, was the cover story. True, the young man could shoot and make bombs. But he was too fond of the girls, and in unguarded moments he had expressed himself in terms less than wholeheartedly committed to Soviet communism.

Later, the young man – who became known as Carlos – turned up in Marseilles, where he got into various scrapes. Then suddenly we find him hitting the headlines in the summer of 1975, with the cold-blooded murder on 27 June in Paris of three French intelligence officers who had been foolhardy enough to call unarmed at his flat. In London, a cache of arms said to belong to him was found in a girlfriend's flat. Then it turned out that he was working for one of the most extreme of the Palestinian terrorist groups, the Popular Front for the Liberation of Palestine (PFLP).

But Carlos's biggest exploit was still to come. On 21 December 1975, with the police of several countries after him, he led a group of terrorists who coolly kidnapped eleven leaders of the oil-producing states in a meeting in Vienna. (Some of the hostages were released in Libya and the rest in Algeria.) For this contribution to the Arab cause, Libya's strong man, Colonel Khadaffi, is said to have given Carlos a $2 million reward.

Even at the time of the murders in Paris, it was known that Carlos had been trained in Russia, but it wasn't certain whether he was actually working for the Russians, or whether, having trained him, they had simply turned him loose on the world. Details of his original recruitment in Venezuela came to light more recently, and the consensus among security services early in 1977 was that Carlos, whatever his Palestinian involvements, was still a conscious agent of the KGB.

It is fair to say that without Soviet help a number of terrorist movements in various countries would have been either insignificant or at least a good deal less troublesome than they were. Quite apart from Carlos, where would the Palestinian terrorists be without the Soviet weapons freely made available to them, either directly or through such Soviet-supported countries as Iraq and Libya? The young terrorists of the Turkish People's Liberation Army (TPLA), who flourished until the Army cracked down on them in the early 1970s, received arms from Bulgaria across the Black Sea; and had propaganda facilities in East Berlin. Even the anti-Marxist wing of the Irish Republican Army (IRA) – the Provisionals – received Soviet arms, though in what quantities it is hard to say. A large consignment destined for the 'Provos' was seized at Schiphol airport (Holland) in October 1971, and it would be surprising if it were the last. Other Soviet arms were sent to the official IRA by the Libyans.

Such examples could be multiplied. But the ones I have quoted are sufficient to show that the Soviet investment in terrorism is major in scale and of long standing. Indeed, it is, from the Soviet standpoint, a remarkably cheap investment. The selective training of terrorists is relatively inexpensive. As for arms, that is one commodity of which there is no shortage in the Soviet Union. Indeed there is a glut of them. With the heavier weapons – missiles, tanks, planes and artillery – the Russians can buy governments. With the smaller arms – including Kalashnikov assault rifles and portable rockets – they can feed and ultimately control terrorist groups.

What of the return on the investment? Well, as with other forms of investment, it depends how you measure the return. Some of the transnational terrorist groups (so called because they operate in countries other than their own) are hard to control, even with Russia's vast resources. But even if they are not under Soviet control, and even if they don't actually gain power through terrorism, their work of destruction and disruption suits the Russians nicely. Western societies are weakened and the authorities are discredited. Moreover, the local Communist parties, by staying out of it (though there have been some exceptions, such as Portugal), begin to look relatively moderate and sensible, in comparison with the bomb-throwers and assassins.

It is the kind of situation in which it is hard for the Russians to lose. And there is always the chance that a Soviet-supported terrorist group will actually come to power and that thereafter the country concerned will be ripe for satellisation. And so World War III goes on, while in general public opinion in affected countries thinks of terrorism as just something that 'happens', because of social conditions or racism. Terrorism never 'just' happens: terrorists everywhere know that they can look to Moscow for the weapons and know-how of violence.

5

Operation 'Détente'

In their weakness and confusion, the Western Allies handed 'détente' to Brezhnev on a plate. That is, they gave him the opening the Russians had been waiting for, for nearly twenty years. He was ready for it, but some of his colleagues and allies were highly suspicious of this unsolicited gift, and he had to persuade them that it was worth accepting. Having disposed of the reservations in his own camp, he conducted 'détente' in the best Soviet style, as an operation in World War III.

In my vocabulary, 'détente' is nearly always in quotation marks. That is, when it refers to what the Soviet leaders *call* 'détente'. Occasionally, the inverted commas can be dropped, when the word refers to the real thing. Let us, then, deal with the semantics first.

A great deal of sentimental nonsense has been written about 'détente', much of it deliberately aimed at deceiving. The first question to ask is: What is 'détente'? The word is French, and is generally taken to mean a relaxation of tension. (Ominously, one of its meanings in French, is 'the trigger' of a gun; and indeed the release of the trigger, while it may cause instant death, does relax tension at the firing end.) In the shadowy world of political semantics, words mean different things according to which side of the iron curtain you are on.

In the West, we are quite clear what we mean by détente. There has been tension between two countries or groups of countries; perhaps a war or two. Then relations improve; governments are no longer at each other's throats; any threat of war recedes and vanishes. The perfect example is France and Germany. I spent my childhood in France, and at that time Germany was looked on as the hereditary enemy. Germans were 'Boches', and the Kaiser's atrocities, real or false, were retold in children's picture books. Three times in a lifetime the Germans and French have killed each other in uniform, and even out of it. Yet look at them today – or rather, look at France and the Federal German Republic, since what I say is true of West Germany but not of the Communist regime in East Germany. France and West Germany are founder-members of the European Economic Community (EEC) and allies within NATO, although France under General de Gaulle left the integrated allied command. If a French girl wishes to marry a German boy and he is willing, there is nothing to stop them in the relations between their two countries. People and ideas move freely from one country to another. There is no mutual censorship. No visas are needed in each other's passports. And war has become 'unthinkable' between these two hereditary enemies. *That* is détente.

But that is not what the Russians mean by 'détente'. If a Soviet citizen wishes to marry a German or a French man or woman, although it has been known to happen, it is not at all easy. You cannot buy the *Daily Telegraph* or *Die Welt* freely in Moscow and you can buy only such Western books as the authorities will allow in, and see such films as are deemed fit for Soviet audiences. Nor has war become unthinkable between the USSR and Western countries. On the contrary the enormous growth of Soviet armaments has revived fears of a military clash.

What, then, *do* the Russians mean by 'détente'? To get the answers, you not only have to study Soviet statements, both for home consumption and for abroad, you also have to note Soviet actions. What it comes down to is this. The Russians want the West to recognise Stalin's conquests during and after the Second World War. They want an end to what they call the cold war: that is, anti-Soviet words and deeds in Western countries, whether from governments or private individuals or groups. They want the West to believe that there isn't going to be a war between the Warsaw Pact countries and NATO. They want access to Western food and technology, and easy credit terms to meet the bills. They also want some kind of arms limitation agreement with the United States that will allow the Soviet side to keep the lead it has gained during the past decade. With all this, the Russians absolutely rule out any 'ideological' détente. The West must not attack them (and if anybody in the West is unfriendly enough to point out that Soviet dissidents, for instance, are sent to psychiatric hospitals and hideously maltreated, it is regarded as an attack), but they, the Russians, can say what they like about Western 'imperialism', 'capitalism', 'racism', 'neo-colonialism' and the rest. Détente, in Soviet eyes, is rather like heads we win, tails they lose.

The prehistory of 'détente' goes back to the beginning of 1954, when the Big Four of those days (US, Russia, Britain and France) met in Berlin. For the USSR, Mr Molotov, notorious for his stonewalling diplomacy, proposed a 50-year collective security pact, with Germany neutralised and divided. In those days, the Western powers were rather more determined, and clear-sighted, than they have since become, and nobody on the Western side was going to buy that kind of package.

To tell the whole story of 'détente' diplomacy in the intervening years would be unnecessarily lengthy. From time to time over those years, the Russians came out with their stock proposals for a European Security Conference. Usually, these were coupled with suggestions that NATO and the Warsaw Pact should both be dissolved – which would mean the withdrawal of the American troops in Europe, and of America's protective umbrella over the Alliance. The Americans, then, would be back home 3,000 miles away, and the Russians would be just where they had been all along, with little to stop them should they wish to occupy Western Europe.

The Russians launched their proposals yet again in 1969, when the West's first wave of indignation over the occupation of Czechoslovakia the previous August had spent itself. Later that year (1969) the NATO powers dropped hints that they might, after all, be interested in a European Security Conference. By that time, Willy Brandt's Social Democrats were in power for the first time in West Germany.

Brandt wanted to break with the rigid foreign policy introduced years earlier by the Christian Democratic leader, Konrad Adenauer, from which his successors had not deviated. After all, he could argue, the war had been over for 24 years, yet Germany remained a divided country. Perhaps a more flexible policy would further reunification, or at least remove some of the barriers on the reuniting of divided German families. So he launched his *Ostpolitik*, best described perhaps as a West German form of détente.

Meanwhile, in America, Richard Nixon had come to power, and he too, despite his anti-Communist past, seemed determined to seek some kind of understanding with the Soviet leadership. And not only with the Soviets, but with the Chinese as well. After the years of rigidity in foreign matters, the Americans seemed in a mood for change. Moreover, it was already clear, in 1971, that whatever the Americans were heading for in Vietnam it was not victory.

In February that year, President Nixon presented his annual foreign policy report to Congress, and although he was cool on the Soviet proposal for a Conference on Security and Co-operation in Europe (CSCE), he did not reject it either. In Moscow, Brezhnev correctly read the signs and in April, at the 24th Congress of the Soviet Communist Party, he launched his famous 'Peace Programme'. The old refrain came out again: 'Dissolve NATO and the Warsaw Pact.' And he called once more for a Conference on Europe. As an *operation*, this was the start of 'détente'.

In February 1972, President Nixon created a world sensation by visiting Peking with Henry Kissinger. He wanted to complete his balancing act by going to Moscow as well, and Brezhnev was all in favour. But within the ruling Politburo the Ukrainian Shelest was strongly against a visit from the President of the 'imperialist' United States at a time when American bombs were being showered on North Vietnam. In this kind of situation, it was either Brezhnev or Shelest, so the unfortunate Shelest had to go, and was simply dropped from the Politburo after losing his job as First Secretary of the party in the Ukraine.

Strange as it now seems, Brezhnev had some trouble 'selling' his idea both to his Kremlin colleagues and to his Warsaw Pact allies, according to accounts that appear to be well-founded. Shelest and those who thought as he did may have feared that 'détente', if followed through to its logical conclusion, could spell the end of the struggle between 'socialism' and 'capitalism', leaving the Communists with no particular justification for their permanent hold on power. As for the

Warsaw Pact party bosses, the same question took a slightly different form. All of them knew that without Stalin and the power of the Red Army, not one of them would have been in power; and that given half a chance the people in all their countries would kick them out, as clearly shown in Hungary in 1956 and in Czechoslovakia in 1968. Where would a security pact in Europe lead? They reckoned they had a right to proper answers from Brezhnev.

The Soviet party boss duly reassured the dubious and the timid. In 1973, he summoned East European Communist leaders to a meeting in Prague, and said (in more or less these words): 'Trust us, comrades. For by 1985, as a consequence of what we are now achieving with détente, we will have achieved most of our objectives in Western Europe. We are achieving with détente what our predecessors have been unable to achieve using the mailed fist . . . We have been able to accomplish more in a short time with détente than was done for years pursuing a confrontation policy with NATO.

'[By 1985] we will have consolidated our position. We will have improved our economy. And a decisive shift in the correlation of forces will be such that, come 1985, we will be able to exert our will whenever we need to.'

That Mr Brezhnev did indeed express himself in these terms became known to Western intelligence services shortly after from the report of an informant who was present at the meeting. The information, however, was ignored by Dr Kissinger, the American Secretary of State. That he did ignore it could be deduced from the visible fact that it very patently did not affect his conduct of American policy in its strenuous pursuit of the thing called 'détente'. But more recently the story was told by Mr William Beecher, who was assistant secretary for Public Affairs at the Pentagon at that time, in an article in the *Boston Globe* of 11 February 1977. This account, which was authentic, confirmed the previous reports.

Although Brezhnev got his own way (as the boss of the Soviet Communist Party usually does), the doubters had a point or two in their favour. Even before Brezhnev had launched his Peace Programme Willy Brandt had been going out of his way to give the Russians what they wanted. If that was the way things were going anyway, the critics argued, all the Soviet leaders needed to do was sit back and wait for the

good things to come their way. What, then, was the point of
giving anything away at all (even verbally) and running the
risk of further splits within the international Communist
movement?

Brezhnev turned out to be right, but there was some sense
in what the critics were saying at the time. Ever since Stalin
had grabbed eastern Europe at the start of World War III, the
major Soviet objective for that part of the world had been
Western recognition of his conquests. *De facto*, of course, the
West already did recognise them, since the Western countries
had diplomatic relations with all the satellites except East
Germany. But East Germany was of special importance to the
Russians, for this was the ultimate example of what has been
called the 'systemic' dividing line. In other words, Germany
was one nation, but there were two German states – one of
them free and 'capitalist', the other Communist and enslaved.
Moreover, as a result of Stalin's grab of eastern Poland at the
start of World War II, when he and Hitler were on the best of
terms, the Polish Communists (at the end of the war and with
Russian backing) had driven the German population out of
eastern Germany, so that the *de facto* eastern border of East
Germany now ran along the line of the Oder and Neisse rivers.
This 'Oder-Neisse line' had been recognised by the Big Three
(Russia, America, and Britain) at the Potsdam conference in
1945, but only as a 'temporary boundary'. What the Russians
were after was recognition of the post-war boundaries of
Europe as permanent; recognition of the German Democratic
Republic (East Germany); and indeed *de jure* recognition of
the whole Soviet empire in eastern Europe – meaning not only
that the Western allies acknowledged the facts of the situation,
but that they should *approve* it as well.

During the whole of the Adenauer period in West Germany,
there was not the slightest chance that the Russians would
achieve these World War III objectives. The 'iron chancellor'
of the Federal Republic, who was in power from 1949 till
1963, was inflexibly opposed to recognition of East Germany
and the Oder-Neisse Line. (For years, the information
bulletin of the West German embassy in London, and
doubtless of German embassies elsewhere, was adorned with a
map of Germany showing its pre-war frontiers, and German
spokesmen referred to what we called 'East Germany' as

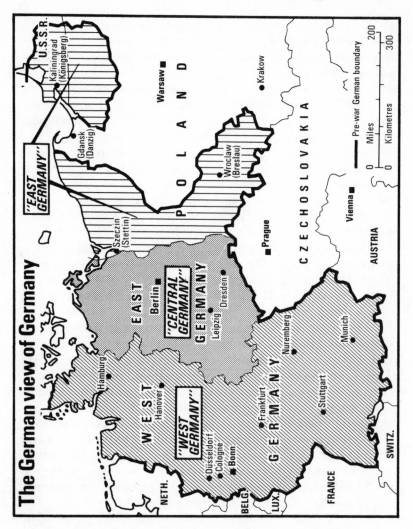

The German view of Germany

'Central Germany', while the term 'East Germany' referred to the Polish territories east of the Oder-Neisse.)

Professor Walter Hallstein, a former German Foreign Office official who became President of the European Economic Community, gave his name to the 'Hallstein Doctrine', under which no country that had diplomatic relations with East Germany could also have them with West Germany. Everybody had to choose between one and the other.

And the Federal government claimed to speak for all Germans, including those in Communist Germany.

In this situation, the status of the pre-war capital of Germany, Berlin, remained a bone of contention and the western part of the city a hostage to fortune, as an enclave in hostile Communist territory. At any time, the Russians and their East German satellite could make life difficult for the people of West Berlin, and for the American, British and French garrisons. It was therefore another aim of World War III to get the Allies out of West Berlin, so that in time it could be absorbed into East Germany.

In its inflexible line during the Adenauer years, and for some time after the Chancellor stepped down in 1963, West Germany had had the full support of successive American governments. Indeed, an uncompromising American policy for eastern Europe as a whole was enshrined in the famous 'Captive Nations Resolution' adopted in 1959 by the US Congress, which committed the US to work for the freedom and independence of Russia's satellites.

Now consider what Chancellor Brandt 'gave' Brezhnev:

Recognition of the borders of East Germany, and of Poland's Oder-Neisse frontier: under the Bonn-Moscow and Bonn-Warsaw treaties (August and December 1970), respectively.

New opportunities for espionage in West Germany through the opening of a Soviet consulate-general and a trade mission in West Berlin and of a large East German mission in Bonn: under the Four-Power Agreement on Berlin (September 1971) and the General Treaty between the two German governments (November 1972).

West German recognition of Communist East Germany: under the General Treaty of November 1972 between the two German governments, which provided that both should seek admission to the United Nations.

Thus all that Adenauer had fought to preserve was gone, and the Hallstein Doctrine was in shreds. We are not concerned in this context with the rights and wrongs of the frontiers of Germany and Poland, among the thorniest questions of modern and contemporary history. The point is that the three

results of the *Ostpolitik* treaties listed above were Soviet objectives in the Third World War; and all three were given to
Brezhnev by Willy Brandt.

And in return, what did Brandt and his allies get? For the
first time the Soviets gave a written undertaking to facilitate
surface transit of West German traffic to West Berlin through
East German territory. In a formal sense, this was something.
But of course it left West Berlin just as physically and
militarily vulnerable as always. And the infamous Berlin Wall
stayed where it was, and indeed was later provided with new
electronic devices to bring instant death to any East Germans
foolhardy enough to seek refuge in West Berlin.

It will be noted that the first two *Ostpolitik* treaties – with
Moscow and Warsaw – were concluded *before* Brezhnev had
launched Operation Détente. Doesn't this prove that the
critics were right, and that all the Russians needed to do was
sit and wait for the unilateral concessions to come, without
making even verbal ones themselves? The answer is No, for
Brezhnev was to show, conclusively, that where ideology was
concerned, the circle could be squared. In other words, he
could get what he wanted out of the West while continuing to
attack everything the West stood for and openly aiming at the
destruction of Western systems and societies. In this belief,
Brezhnev was showing himself to be a good Leninist, for Lenin
had boasted that the 'capitalists' themselves would provide
the rope with which to be hanged. What Brezhnev was doing
was to show that, with a little encouragement, the 'capitalists'
would even let the Russians have the 'rope' on easy terms.

Besides Brezhnev knew better than his critics could that
when it came down to hard facts the Soviet Union couldn't do
without 'détente'. So many things had gone wrong – not outside but inside the USSR. Stalin had given the Russians a big
steel industry and the means of war. Under Khrushchev, the
Russians had put cosmonauts into space. Under Brezhnev,
the war economy had gone from strength to strength. But
visitors from the poor countries of the Third World could see
for themselves that in the material comforts of peace,
'capitalism' was leaving 'socialism' far behind. America and
Japan, and some of the countries of Western Europe, were
moving into the computerised, high-technology affluence of
the post-industrial age. On the civilian side, the Soviet

economy offered very little. And after more than half a century of communism, the system still could not guarantee to feed the people. In good years, yes; in bad years, the Russians had to shop for grain abroad, mostly in despised capitalist America.

The Soviet leaders knew that if economic development towards theoretical 'communism' – affluence for all – was the top priority, they could go a long way towards it by slashing 'defence' expenditure, demobilising enough men to exploit un-tapped resources in Siberia, and diverting technology from military to civilian uses. They could feed the people by de-collectivising agriculture, for after all tiny private plots allowed under the system made an altogether dispropor-tionate contribution to national food supplies. But to cut on defence would be to risk Moscow's hold on the East European empire, and, in time, even on the non-Russian republics of the USSR itself. As for agriculture, a public admission that the system did not work in this domain could call in question the system as a whole, and therefore the right of the ruling group to stay in power.

That was the dilemma which faced Brezhnev and his team. The easiest way – indeed the only visible way – to resolve it was to cultivate the *illusion* of 'détente' and entice the West and Japan with visions of an enormous Soviet market, wide open for products of the hated capitalist system. There were a number of side advantages, besides the fundamental one of keeping the system intact. If Western governments (and to a large extent public opinions) could be persuaded that there was not going to be a third world war (World War IV, by the criteria of this book), they could be made to 'buy' the idea of helping to develop the Soviet economy, so that the Russians, ever richer, would continue to take all the West and Japan could offer. Meanwhile, the Soviet leaders could continue to add to their already preponderant military strength, thus fostering the notion, especially in Western Europe, that there was no point in standing up to the Russians anyway, since they were too strong to be defied. (Heads we win, tails they lose.)

This was the logic of Operation Détente, and it worked almost to perfection.

'Détente' became a prodigious exercise in public rela-tions. Brezhnev – the dour, dull, plodding party boss, the apparatchik – was suddenly seen to be human after all. Instead of scowling, he and the equally dour Premier, Aleksei Kosygin, went around smiling and making speeches about peace. Brezhnev turned out to be a rather amiable old chap, fond of the ladies and with a dashing taste for fast cars. The new Brezhnev gallantly raised Frau Brandt's hand to his lips, and allowed himself to be picked off the ground by the giant American film actor, Chuck Connors. As for the cars, as soon as the Western leaders learned about the Soviet leader's little foible, they tumbled over each other to gratify it. President Nixon presented him with a Lincoln, President Pompidou of France with a special Citroen, and Chancellor Brandt with a Mercedes. In June 1977, President Giscard d'Estaing enriched his stable by two more cars, one of which was resprayed in blue instead of the original green to please his Soviet guest.

All this – the summitry, the bonhomie and the PR job – came to be known as Brezhnev's *Westpolitik*, although this was not what the Russians called it. 'Détente' summitry meant high technology on the cheap for the Russians. In May 1973, *Ostpolitik* and *Westpolitik* joined hands when Brezhnev visited Bonn and signed a ten-year agreement on the intensive development of economic, industrial and technological co-operation, as well as a cultural pact. So effusive were the handshakes when Brezhnev and his party took their leave at Cologne airport that take-off was delayed by 35 minutes.

The Russians did similarly well in harnessing French industry and technology to Soviet needs. Brezhnev visited France at the end of June 1973, and spent seven hours in *tête-à-tête* with President Pompidou (plus interpreters) in the elegant Château de Rambouillet outside Paris, where General de Gaulle used to entertain the mighty from other countries. The pay-off came within a fortnight when, on 10 July, the Soviet Foreign Trade Minister and Valéry Giscard d'Estaing signed two ten-year programmes. Under the first, the French were to invest between 5,000 and 7,000 million francs in the USSR. For a start, they would build a cellulose factory at Ust Ilim in Siberia, and *the Russians would pay them back in cellulose from the factory*. The other programme provided for a joint space exploration programme and co-operation in atomic energy, colour television and various industries. The French would also help to develop the Siberian gas fields and get some of the gas in return.

Brezhnev did not bother to come to London, but Britain was given its chance to develop the enemy economy in February 1975 when Prime Minister Harold Wilson visited Moscow, announcing on his return a British line of credit to the Soviet Union totalling nearly £1,000 million. The interest rate was left unstated, but was believed to be about $7\frac{1}{2}$ per cent, at a time when Britain was borrowing from Iran at nearly twice that rate.

From the Americans, the Russians received not only technology and grain, but gratuitous and one-sided political and military concessions. During Operation Détente, Brezhnev met Nixon three times and President Ford once. The United States got nothing of value out of these exchanges, although Nixon may have reckoned that they contributed to the image he had been cultivating as a man of peace and may, however marginally, have delayed the Nemesis fast overtaking him in the latter stages, as a consequence of the Watergate affair.

To understand the Soviet-American summits, one has to see them as part of the whole paraphernalia of 'détente'. I am not at this point talking about Operation Détente, but about the broader picture as it looks from the outside. In these terms, 'détente' is about three things: trade, arms control, and relations in general. Brezhnev's European summits were mainly about trade (meaning, Western capital, credits and technology), and to a lesser extent about relations between the USSR and the various Western countries. The Soviet-American summits were about both these things, but arms control also played an important part in them. Then there were the series of multilateral talks and conferences, especially those about Mutual and Balanced Force Reductions (MBFR), and the Conference on Security and Co-operation in Europe (CSCE). Finally, there were the Strategic Arms Limitation Talks between the USA and USSR.

The first Nixon-Brezhnev summit, in May 1972, yielded a treaty limiting Russia and America to two defensive missile sites, and an agreement freezing land and sea-based offensive missiles; in the strategic jargon of the nuclear age, defensive missile sites for ABMs (Anti-Ballistic Missiles): in other words, a country sets up a missile site to shoot down another country's missiles. Even, in the financial arithmetic of nuclear weaponry, this is a hideously expensive proposition, for to be useful the ABMs must be able to detect even multiple nuclear warheads detaching themselves from enemy rockets and destroy all of them high in the sky.

The Russians had made a start with an ABM system in the 1965–6 period, while they were doubling their strength in intercontinental ballistic missiles. The Americans, reluctant to sink so much money into an apparently bottomless pit, were slow off the mark. They didn't commit themselves to an ABM until a vote in the Senate on 24 June 1968. Now came an interesting case of cause and effect, for within three days, the Soviet Foreign Minister, Andrei Gromyko, announced that his country was now ready to discuss Strategic Arms Limitation. That was how SALT began.

Having decided to built an ABM, the Americans went ahead and built one. But whereas the Russian one protected Moscow, the American one was at Grand Forks, North Dakota, and therefore mainly protected itself, leaving Washington uncovered. The agreement to limit the number of ABMs to two on either side was pretty meaningless, and it soon became apparent that neither country was going to build more than one anyway.

As for the other 1972 summit agreement – freezing the numbers of offensive missiles on either side – it sounded more reassuring than it was in practice. The Russians have always concentrated on more powerful rockets and bigger nuclear warheads than the Americans. In time, therefore, the Russians would gain a 'throw-weight advantage'.

The second Nixon-Brezhnev summit started in Washington and continued in the American President's West Coast home at San Clemente, California. The final communiqué came on 25 June 1973 and was hailed by both sides as a great contribution to world peace. Indeed, so keen was President Nixon to contribute to world peace that he accepted a position of slight strategic inferiority relatively to the Russians – so that the great arms race could at last be ended. At this meeting, as at all previous talks on disarmament and arms control, the Russians again flatly refused to allow any inspection on the spot. The new Soviet-American agreement on the limitation of strategic arms (published as a separate document on 22 June) provided that such limitations 'must be subject to adequate verification *by national technical means*'. What this meant was that spy-in-the-sky satellites and long-distance detection devices would have to suffice. With the astonishing progress in technology in both these spheres, the Americans evidently felt confident that they would be able to see or hear for themselves whatever the Russians were up to.

The final communiqué at San Clemente called for a tremendous expansion of trade between the two super-powers, to reach a total of $2,000 million to $3,000 million over the next three years. American companies would help develop Siberian natural gas installations; and America would get some of the natural gas – a good point, this, for American public opinion at a time of looming oil shortages. To help all this new trade along, a joint American-Soviet Chamber of Commerce was to be set up. Fresh from this triumph of Operation Détente, Brezhnev went on to Paris for his further triumph with President Pompidou.

By now, the stage was set for the grand opening of the European Security Conference (CSCE). Like Alice in Wonderland after eating her mushroom, the idea had grown and grown. When the Russians and their satellites had revived the idea of a security conference in 1966 and 1967, they had tried to keep the Americans (and the Canadians) out of it on the ground that European security was of interest to Europeans and nobody else. But this was just an opening gambit, and the Russians cannot have been serious in supposing that the Europeans and Americans would fall for it. When the Warsaw Pact foreign ministers met in Budapest in June 1970, they announced that participation in the security conference would be open to the North American States. They also wanted East Germany to take part. But as time went on, more and more countries wanted to be in on the act. These included non-European countries, such as Algeria and Tunisia, which argued that peace in Europe was of concern to them as well as to Europeans. The Yugoslavs, although claiming to be 'non-aligned', didn't want to be left out either, so when the preparatory talks began in Helsinki in November 1972, 34 nations were represented. (In the event neither Algeria nor any other non-Europeans apart from North Americans were in-

cluded.) By June 1973, they had talked themselves out, and on
7 June it was agreed that the great conference should be held
in three stages: a meeting of foreign ministers in July 1973 in
Helsinki (Stage 1); a longer meeting of diplomats and other
officials to consider the details, to start in Geneva in September 1973 (Stage 2); and a final meeting in Helsinki in the spring or summer of 1974 (Stage 3). There was some ambiguity
about the level of Stage 3: should it be a summit (as the Russians wanted)? Or should it be simply a meeting at ministerial
level to adopt – or reject – the recommendations of Stage 2?

In Stage 1, the foreign ministers got down to work briskly
and finished in five days (3–7 July). The hard grind fell to
Stage 2, which began in Geneva on 18 September 1973. After
some months, it became apparent that the original hope that
Stage 3 would take place in the summer of 1974 was misplaced. In the end, it was delayed until July 1975. Soon after
the start, the hundreds of assembled diplomats and other
officials split up into four committees, each one considering a
'basket' of proposals. *Basket I* was about 'confidence-building
measures' – such as prior notification of major military movements and manoeuvres in specific areas. *Basket II* was about
trade and economics. From the outset, the Soviet side pressed
the European Economic Community to remove quota restrictions and confer most-favoured nation treatment on the Communist countries. But no concessions were offered in return:
the Soviet bloc was to remain a closed economic system under
centralised control.

From the Western standpoint, by far the most important
committee was that concerned with *Basket III* – dealing with
human rights, freedom of information, cultural exchanges and
the like. During the long build-up to the CSCE, public-
spirited citizens in a number of West European countries had
drawn attention to the Soviet Union's dismal record in these
spheres. A true détente, they argued, implied opening up the
frontiers between Eastern and Western Europe, giving
freedom of travel to individuals (instead of to groups under
secret police supervision), allowing citizens of Eastern Europe
to marry those of Western Europe, bringing divided families
together again, allowing Soviet citizens to read *The Times*, *Le
Monde*, and other Western newspapers as well as the *Morning
Star* and *L'Humanité*, and to listen freely to Western broadcasts

and read Western books, watch Western television and see Western films of their choice. This was undoubtedly the area in which the Soviet Union was most vulnerable, and the Communist negotiators fought every inch of the way – in the end yielding very little of real substance.

Basket IV was the 'follow-up' basket. The Russians had kicked off in their usual style, by proposing an All-European Commission, to make sure the recommendations of the conference were observed on either side. This neat device for excluding the Americans and Canadians, and creating a body which the Soviets would inevitably have dominated, was fortunately shelved.

Stage 2 of the CSCE, incidentally, gave some of the non-European Mediterranean countries a chance to be heard after all. It was Malta's irrepressible Prime Minister, Dom Mintoff, who had first pressed that Algeria and Tunisia should be heard in Geneva. From 9 October 1973, not only were the Algerians and Tunisians allowed in, but they were joined by Israelis, Syrians, Egyptians and Moroccans. 'Europe' turned out to be bigger than had been supposed. By then, well over 600 delegates were assembled in various Geneva hotels and villas. In scale, if not in final achievement, this was an impressive tally.

By the time of the third Soviet-American summit at the end of June 1974, President Nixon was in serious trouble – his impeachment seemed a distinct possibility. Summitry had become of no little importance to his survival. He had argued all along that there were more important things in the world to deal with than Watergate, and that he was the man to deal with them. Even Brezhnev, despite the absence of pressure from public opinion in the USSR, must have been under pressure from his colleagues to bring home results. After all, Operation Détente was very much his own creation, and he had sold it to his colleagues and satellites in the face of considerable reluctance. Both men, then, were building up to a mood of suitable euphoria. Of the two, however, Nixon was by far the more vulnerable. It was already plain for all to see, except possibly himself, that he was on his way out: no summit euphoria was going to save him. But Brezhnev already had several juicy Western trade deals in the bag, and spoke from a position of fast-growing military strength: indeed, during the

past eighteen months or so of 'détente', the Russians had added a further, 1,500 tanks to their armour in Europe, which
now out-numbered NATO's 3:1. In the air, their lead was
twofold. There was no need for him to make any concessions,
and he didn't.

The 1974 summit yielded two points – claimed to be of substance – and a great deal of disquieting verbiage. The points of
substance were:

1   A Treaty on the Limitation of Underground Nuclear
Tests, stipulating a new limit of 150 kilotons on underground nuclear tests (the atomic bomb that destroyed
Hiroshima was of 20 kilotons), but not until 31 March
1976.
2   A new protocol on the 1972 Anti-Ballistic Missile
Treaty, limiting Russia and America to one defensive missile site each, instead of two.

The sceptics (including the author of this book) pointed out
that since the new underground testing limit would not come
into force until the spring of 1976, the Russians would have all
the time they needed to fix six accurate independently
targetable warheads – each of a megaton (fifty times the
blasting power of a Hiroshima-type bomb) – on to *each* of their
awesome SS-9 and SS-18 missiles. The Americans, too, were
presumably not going to stand still, but at that time their
Minutemen missiles carried only three independently
targetable warheads, and each delivered only 200 kilotons, or
ten times the Hiroshima load.

As for the anti-ballistic missiles, time had confirmed that
neither super-power particularly wished to build more than
one site anyway. So the agreement not to build two, as
provided by the 1972 Treaty did not mean much.

The rhetoric of the final communiqué on 3 July 1974 was
disturbing in its implications. In the interminable negotiations
at Geneva, the West European officials had, on the whole,
behaved with commendable firmness and fortitude. Time and
again they had insisted on the importance of human rights in
the USSR and other Communist countries. In the face of all
rebuffs, they had continued to insist on the importance of
access to information – in other words, to the free flow of men

and ideas, as well as goods, across the Iron Curtain. Their firmness had delayed Stage 3 of the conference. The British and French high officials, in particular, had consistently argued that there was no point in going on to Stage 3 unless Stage 2 could show substantial progress on the points at issue. Moreover, they had consistently resisted the Soviet proposal that Stage 3 should be a summit meeting of all the Heads of all the States participating in the conference. And now, in Moscow, President Nixon was selling the pass. For the communiqué which he signed:

1 Called for an *early* final stage to the Conference on Security and Co-operation in Europe and spelled out the assumption that it should take the form of a summit meeting.
2 Committed the American side to an inevitably one-sided declaration of 'non-interference in internal affairs'.
3 Called for an 'irreversible' improvement in US-Soviet relations.
4 Reaffirmed American (and of course Soviet) support for the quadripartite Berlin Agreement of 3 September 1971 as crucial to stability and détente in Europe.
5 Recorded the signing of a further agreement on industrial, economic and technical co-operation.

The commitment to a quick summit as Stage 3 of the security conference did less harm than it might have, as Nixon had to step down before it could be implemented. The agreement not to 'interfere' in each other's internal affairs was absurd, as all such agreements are with a totalitarian State. The Soviet Union was, and remained, virtually a hermetically sealed society. Interference in its internal affairs was almost impossible, although the broadcasts of the American-financed Radio Liberty or the Voice of America, or television programmes beamed by communications satellites, were held by the Russians to constitute just such interference. In contrast, the societies of the West – and especially that of the United States – were wide open to Soviet subversion. True, certain restrictions were placed upon the movements of Soviet diplomats and journalists (on a tit-for-tat basis for restrictions on American and other Western envoys or journalists in

Russia). But in the USA at least, the special privileges available to diplomats accredited to the United Nations (with its headquarters in Manhattan) largely nullified such restrictions. In this context, a further provision of the Moscow communiqué gave cause for concern. A Soviet consulate-general was to be opened in New York; and simultaneously an American consulate-general would be opened in Kiev. This may have looked like a reasonable balance of conveniences, but only to the uninitiated – among whom it was hard to include either President Nixon or Dr Kissinger who accompanied him to Moscow. How many of the Soviet personnel staffing the new consulate-general in New York would be officials of the KGB or of military intelligence (GRU)? How many would be directly responsible to the International Department of the Central Committee of the Soviet Communist Party – whose head, Boris Ponomarev, had lately led a delegation of the Supreme Soviet on a visit to the US Congress?

But, the uninitiated might well ask, what about facilities for the CIA in the American Consulate-General in Kiev? The answer to this question is simply that there is no comparison between the two cases. Any CIA personnel operating on Soviet soil are under constant surveillance from the all-pervasive KGB, and contacts with the local population are virtually impossible. In New York, in contrast, although one might expect the FBI to do its best, contacts with Americans, or indeed with people of all countries who flock to Manhattan, either on their own business or because they live there, or because they belong to one of the delegations of the United Nations, are free and unfettered. The espionage work of the Soviet Consulate-General – although freedom of travel would be restricted in line with similar restrictions on the movements of diplomatic and consular personnel in the USSR – would usefully supplement the work of the Soviet spy centre in the UN itself, where Soviet diplomats accredited to the international organisation could travel to all parts of the United States unhindered. This, then, was another unequal deal.

Nor was there any cause for rejoicing in the communiqué's reference to an 'irreversible' improvement in US-Soviet relations. If these relations were to be improved at the expense of European security, there could be little joy in the thought that the improvement was to be irreversible. To the beleaguered President Nixon, however, the phrase undoubtedly had a musical ring, for on his return to America and on his way to a holiday in Florida, he made a statement to the press in which he echoed the communiqué with a reference to new patterns of co-operation that would create 'an irreversible momentum which will lead to permanent peace'. To those of us old enough to remember the newsreels of Neville Chamberlain returning from Munich in 1938 after his meeting with Hitler and Mussolini and proclaiming his belief that the piece of paper he had signed there meant 'peace in our time', the President's words had an ominous familiarity.

There was further cause for disquiet in the endorsement of the Berlin Agreement of September 1971. Under this agreement, the Russians guaranteed in writing for the first time transit facilities and rights between the German Federal Republic and West Berlin. As I have argued, this was not a negligible concession, but it was more than balanced by the implied recognition of the German Democratic Republic by America, Britain and France. No one, of course, would have expected President Nixon to denounce the Berlin Agreement, but his approval of a Soviet-drafted phrase referring to the 'key rôle' of the Agreement was surely unnecessary. The point is that virtually the only progress recorded at that point in the CSCE was on the 'inviolability of frontiers'. One of the key Soviet objectives in the conference – *de jure* Western recognition of the permanent division of Europe on ideological lines, with the Eastern part under Soviet control – was thus within sight. No Soviet concession had been exacted by the Western negotiators in return for this 'progress'. (Actually, all was not lost on this vital point, for the Western negotiators were rightly insisting on a stipulation that frontiers *could* be changed by peaceful means and by agreement, in the face of Soviet insistence that they should be 'immutable'.)

The provisions for industrial, economic and technical co-operation were of a general nature, but confirmed American readiness to help develop the Soviet economy.

The only bright spots in this gloomy phase of World War III were provided by the US Congress. On the one issue of aid and trade for the Soviet Union (though not on other issues) the legislators showed greater sense and realism than the Executive. Quite the most forcibly sensible of the legislators was Senator Henry ('Scoop') Jackson, Chairman of the Senate Subcommittee on Arms Control, who lost no opportunity for exposing the hollowness of Soviet professions of good faith and violations of human rights. In a speech on 22 April 1974, he had said: 'So long as the Soviets support the greatly exaggerated military sector of their economy at anything approaching current levels, an American programme of subsidised economic transactions and the transfer of sophisticated technology, whatever its intended purpose, will inevitably amount to aid to the Russian army, naval and air forces. At a time when the Soviet economy is in great difficulty, we ought to be able to persuade them that a re-ordering of their priorities away from the military sector is the best way to achieve economic well-being.'

The Senator had been one of the most outspoken critics of the great grain deal of 1973 under which the Russians, after a particularly disastrous harvest, had bought $750 million worth of American wheat at an artificially low price – leaving the Americans short on the home market, forcing up the price of grain and in general contributing to inflation throughout the Western world. Now, towards the end of 1974, Senator Jackson made a determined effort to tie any major extension of US-Soviet commercial relations to the easing of Soviet restrictions on emigration from the USSR. His campaign greatly embarrassed Henry Kissinger, and Brezhnev – who at the end of the year denounced the 1972 Soviet-American trade agreement.

At about the same time, Congress took the important decision to limit credit to the USSR at low interest to $300 million over four years. This decision dashed Soviet hopes of a large-scale American participation (with Japan) in a gigantic project for the development of Siberian natural gas in the Yakutsk region. But the Russians had already done pretty well out of American generosity over the previous two or three years. Indeed, between March 1973 and March 1974 alone the American Export-Import Bank – a government agency – had issued credits totalling $400 million at the generously low rate of interest of 6 per cent. The actual money had come from private banks, and it was astonishing to see the haste with which such citadels of American capitalism as the Chase

Manhattan Bank, Bankers Trust, Bank of America, Wells Fargo and others fell over each other to help a regime dedicated to their collective destruction. Highly sophisticated technology was made available – in the Kama River Truck Plant, in acetic acid plants, piston manufacturing machinery, iron ore pellet plant, gas reinjection compressors, and submersible electric pumping units. All this amounted to a veritable Marshall Plan in reverse – for the benefit of the main citadel of Communism, whereas the original Marshall Plan was designed to strengthen Western Europe against Communism. The high point of this capitalist aid programme was the sale of an astronaut's space suit to the Russians for $180,000. The space suit had cost the Americans $20 million in research and development costs.

Unfortunately, the departure of Richard Nixon did not put an end to this madness On taking over as America's unelected President, Gerald Ford decided to keep Henry Kissinger as his Secretary of State. (A year later, in November 1975, President Ford was to give the Russians a gratuitous political victory by removing his Secretary for Defence, James Schlesinger, who had been outspokenly sceptical on détente, while Kissinger stayed on.) A year earlier President Ford had also partaken of the joys of summitry – this time at Vladivostok in the Soviet Far East, in November 1974. To the surprise of most observers, the outcome was a joint statement on the Strategic Arms Limitation Talks, which American spokesmen hailed as 'putting the cap on the arms race'.

It did nothing of the kind, however, for it authorised very high ceilings for 'multiple independently targeted re-entry vehicles' (known in the strategic jargon as MIRVs). More ominously, it gave the Russians a built-in advantage over the Americans, for it imposed no limitations on either throw-weight or qualitative improvement. At the time the agreement was signed, the Soviet missiles had up to *six times* the payload capacity of the American ones. Interestingly, the United States already had 918 MIRVs on deployment at the time, and the USSR had none. The Vladivostok agreement therefore gave the Russians the time they needed to catch up on deployment, as well as guaranteeing their throw-weight superiority. The absence of a qualitative stipulation is also significant, for the conventional wisdom was that the

American side compensated for the relatively low throw-weight by greater technological sophistication, notably in accuracy of delivery. But the agreement had nothing to say on technological improvement, and since the Russians spend a good deal more on 'defence' than the Americans, Vladivostok virtually guaranteed Soviet qualitative, as well as throw-weight, superiority within the next decade.

Against these massive disadvantages were two small advantages. One was that a ceiling (although a very high one) *was* set, so that the Americans at least knew where they stood (subject to verification). The other was that the agreement allowed the United States to shift from the highly vulnerable missile force to a sea-based one.

As usual, Senator Jackson made the most pungent comment on this further Soviet victory in World War III. 'Considering,' the Senator said, 'that the Administration has requested unlimited authority to extend low interest, subsidised loans to the Soviets, it [the agreement] is tinged with this irony: we will end up subsidising the Soviet strategic weapons programme as well as financing our own.'

The crowning ritual of Operation Détente was the summit conference at Helsinki in July 1975, which delivered itself of a massive document styled the Final Act. This is not the place for an extensive analysis of this curious document, hailed on all sides as of historic importance, but unlikely to affect the course of history to any great degree. It is more relevant, from the standpoint of this examination of the course of the Third World War, to look at security conference as a whole in terms of Soviet objectives in Operation Détente

What did the Russians hope to get out of 'détente'? I have mentioned some of the objectives, but not all of them. Seven can be pin-pointed – three of them explicitly stated time and again, the others left unstated but easy to deduce from Soviet actions or statements or known as such from intelligence reports.

The three stated objectives were: the dissolution of NATO and the Warsaw Pact; the immutability of frontiers in Europe; and a final document with the force of a peace treaty. The Russians did not do very well on these stated objectives. NATO and the Warsaw Pact were still in existence at the end of the Helsinki summit; and the American forces were therefore still in Europe. The removal of the Americans was, of course, a main unstated objective, and would have been a disastrous consequence of any decision to dismantle the rival military organisations.

On European frontiers, the Russians did achieve partial success, in that the conference recognised the 'inviolability' of these frontiers. Looking at it one way, it meant that the Western signatories would not resort to force to change existing borders – for instance, West Germany bound itself to resist any temptation it might feel to cross the East German border and re-unite the German nation. But there was nothing to prevent the West Germans and East Germans getting together and deciding on reunification (unlikely though this prospect might have seemed). This might be regarded as about half of what the Russians were after. Time and again, the Russian negotiators had pressed for the 'immutability' of frontiers; and to their credit the Western officials (who were just as able as the Russians to look up a dictionary) stuck to 'inviolability'. Had they agreed to the Soviet wording, the Russians would have taken it as Western recognition of the permanence of Stalin's conquests and of the ideological division of Europe. In effect, the West would have recognised the Brezhnev Doctrine, under which the Russians claimed the right to intervene militarily (as they had done in Czechoslovakia) in 'socialist' countries that might wish to depart from socialist principles as defined in Moscow. (For after all, even though the Soviet troops remained in Czechoslovakia after removing Dubcek and his 'Communism with a human face', the frontiers of Czechoslovakia remained unchanged.) However, on the way to the security conference, Willy Brandt had given the Soviets most of what they wanted with his *Ostpolitik*.

Against this, the Final Act at Helsinki did not have the force of a peace treaty, as the Russians had hoped. So to that marginal extent, the conference had not 'delivered the goods'.

When it comes to the *unstated* objectives, the Russians did a good deal better (apart from the withdrawal of US forces). One of these was to contribute to the military, political and psychological disarmament of the West. There, no doubt about it, Operation Détente brought considerable success.

Before the end of the year, for instance, both the American and British governments announced large defence cuts.

A third unstated objective is generally held to have been the 'Finlandisation' of Western Europe. This ugly word calls for some explanation. In November 1939, Stalin's Red Army invaded Finland, and after three months of a bitterly contested winter campaign forced the Finns to accept rather harsh peace terms under which they ceded a good deal of territory. The Finns are a proud and tough people who are attached to the Western democratic way of life. The long-term consequences of Stalin's aggression, however, are that in return for continued freedom to run their own affairs at home, they cannot run an independent foreign policy. There could be no question, for example, of Finnish membership of NATO, or even of the European Economic Community, for the Russians would not stand for it.

That is what is meant by the term 'Finlandisation', which of course greatly irritates the Finns but does describe an unpleasant reality with which they have to live. Now if the Americans withdrew from Europe, and if NATO were dissolved, Western Europe would be Finlandised pretty rapidly, and in time, no doubt, would 'go Communist'. This had not happened when these lines were written, but the question is whether Operation Détente furthered 'Finlandisation'. To that the answer can only be that it did. You have only to study the pronouncements of Western governments on issues to which the Russians are known to be sensitive to see how relatively deferential they became during Operation Détente.

Here is an example: on 21 May 1975, in a press conference, President Giscard d'Estaing declared that he understood Soviet concern over ideas, current at that time, for a common European defence structure. He had said as much to Brezhnev at their Rambouillet meeting. And he added that French diplomacy had erred in the winter of 1974 in discussing such ideas, which had caused a sharp Soviet reaction. (In other words, if the Russians don't like something, don't even talk about it: what is this if not the deference of the Finlandised?)

Another example: during the German federal election of 1976, a constant refrain in speeches by the ruling Social Democratic leaders was that to elect the opposition Christian Democrats would be a 'security risk' on the ground that they were nasty to the Russians. The psychology of Finlandisation again.

The American and British invitations to Ponomarev in 1975 and 1976 respectively were 'Finlandistic' with a vengeance; and even more so, if possible, the welcome given to Shelepin, the ex-KGB head of Russia's 'trade unions', by the British Trades Union Congress.

Last but not least, a major unstated objective of Operation Détente, as we have seen, was the harnessing of Western technology to Soviet needs, without reducing Soviet 'defence' spending. Towards this objective, of course, the Russians made spectacular progress, as the above examples demonstrate.

The Security Conference and the Final Act have their Western apologists, not least among the able and patient high officials who spent so many career-man-hours inching back and forth in tedious word battles with the Communist negotiating battalions. Look, they say in effect, the Russians wanted 'immutable' and all we gave them was 'inviolable'. Besides, they go on, we obliged the Russians to discuss human rights and contacts, and freedom of movement for people and ideas, thus forcing them for the first time to submit their domestic policies to international scrutiny.

Well, the negotiators had a point there, though less of a point than they claimed. Certainly it was marginally useful that the Russians should be on record as supporting various rights and freedoms, if only so that they can be shown up as not observing them in practice. Against this, Soviet spokesmen and commentators never admitted that they had made any concessions at all on Basket 3 of the security conference (the one dealing with human rights and East-West contacts). Georgiy Arbatov, head of the Soviet Academy's Institute for the Study of the USA and Canada, specifically denounced Western claims that Basket 4 constituted a price to be paid in return for Western concessions, in a much-quoted article in *Izvestia* on 4 September 1975. The notion that 'détente' implied any relaxation of anti-Western activities was repeatedly denounced. When Giscard d'Estaing, on his visit to Moscow in October that year, publicly interpreted détente as implying a relaxation of ideological tensions, Brezhnev snubbed him by cancelling part of the arranged programme.

Nor did 'détente' have any discernible effect in inhibiting
the Russians. For example, they blatantly intervened in Portugal before and after the military coup of April 1974, and
continued to do so while the security conference was in
progress. In Angola, their intervention was still more flagrant.
Moreover, throughout the period of the conference, in all three
stages, and since then, the Soviets went on training terrorists,
the KGB carried on spying and subverting, and indeed the
unilateral cold war (World War III) went on exactly as
though 600-plus officials had not consumed so much time in
Helsinki and Geneva.

It would be unfair to blame officials for the successes of
Operation Détente. The blame rests squarely on the shoulders
of the elected leaders of Western governments who preferred
illusion to reality, and settled for retreats and wholesale
deception of their peoples in preference to defending their way
of life and protecting their future.

Let a Soviet publication have the last word on Operation
Détente. I don't know who Y. Molchanov is, but I do know
that in the December 1976 issue of *International Affairs*,
published in Moscow, his masters allowed him to write:
'Détente serves as a basis for peaceful competition between
socialism and capitalism on a world-wide scale, and is a
specific form of the class struggle between them.' He went on
to say, in the standard form, 'The final victory of socialism
over capitalism in this competition is objectively inevitable.'

Nothing new in this, of course. Lenin was saying it in the
1920s. Stalin also said it, and Khrushchev and Brezhnev.
Knowing this, why did the Western leaders go along with the
sinister farce of 'détente'? Why were they so eager to bolster
the flagging economy of a regime committed to the destruction
of their own free systems? Why did they encourage Western
companies to do likewise? Why did Western capitalists rush to
provide technology to the super-power that advertises its intention to destroy them all? Are they all mad, or merely
stupid? Or are they something worse than mad or stupid?

There appears to be no satisfactory answers to such questions.

Before closing this chapter, let me draw attention to two
items that illustrate the very special character of the regime

that confronts the West. One of them concerns the strange rôle of the Hammer family in Operation Détente. Dr Julius Hammer was a Russian émigré in the United States. He was a founder member of the American Communist Party, but he was also a successful businessman. In the 1920s, his Allied American Company made him and his family a fortune in trade with Lenin's Russia, then a starving revolutionary state. This was at the time of Lenin's famous New Economic Policy, when the Soviet leader briefly allowed a return to free enterprise to inject a little prosperity into the prevailing revolutionary misery. Later, when the NEP was abandoned, the Hammer family turned over their assets to the Soviet government, which in return gave them a fabulous collection of art treasures, later to form the basis of the famous Hammer Gallery in New York.

Fifty years later, Julius Hammer's son, Armand, by then in his 70s, spearheaded the American drive to rescue the Soviet economy from its socialist doldrums. As chairman of Occidental Petroleum of Los Angeles, Hammer was offered deals worth between $1,200 million and $2,500 million (the exact amount was obscure) in fertilisers, the Yakutsk gas fields, and the construction of a hotel and trade centre in Moscow.

The other item is really part of the same story. When Lenin embarked on the NEP in 1921, he gave a special rôle to Felix Dzerzhinsky, first head of the cheka (forbear of the KGB). He was to force Western capitalists to co-operate with Soviet intelligence, if necessary through economic or personal blackmail.

History repeated itself in the 1970s, when a KGB general, Yevgeniy Pitrovanov, was appointed deputy chairman of the Moscow Chamber of Commerce. How many of the Western businessmen whose arrangements on business trips to Moscow were supervised by Pitrovanov realised that he was a KGB general?

Let Nikolai Bukharin cap these two stories. Bukharin was a Bolshevik and close associate of Lenin's; which did not stop Stalin executing him as a 'Trotskyite' in 1938. Defending Lenin's New Economic Policy at the time, he said: 'On the one hand, we admit the capitalist elements, we condescend to collaborate with them, but on the other hand our final goal is to eliminate them radically, to vanquish them, to cancel them

out both economically and socially. It is a type of collabora-
tion which presumes a bitter fight, but not necessarily the
spilling of blood.'

Do the rich and powerful men who run the giant enterprises
that help to keep their moral enemies in power know this? Do
they know the policy is unchanged? What motive, other than
the death-wish, drives them on? If the profit motive, what
short-term profit can be worth their own extinction? I have
put these questions in various forms to groups of leading
businessmen in several countries and have had only evasive
answers.

6
Where Did We Go Wrong?

Somewhere along the line, a wrong decision was taken. Either there was a failure of analysis, or the analysis was impeccable but the decision-makers couldn't bring themselves to face the dreadful reality. That one or the other must be true is surely obvious from the developing situation described thus far. Which was it?

The question is really not very difficult to answer. In the public life of the democracies, courage is a rarer attribute than intelligence, although neither is as plentiful as might be wished. If you are old enough, cast your mind back to the thirties. If not, read yourself in and try to recapture the mood of the times. In 1930, the Great War was a recent memory, only twelve years back. Only thirteen years earlier the Russian Revolution had been taken over by the Bolsheviks. There was a great economic depression, and the Wall Street crash was still a daily topic of conversation, along with the British general strike of 1926 and the lengthening dole queues.

Familiar names in the conversation of adults were Mussolini, Lloyd George, Ramsey MacDonald, Stalin . . . and a strange German fanatic called Hitler. I am not going to repeat the history of the 'thirties. I just want to recall one thing. In the 1930 elections in Germany, Hitler's National Socialist Party polled 6 million votes. He was becoming too strong to be ignored, and the able and educated men in the Chancelleries of the West began to read the extraordinary book he had written in gaol some years earlier, under the title *Mein Kampf* ('My Struggle'). What were they to make of these apparently demented ravings, about Jews and Aryans, about the German master race, about the injustices of the Versailles Treaty? Here was something new and unwelcome. It was not a statesman's book, but the work of a fanatic with clear symptoms of mental derangement. Yet this man, in 1930, already had a mass following in Germany. He was going to come to power and Western governments were going to have to deal with him, since he couldn't be wished away.

We know now that even at that time there were men of courage and intelligence who knew where Hitler was going to take Germany, Europe and the world. Among them, for instance, was the Permanent Under-Secretary of Britain's Foreign Office, Sir Robert Vansittart. But in general the elected leaders of Western political parties and governments simply refused to face the evidence. It was too monstrous for their gently nurtured and educated minds to take.

If these men – Baldwin and Chamberlain, Blum and Daladier and the rest – had absorbed the evidence and drawn the right conclusions from it, they could have stopped Hitler in his tracks (for instance when he ordered his troops into the Rhineland in 1936) and prevented World War II. Alternatively, they could have entered the war fully armed and prepared, and prevented the disasters of the Blitzkrieg, Dunkirk and Norway. But they did none of these things, either because they did not believe Hitler's ravings in *Mein Kampf*, or because, believing them to be the awful truth, they lacked the courage and will to take the necessary decisions. So we had the long and shameful futility of Appeasement and the brief and shameful absurdity of Mr Chamberlain's 'peace in our time' in the wake of a great betrayal in Munich. In England during those years of weakness and indecision, the lone voice of Winston Churchill spoke the truth about Hitler and German rearmament. But he remained in the political wilderness until war broke out, and did not become Prime Minister until Chamberlain was forced out in the wake of the continental disasters of 1940.

All this is well known, but I recall it now because the lessons of the Nazi period have *not* been learnt. *The Communist Manifesto* (by Marx and Engels) was published in 1848 and has been available in English since 1888. Lenin's writings have been around for decades. *What is to be Done?* was published in 1902 and has been available in English since 1931. *Imperialism: The Highest Stage of Capitalism* came out in 1917 (in English, 1933), and *'Left-wing' Communism: an Infantile*

Disorder in 1920 (1934). At least as important as these key works is the *Programme of the Communist International*, drafted in 1924 and adopted in its final form at the Sixth Congress of Lenin's Comintern in 1928. All that has happened since is in such writings: the nature of Communist Parties everywhere and of the totalist tyrannies they invariably establish; the subversive techniques of Soviet imperialism; indeed, the whole sorry and predictable course of the Third World War.

Moreover, in all Western countries, intelligent men in considerable numbers have waded through these turgid works and grasped their inner meaning. In many cases known to me, and doubtless in countless others, these wise men – scholars, journalists, high officials – have passed on their wisdom to the politicians and statesmen of the day. But the elected leaders, brought to power by the votes of the people they rule over, have failed to take the unified strategic decisions that could have stopped the aggressors. Such decisions as they have taken have been piecemeal, never dealing with more than one or two aspects of the problem at once. Latterly, they have not even done that: not only have they stood by and watched the ever-quickening erosion of the Target Area, they have gone further by giving the enemy the means to complete our destruction. In Lenin's words, What is to be done?

I shall answer Lenin's question in the later passages of this book. But first, let us deal more precisely than we have done so far with the question that forms the title of this chapter: Where did we go wrong?

In the open societies of the West, the mood of the moment is always important. In 1945, when the Third World War was just beginning, the mood was euphoric. The dominant emotion was relief that the long nightmare was over. Mothers and children wanted the man of the house back. The men (and women) who had been in uniform wanted to get out of it. There was a lot of idealistic talk – and of course some practical talk as well – about post-war reconstruction. For a time, the most familiar set of initials was UNRRA, the United Nations Relief and Rehabilitation Administration. The UN was the focus of youthful idealism and misdirected mature energies. Misdirected, because the underlying assumptions of the world organisation – that the nations who had fought together would remain 'united' and that the fascist enemies (Germany, Italy and Japan) must never be allowed to rise again – were false or irrelevant. Fascism, Nazism and Japanese militarism were all dead and *hors de combat*. Soviet imperialism was terribly alive, yet a major share of responsibility for the peace of the world was being entrusted to those who had just (only very few noticed it) started World War III.

There was to be no return to the miseries of the 1930s. Capitalism was to be revitalised and purged of its sins, with the brand-new international monetary system being worked out at Bretton Woods, a welfare state in Britain and limitless expansion without unemployment as promised by the then fashionable sage, John Maynard Keynes.

In the middle of the Potsdam Conference of 1945, on the fate of the defeated Axis powers, the British voters threw out Churchill, the man who had led them to victory against the Nazis. A lot has been written about this verdict (to which I contributed in a minor way by voting Labour), but I think that in the end it boils down to this: that the mass of British voters, while genuinely grateful to Churchill, saw in him the symbol of warrior leadership, which they would not trust to manage Britain in peacetime. And in practical terms, they saw him (however unjustly) as the leader of that Tory party which they held responsible for the miseries of the 1930s and for Appeasement. They had fought bravely and stood up to hardship and bombardment, and now they wanted peace. They also wanted (let there be no mistake about it) a hefty dose of welfare socialism. As for the communist threat, few people thought about it. The Germans had to be kept down. The Russians were our glorious allies and had made a mighty contribution to the allied victory.

In America, the mood was still more escapist and un-realistic. So little understanding did President Roosevelt have of the nature of Marxism-Leninism and of the character of his Russian ally that at the Yalta conference in February 1945 he had given Stalin virtually a free hand to enslave Eastern Europe. He was seriously ill at the time, as the shocking official pictures of the time made clear, and in April he died, making way for his Vice-President, Harry Truman – the un-derestimated haberdasher from Missouri, who was to become one of America's greatest presidents. Thus at the Potsdam conference later that year, where Germany's fate was decided, the Big Two of the West were each represented by relatively untested men – Clement Attlee for Britain and President Truman for the USA.

But we are talking about prevailing moods. The great American public was in no mood to face fresh menaces or even to admit that there might be fresh menaces to face. When the Potsdam conference began, there was a little unfinished business to attend to in the Far East, but it did not take long. On 6 August the first atomic bomb detonated in anger obliterated Hiroshima. Three days later, it was Nagasaki's turn. On the twelfth the Japanese offered to surrender, and on 2 September they signed the instrument of surrender aboard the USS *Missouri* in Tokyo Bay.

The point to remember is this: America began to demobilise immediately, and went on doing so even when the nature of Stalin's plans became clear beyond a doubt. By the end of 1946 the US Army (which included the Air Force) was down to $1\frac{1}{2}$ million men and the Navy to 700,000 (from a war-time peak of nearly 15 million for both services). By the spring of 1950, the height of what had come to be known as the Cold War, the army numbered only half a million. Not that the US was defenceless, for air power and a monopoly of atomic weapons protected the great Republic and its European allies. But there had been no answer to the things that Stalin had been doing in eastern Europe during Operation Satellite 1. And the Soviet Union had *not* demobilised.

Paradoxically enough, some of us who lived through the early years of the Cold War (the start of World War III) now look back with some nostalgia to what seems in retrospect an era of American realism and determination. And yet it was in those post-war years that the wrong turning was taken – that 'things went wrong'.

It was all done with the best of intentions and for a while it even seemed to be working. I am referring to the policy of 'containment' adopted by the Truman government in 1947. It is a measure of the catastrophic decline of leadership in America and the West as a whole that one should look back nostalgically to the containment period as the time when the Americans stood up to the Russians and to Communism.

Once again, the public mood is important. After the euphoria of 1945, the mood had changed rather sharply in

America, Britain and France. And it was Stalin who had provoked the change. No amount of residual gratitude and solidarity could obscure the fact that he was grabbing Eastern Europe, that China was being taken over by the Communists and that a Communist was leading an 'anti-colonial war' against France in Indochina (although the full significance of these events and the connection between them were not immediately apparent).

The policy of containment was triggered by events in Greece and Turkey. In 1946 and early 1947, the Soviet Union had supported Communist terrorists and guerrillas in what turned out to be an abortive attempt to seize power. Turkey was at the receiving end of threats and diplomatic pressures from Moscow, and it began to look as though Stalin was going to expand his power into the Mediterranean. The burden of economic and military assistance to the two threatened countries rested entirely upon an exhausted and impoverished Britain. In February 1947, the Attlee government decided it could go on no longer. On 21 February, the then Foreign Secretary, Ernest Bevin, said so in a note to the US government and touched off a flurry of consultations and heartsearchings in Washington.

Truman rose to the occasion, demonstrating that those who had spoken disparagingly of him were wrong and that he had the makings of the great President he undoubtedly became. On 12 March, he asked Congress for $400 million to cover economic and military aid to Greece and Turkey. The 'Truman Doctrine' of help to nations struggling against Communist take-overs was born.

It was a splendid moment, to be remembered with pride by Americans, by the British whom they were relieving, and by free or relatively free peoples everywhere in what I call the Target Area (which was so much vaster then than it has since become as a result of Soviet victories in World War III). The vacuum in Western leadership was being filled by a clear-sighted and resolute man.

Yet the new doctrine rested on shaky intellectual foundations. The President had pledged support to 'free peoples who are resisting attempted subjugation by armed minorities or by outside pressures'. The said free peoples could breathe more easily, and did, secure (at least for the foreseeable future) in the belief that the West's super-power, the USA, would henceforth protect them from the new totalitarians.

Yes, but for how long? For ever? Clearly not. For ten years? Twenty years? And what would happen if the Americans lost interest, or returned to 'splendid isolation'? There were no clear answers to such muted questions. Nor indeed were the grateful 'free peoples' likely to formulate them out loud at that time. All they could think about was their relief that help was on its way.

Today, thirty years on, it can be seen quite clearly that 'containment' carried the seeds of its own decay. It was not Truman who conceived the policy of containment: what he did was to provide swift and resolute leadership when it was needed. 'Containment' was the work of a very different kind of man: George Kennan, diplomatist and scholar. Whatever the criticisms now levelled at him (by others besides myself), Kennan can take legitimate pride in having written what was possibly the most influential article in history. Ironically, the article was unsigned, for at the time, Kennan was head of the Policy Planning Staff in the State Department and required to preserve formal anonymity. It appeared in the July 1947 issue of the American quarterly *Foreign Affairs* under the title 'The Sources of Soviet Conduct', and was attributed to 'X'.

For many years, it was considered bad form to criticise Mr X. It still is today, though to a lesser degree. His identity became known soon enough, and George Kennan rightly commanded a good deal of respect. As a professional diplomat and a student of history, in particular of Russian history, he was (and is, as these lines were written) a man of calibre, and certainly of integrity. When a much greater thinker, James Burnham, tore the containment policy to shreds in 1953, in his book *Containment or Liberation?*, there was a roar of outrage from the liberal establishment on the American East Coast. For not only was George Kennan an almost venerated figure, but wasn't Burnham that ex-Trotskyite who had failed to denounce McCarthyism?

I am not concerned here with the great Burnham controversy which I have written about elsewhere (in the *New Lugano Review*, 1976/11–12) but simply with what Burnham had to say about Kennan and containment in 1953, because events have proved him right. The policy was 'designed to confront the Russians with unalterable counter-force at every point where they show signs of encroaching upon the interests of a peaceful and stable world.'

Commenting on these words of George Kennan's, Burnham remarked that the policy appeared to commit the Western world to a protracted period of vigilance. However, no positive steps were apparently required of the American people and their governments. There was to be no encroachment on Soviet territory and no military aid to assist what Kennan described as 'the violent upthrust of liberty'. In the end, the Soviet regime would collapse because it was evil. All that was needed was the persuasive power of America's good example. Although any military aggression from the Soviet side would be met with counter-force, there was no provision to meet subversion and political action by Soviet proxies.

Let us be fair to Kennan and to containment. When he wrote his original article in *Foreign Affairs*, the Soviet regime had 'only' been in existence for thirty years and there was no very good reason to suppose that it was permanent. The Chinese were engaged in a civil war, but Mao Tse-tung was still not in sight of victory. Stalin was getting old, and it was not altogether unreasonable to hope that in his decline or after his death some upheaval would put an end to the tyranny he had imposed on the Soviet and conquered peoples. The dictator died in March 1953, and three years later Khrushchev did indeed denounce the abominations of his regime (some of them, at any rate), before the assembled Communists of the world. But the regime itself went on, even if the personal dictatorship had ended. It was really only in the post-Stalin period that it was possible to understand that the Soviet autocracy was self-perpetuating. (Of course this could have been deduced theoretically from the sacred texts of Leninism, but practice is so much more conclusive than theory.)

Moreover, Kennan wrote his article, as I have already mentioned, at a time of optimism, commitment and moral fervour in the United States, with Truman ready to pick up the torch of freedom from Britain's faltering hands. Very soon, the Marshall Plan – named after Truman's Secretary of State, General George C. Marshall – would speed Europe towards economic recovery after the devastation of World War II. In these circumstances, 'containment' was a message of hope and an inspiration.

But when all these things have been said, we cannot escape from the logic of Burnham's analysis. As he pointed out, in the years after the fighting stopped in 1945, the American policy-makers had three options. One of them was appeasement: giving Stalin what he wanted, as Chamberlain and Daladier had tried to give Hitler what he wanted. That option, though a real enough possibility intellectually, was not 'on' politically. Munich and Chamberlain were dirty words, and few people were aware that at Yalta, appeasement was just what Roosevelt had offered Stalin.

The second option was to take the offensive, or counter-offensive. But that would have been against the American tradition, and wildly unpopular. So, instead, the Truman administration, counselled by George Kennan, opted for 'containment', which was neither fish nor fowl, but suggested firmness without giving offence to peace-loving liberals. It was a 'hope for the best', Micawberish policy. It was not a strategy, for it neither stated a goal nor proposed means of reaching one.

What, asked Burnham, was the goal of containment? A deal with Moscow? Hardly, for that would be appeasement. To overthrow the Kremlin? Hardly again, for that would imply war. Well, then, what was it? Let Burnham sum up: 'The policy of containment, stripped bare, is simply the bureaucratic verbalisation of drift.' The problem was too big, so 'let's duck the responsibility ... and slip the ball to old mother history.'

Two fatal flaws lay at the heart of containment. One we have already met: the inability to accept as true the reiterated Soviet expressions of confidence in the ultimate victory of the 'socialist system' over rival systems, and act accordingly. The other was the unfounded optimism of Kennan's approach, the naive belief that if America set a good example, the Russian people would rid themselves of their nasty rulers. When optimism is shown to be misplaced, it usually yields to an equally irrational pessimism: 'We can't win, so we might as well not try.' Looking back over the decades of the Third World War, it is easy to see that there have been alternations of excessive optimism and of depressing pessimism, both born of a reluctance to face the facts and of a deficiency in the courage of true leadership.

Containment ruled out victory and hoped only for the avoidance of defeat. It was thus purely defensive and, as Burnham had foreseen, it turned gradually but relentlessly into new forms of appeasement.

For some years, however, it had its moment. One of its high points was the Marshall Plan; another was the successful 'containment' of Communist aggression in the Korean war (although the North Koreans and their Chinese big brothers were by no means defeated). Indeed, the Korean war showed exactly what could and could not be expected of Kennan's policy. The optimum hope was stalemate, and when General Douglas MacArthur wanted to go for victory and bomb military targets in China, Truman sacked him. What else? Containment allowed China to pass into Communist hands, and initially at least into the Soviet camp. And containment had no answer when Stalin swallowed Czechoslovakia in 1948. And when Stalin in effect declared political war on the West by setting up his Communist Information Bureau (Cominform) in 1947, then blockaded Berlin, the response of containment was the Berlin airlift (magnificent but not aimed at victory) and the signing of the North Atlantic Treaty in 1949.

NATO was and remains a great and glorious thing, a bulwark against the constant and growing danger of military aggression from the Soviet Union. But it is important to realise that it was in no sense an answer to the challenge of Lenin's Comintern and Stalin's Cominform. It offered no concerted plan to resist and defeat subversion, disinformation and revolutionary war. It was the purest child of containment in that its purpose was entirely defensive. It made no provision for carrying a war into enemy territory. And it exposed a fundamental weakness of American (and to a lesser extent West European) strategic thinking, in its underlying assumption that the Soviet threat was purely military. To be sure, the famous Preamble to the North Atlantic Treaty had an ideological tone. But America and its allies did not propose any common policy or action to counter the non-military aspects of the Soviet threat. Did any of the politicians, officials and servicemen concerned at that time with the defence of the 'free world' have any inkling that the Third World War was in progress? I can't think of any evidence that they did. On all the visible evidence, World War II was the armed conflict that ended in 1945, and World War III was the armed conflict with Russia which they hoped (as we all did) NATO would, by its very existence, prevent.

Truman was well served by his Secretaries of State: first Marshall (let us overlook some blunders of his in China before he became Secretary of State), then Dean Acheson. Both were men of character, but Marshall impressed more by natural dignity and a kind of monumental quality, and Acheson by dazzling wit and intellect. The real author of the Marshall Plan and the Truman Doctrine was Acheson. Between them these men lent lustre to Truman's presidency and contrived to disguise the shortcomings of 'containment'.

The Truman-Acheson partnership yielded in 1952 to that of President Eisenhower and John Foster Dulles. Although President Eisenhower was a five-star general and had commanded the Allied Forces in Europe during the decisive last phase of World War II, he did not think strategically as far as the Soviet Union was concerned. Dulles prided himself on so doing, but he was an impulsive man who tended to speak rashly and compose and deliver his speeches without prior consultation. Some of these speeches, in consequence, burst like bombshells on a startled public. He peppered them with such phrases as 'massive retaliation' and 'brinkmanship', which probably scared his allies more than his enemies. To his credit, he made an energetic attempt to guarantee the security of the 'free world' by extending the American chain of defensive alliances on a world scale. In the Far East it was SEATO (South-East Asia Treaty Organisation) and in the Middle East the Baghdad Pact (which Dulles inspired although his country initially stayed out of it), which became CENTO (Central Treaty Organisation). SEATO and CENTO were supposed to complement NATO, although their value was largely psychological in the absence of a joint military structure. The ANZUS Pact with Australia and New Zealand, and mutual security treaties with Japan, the Philippines and Taiwan were part of the interlocking structure. These pacts brought aid and comfort to America's allies, but of a limited kind.

All this was good, but at times of crisis Dulles revealed himself time and again as a man of words rather than action. He
talked of dropping an atomic bomb as part of an air-naval intervention to save Dien Bien Phu, but nothing came of it. He
was inactive, too, when the Soviet army invaded Hungary in
1956, and sided with the Soviet Union and against his British
and French allies in the almost simultaneous crisis of the Suez
expedition.

To sum up: John Foster Dulles was as much a child of 'containment' as Truman and Acheson. To quote a well-known
American observer (Professor Louis J. Halle): 'In fact, the
United States cannot be said to have ever had a policy of
"massive retaliation", any more than it ever had a policy of
"liberation" as opposed to the policy of "containment".' Indeed, when you look closely at Dulles, you discover that for all
his vehement anti-communism, he mostly delivered hot air.
And yet, looking at the shrinkage of the Target Area since the
days of Dulles, and remembering how 'protected' we felt when
he was around, I must confess that my nostalgia extends to the
Dulles era as well. It was bad enough then. How much worse
it is now!

Two of America's Presidents appeared to depart from the
principles of containment, but not for long in either case. One
was Kennedy, who approved a clandestine invasion of Cuba
by a small army of exiles with CIA support. But an exception
this certainly was, for the invaders were denied sufficient support, and the outcome was the fiasco of the Bay of Pigs in
April 1961.

The other President who appeared to stretch the book of
rules was Lyndon Johnson, who sanctioned a successful
landing of American marines in April 1965 in the Dominican
Republic. A civil war had just started, with the Dominican
army split down the middle – and one half of it controlled by
revolutionaries, some of whom had been trained in
Czechoslovakia and Cuba. The Dominican landing was
almost as controversial as the Bay of Pigs, but the outcome
was far more successful. I myself believe that it avoided a
Communist take-over which would in time have given
Moscow another island base from which to threaten the
Americas. Strictly speaking, holever, President Johnson did

not break the rules of containment, since the Dominican Republic had not, at the time of the intervention in 1965, actually passed under Communist control.

Both Kennedy and Johnson involved American forces in Vietnam, but neither broke the rules of containment, and in time President Nixon withdrew them, still observing the self-denying ordinance that enemy-held countries were out of bounds, that is, to the US land forces, for it was considered acceptable within the rules to bombard North Vietnam from the air or the sea.

Before the Bay of Pigs, long before the Dominican landing and more than a decade before the terrible crux of Vietnam, the Russians had tested American nerve to the limit. For years, tens of thousands of refugees from East Germany and East Berlin had 'voted with their feet', by seeking temporary protection in West Berlin and permanent refuge in West Germany. Among them were certainly some thousands of well-placed Soviet or East German spies. But the flow was draining East Germany of its life-blood and stood as a constant reminder of the superior attractions of a successful free enterprise, market economy in West Germany.

In the summer of 1961, Khrushchev decided to put a stop to this intolerable situation. During the night of 12–13 August, teams of East German navvies built a hideous grey structure of bricks and concrete, to divide the slaves from the free – the infamous Berlin Wall. More than ever, West Berlin was an isolated enclave in Communist territory. The point, however, was that the Allied authorities in West Berlin – Americans, British and French – stood idly by and did nothing. The wires hummed between West Berlin, Paris, London and Washington in criss-cross traffic that yielded much nervous cogitation but never a positive decision. As at Pearl Harbour twenty years earlier, the news came through on a Sunday morning, and found the Americans unprepared. The US Secretary of State, Dean Rusk, met with his officials in the State Department. Rusk feared war, should any attempt be made to interfere with the building of the Wall. He favoured no special action. President Kennedy was about to go sailing in his sloop, the *Marlin*, and did so after conferring with Rusk, advising the Secretary of State to go ahead, as he had planned, and attend a ball game. The German Chancellor, Konrad

Adenauer, wanted to go to Berlin and 'show the flag', but was talked out of it by his advisers. An American protest note was drafted, but not delivered for several days.

Was Rusk right? A quick decision to bulldoze the structure from the Western side of the city might indeed have risked war, but even then, war would not have been inevitable, for it would have been open to the Allies to retreat before a Soviet ultimatum. But then again, the ultimatum might never have come: a show of boldness and decisiveness might have called the Soviet bluff. As it was, the West conceded a walkover victory.[1] The following Saturday, 19 August 1961, President Kennedy did take a decision: he sent Vice-President Johnson (as he then was) to Berlin, where he made a suitably rousing speech. About the same time, a belated protest Note from the State Department reached the Russians, who already knew they had got away with it.

The Wall stood, and still stands as an accomplished fact. As a symbol of tyranny it certainly presented the West with propaganda advantages, but make no mistake about it: it made a vital contribution to the stability of the Soviet bloc. Many were the consequences of the Berlin Wall. From it – or rather from the failure of the Western occupying powers to remove it – flowed West Germany's *Ostpolitik*, the relevant treaties and recognition of the German Democratic Republic. It could even be argued that the success of the Berlin Wall probably emboldened Khrushchev to take his dangerous gamble in 1962, in installing Soviet missiles on Cuban soil.

Another consequence, incidentally, is that East Germany's growth as a real centre of economic power dates from the Berlin Wall. Before that, too many skilled people, too many brains, were escaping to West Germany. After that, the great majority of those remaining lost all hope and got on with their regulated lives. Occasional foolhardy souls tried to make the attempt to cross the Wall, but few made it to the other side. In time, the resources of high technology contributed to the death-dealing capacity of the Wall. Unmanned machine-guns, activated by radar and electronics, ringed the No Man's Land

1   For a full description of the crisis, see Eleanor Lansing Dulles, *The Wall: A Tragedy in Three Acts*, a fascinating monograph by the sister of John Foster and Allen Dulles (University of South Carolina, 1972).

between the two Berlins, making corpses of those brave or rash enough to attempt to flee oppression. But this was something the Russians and East Germans could live with. For they knew that the Americans and their allies would do nothing about it. Another kind of wall protected them from any retaliation: the Wall of Containment.

Europe's leaders were no more successful than the Americans in assessing Soviet objectives or taking counter-measures. The only Western leaders who attempted to act in-dependently of the United States in important matters of policy were Sir Anthony Eden (later Lord Avon), Guy Mollet and General de Gaulle. Eden and Mollet jointly launched the Suez expedition in 1956 without consulting their American allies. Although Suez was not exactly a World War III battle, it yielded lessons relevant to our theme, if only because of the unfortunate coincidence that the expedition was launched within a few days of the outbreak of the Hungarian Revolution on 23 October 1956.

With greater resolution on the British side and a tighter timetable, the ill-starred expedition could have done what was expected of it – that is, it could have removed the ambitious and charismatic Colonel Nasser from the political scene, and perhaps have delayed the Arab victory in Algeria.

It might have done these things, and then again it might not have. Nobody knows, because the expedition was abandoned suddenly and can be seen now as the last muted roar of the British imperial lion. The Suez expedition was a spectacular failure, partly because of deficiencies in both planning and ex-ecution. It diverted the attention of the American President from the crushing of the Hungarian revolt by Soviet tanks, and temporarily placed Eisenhower and Dulles in the same camp as Khrushchev. The Soviet leaders – Bulganin and Khrushchev – brandished their long-range rockets at Britain and France, and exultantly claimed the credit for the Anglo-French decision to withdraw from Egypt. The truth was that Eden capitulated when faced with a major financial crisis and the denial of aid from the United States to obtain alternative supplies of oil. It was a mess. But in Moscow, those waging the Third World War now knew that they could get away with crushing a satellite people trying to throw off the Soviet yoke, that the West European powers had shown they lacked the will and the nerve to act independently of America, and not least that the Americans would veto any unapproved West European initiatives in the name of public morality. In other words, that 'containment' gave them plenty of latitude.

General de Gaulle's assertion of independence was something else. Unlike the great majority of Western leaders in power after World War II, the General thought strategically. When he returned to power in 1958 he saw himself and his country as one of the Big Three of the Western Alliance, along with the USA and Britain. He proposed a Tripartite Atlantic Directorate, but was spurned by the Americans and British, who didn't want their special relationship to be disturbed, nor to complicate life by parting with their nuclear secrets to the benefit of General de Gaulle. Having been spurned, de Gaulle embarked on a more controversial course. His strategy was based on two illusions – that France and the Soviet Union between them could settle the affairs of Europe without the United States; and that the French could supplant the Americans in relations with Germany and the European Common Market. Almost certainly, in his latter years, he listened to the poisoned advice of a Soviet agent of influence planted in the Elysée Palace. (In his novel *Topaz*, the American writer Leon Uris posits just such a situation, and I believe his account to have been dangerously near the truth. More recently a defector from the Soviet KGB, Aleksei Myagkov, revealed that at the KGB training school he attended, de Gaulle's decision to pull out of NATO in March 1966 was presented as an important KGB achievement.) In the end, de Gaulle got nowhere with the Russians, and during his last few years in office his conduct of policy began to look more and more like a private fantasy. Undoubtedly, he left Europe and the Alliance – though not France itself – considerably weaker than he had found them.

As James Burnham had foreseen, containment turned gradually into appeasement. This happened in Germany as it happened everywhere else. For years, Dr Adenauer stood up to Communist pressures with unyielding firmness. He would not compromise. The rigid Hallstein Doctrine upheld the German Federal Republic's claim to be the only legitimate government for the whole of divided Germany. Under it, Bonn would break off relations with any country rash enough to recognise East Germany. But even Konrad Adenauer yielded in time to age, then to death. Some years later Willy Brandt came to power, determined to seek an understanding with the Soviet and East European Communists. In Chapter 5 (Operation 'Détente') we saw the high price he paid for minimal concessions. There was a certain ironical justice in the curious fact that Chancellor Brandt was forced to resign in the wake of the disclosure that his private secretary Günter Guillaume, was an agent of East German intelligence – itself controlled by the KGB.

In their very different ways, and for reasons that had nothing in common with each other, both President de Gaulle and Chancellor Brandt had contributed to the weakening of the West in the face of the continuing pressures of the Soviet Union in World War III. Let us now come back to the leader of the Western Alliance, the United States of America, and take a further look at the Cuban missile crisis of 1962. Underestimating President Kennedy's character, Khrushchev had installed Soviet nuclear missiles on Cuban soil. As everybody knows, he was faced down in the confrontation of October 1962.

The generally accepted view at the time was that the withdrawal of the missiles constituted a major Soviet strategic setback. Undoubtedly it was an important factor in Khrushchev's downfall two years later, but to see this generally satisfactory outcome as an unqualified victory for Kennedy would be an oversimplification. If, of course, Kennedy had failed to get Khrushchev to take the missiles away, this would have been a grave setback for the United States. But the other side of the picture should not be overlooked. The deal that ended the missile crisis brought the Russians two important advances. One was that President Kennedy was forced to give a solemn undertaking to make no further attempt to remove the Castro regime in Cuba. By chancing his arm, therefore, Khrushchev had consolidated Cuba as a long-term Soviet satellite (which, as we have seen, it became some years later). The price the Americans had paid for

Khrushchev's defeat was thus a guarantee for a Soviet client-State.

So conditioned have we become to the unwritten rules of the Third World War that it is very hard for us to grasp the full significance of these circumstances. Perhaps the point will become clearer if we practise what I call 'substitution'. Imagine that instead of Khrushchev persuading Fidel Castro to allow the Russians to install missiles on Cuban soil it was President Kennedy who had persuaded President Kekkonen of Finland to allow the Americans to set up a missiles base on Finnish soil, targeting the missiles on the USSR. In the face of great outrage in the United Nations and the world at large, Khrushchev would have given Kennedy an ultimatum. Hemmed in by hostile political pressures, Kennedy would have climbed down and agreed to withdraw the missiles. However, in return he would have extracted a promise from Khrushchev that never again would the Russians attempt to impose their will on Finland. Henceforth, Finland would be regarded as part of the Western camp – a shrinkage of the Target Area in reverse. Outrageous? Of course, and that is the point. This is the measure of what Khrushchev got away with in the Cuban crisis.

But Khrushchev got something else out of the missile crisis, an even more important advance. This was the withdrawal of American strategic nuclear missiles from Europe – a supposedly reciprocal arrangement in return for the dismantling of the Soviet missile bases in Cuba. At the time, the Americans had a missiles system based in Turkey. Henceforth, they would be withdrawn and Europe would be left less protected than previously, while of course Russia's intermediate-range missile bases in European Russia were left intact.

It is fair to add that this view, which is that of the brilliant French military polymath, General Pierre Gallois, and which I share, is not universally accepted. The critics of Gallois's view point out quite rightly that the American missiles were obsolescent, so that their withdrawal had little immediate effect on the balance of power. Nonetheless, their withdrawal left the European NATO powers utterly dependent strategically on America's inter-continental missiles. Now suppose the Russians launched a conventional offensive against NATO across the central German plain – the traditional invasion route in Europe's chequered history. Would the Americans in their distant fortress unleash their inter-continental missiles at the Soviet Union – and risk their own nuclear annihilation in return? This was the question Europeans started asking themselves. The net outcome of the Cuban missile crisis was thus a drastic reduction in the *credibility* of the American deterrent in European eyes. Moreover, as we have seen, the removal of Khrushchev two years later was immediately followed by a hardening of the Soviet line.

Let us now turn to a more recent and more controversial President of the United States – Richard Nixon. In the dismal succession of events of the early 1970s, President Nixon and his Secretary of State, Dr Henry Kissinger, played a curious joint rôle. That there were serious flaws in Nixon's character was well known long before he became President. But to dismiss him as a twister ('Would *you* buy a secondhand car from Tricky Dicky?' the cynics asked) would be to miss a major dimension of a complex personality. Nixon may well have been a 'twister'; but he was also a strategic thinker, with a greater sense of the meaning and international uses of power than all his post-World War II predecessors, with the single exception of Truman.

A devoted admirer of General de Gaulle, he had something of the same capacity for spectacular initiatives. One such was his decision to seek a rapprochement with China; another, the decision to intensify the precision bombing of North Vietnam in the closing stages of the Vietnam War; and a third, the temporary invasion of Cambodia in the spring of 1970. Yet another decision of Nixon's was to raise the 'alert status' of all US forces – including nuclear ones – during the fourth Arab-Israeli war in October 1973. The China decision has been praised as 'realistic' in that it helped to remove the anomaly whereby that vast country was 'represented' by the small island of Taiwan in the United Nations. But in the terms of reference of the Third World War, the real significance of the Nixon-Kissinger visits to Peking was that it introduced a new element of uncertainty in the Soviet Union's strategic calculations. The full effects of Nixon's fateful decisions remain to be played out, but the fact that it was a kind of setback to the

Russians in their general war of aggression must go on the credit side.

The intensified bombing of North Vietnam, and the decision to invade Cambodia find little support among commentators. In America, the supporters of Nixon are silenced; only his opponents are vocal. The logic of the Cambodian decision was that for years the Vietnamese Communists had operated against South Vietnam from the safe haven of bases in Cambodia. That decision, and the further decision to treble the quantity of bombs rained down on Vietnamese targets, would have made excellent sense if Nixon was 'playing to win' in Indochina. But he, too, was hampered by containment. A strategy of victory would have involved an American invasion of North Vietnam, which neither Nixon nor American public opinion would have countenanced.

In retrospect, these bold decisions are seen as no more than delaying tactics in a strategy of withdrawal. The shadow of Kennan hung over the White House in 1972 as in 1968, 1961, 1956 and all the other fateful dates of World War III. The nuclear alert decision of October 1973, however, deserves unstinted praise. Almost certainly it prevented a Soviet airlift of occupation forces to Egypt. But by then Nixon was already incapable of following a coherent foreign policy. He and Kissinger presided over the Paris Agreements which abandoned America's protégés in South Vietnam, Laos and Cambodia, and the delayed result was the final Communist conquest in the spring of 1975.

Bold and even far-sighted as he was in foreign policy, Nixon was curiously blind to the consequences of his actions nearer home. The break-in at the Watergate Hotel in Washington during the Democratic Party's Convention was in itself a sordid little incident, of relatively little importance. But Nixon tried, with ever more desperate ineptness, to cover up for those involved on White House instructions. In the much more serious crisis that faced General de Gaulle when members of his secret police kidnapped and killed the Moroccan leftist leader, Ben Barka, no more than a ripple disturbed the centre of power in the Elysée Palace. A few dismissals, a few magisterial words, and General de Gaulle sailed on undisturbed.

For reasons that remain mysterious, in a man who must be

credited with intelligence if not with an unblemished character, Richard Nixon not only recorded the sordid goings-on in
the White House on tape, but failed to destroy the tapes while
he had the chance. In itself, the Watergate scandal is not of
direct concern to this book. The point is that it weakened the
President, in the end fatally, and prompted him to bid ever
more desperately for popular support as a man of peace. As
we have seen, President Nixon gave away far more than he
need have done in his summit meetings with Brezhnev in
Moscow, Washington and Santa Barbara, a process which his
successor, President Ford, with Dr Kissinger's counsel,
carried further at the Vladivostok Summit in November 1974.

The shock waves of Watergate went on and on. At first, the
Russians were thrown off balance. Usually they relished
anything that discredited their major adversaries. But this was
too much: they were being deprived of the man who had given
them so many of the things they wanted. For weeks the Soviet
press stayed silent on the Watergate affair, then when at last it
broke silence, attributed the scandal to 'enemies of détente'.

If the 'investigators' had stopped there, the harm Nixon and
his team had done to themselves and the nation could have
been limited, and the democratic processes of the world's most
open society could have found their vindication. But it didn't
stop there. In an orgy of self-flagellation (aided and abetted by
now by the Soviet subversion machine) the journalists and
their Congressional allies wanted to destroy everything that
might in some way or another have contributed to Nixon's
hold on the White House. Thus, the Federal Bureau of In-
vestigation and the Central Intelligence Agency had to be discredited, along with Nixon, Haldemann, Ehrlichman and the
rest of the White House staff.

True, both these secret organisations had unsavoury
episodes and illegalities in their recent histories. They had
been allowed to get away with too much, and it was right they
should be made more clearly accountable for their actions.
(We return to this point in Chapter 10.) But it was neither
necessary nor desirable that the work of the CIA in particular
should be exposed, month after month, and even year after
year. Many of the 'revelations' were patently untrue or exaggerated, and so served only the special interests of the main
enemy, and of the Agency's ideological defectors, Philip Agee

and Victor Marchetti. By 1975 the CIA had been virtually destroyed as an instrument for the execution of American foreign policy, and indeed the Administration's capacity to sustain a policy had suffered grave impairment. The full extent of the damage was laid bare on 18 December 1975, when the US Senate Foreign Relations Committee decided to block CIA funds destined to help non-Marxist nationalist movements in Angola. To his great credit, Dr Kissinger had been pressing for appropriate support to the non-Marxist guerrillas. The Senate decision allowed the Russians to carry on, almost completely unchallenged, their massive arms build-up for the Marxist MPLA. The Russians and their Cuban proxies thereby gained control over this vitally important territory. For good measure, President Ford and his Secretary of State had obligingly reassured the Russians in public that no matter what they did in Angola, deliveries of grain to the Soviet Union would go on. Was this what containment meant? Or had 'containment' become appeasement?

At about the time of the Senate Committee's decision, the new appeasement was being given doctrinal form at a meeting of American ambassadors in London. Both Henry Kissinger and one of his most senior advisers, Helmut Sonnenfeldt, had much to say. And their remarks, of which an official summary was issued after the customary press leakages, constituted the new 'Kissinger-Sonnenfeldt Doctrine'. By then, most of us were accustomed to evidences of the decline of American will. But I, for one, could not have been as fully inured as I had supposed. And I confess that I read subsequent reports of what went on in London in December 1975 with shock and incredulity.

How far our American leaders had travelled on the downward path since the Truman Doctrine of 1947 had brought hope to the oppressed! The new doctrine invited the peoples of Eastern Europe to bury their hopes. There was no way (the official summary put it) to prevent the emergence of the Soviet Union as a super-power. The real problem was the way Soviet power was exerted imperially and globally, which was crude and based on pure force. There were dangerous tensions both within the USSR, arising out of the treatment of non-Russian nationalities, and in Eastern Europe, which was the Soviet Union's natural area of interest, but which accepted the fact only because of the presence of sheer Soviet military power. Kissinger and Sonnenfeldt saw these tensions as a far greater danger to world peace than the East-West conflict. If nothing was done about them, they could lead to what the summary called World War III – that is to a shooting war in which both super-powers would be directly engaged, in other words to what I call World War IV.

What was to be done? Here is a direct quotation, which sets the flavour of the whole. 'In today's circumstances, neither side can gain a strategic advantage that can be translated into political utility. We are doomed to co-existence.'

After the reference to the inevitable emergence of the Soviet Union as a super-power, the summary went on: 'What we can do is to affect the way in which that power is developed and used. Not only can we balance it in the traditional way, but we can affect its usage, and that is what *détente* is all about.'

Specific recommendations followed:

1 The US must strive for a more organic relationship between Eastern Europe and the Soviet Union, with greater national autonomy 'within the context of a strong Soviet geopolitical influence'.

2 Expansion of mutual trade relations, with most-favoured nation status and adequate credits to facilitate Soviet access to the American domestic market.

3 Such measures will make the Soviet Union peaceful and prosperous, so that it ceases to be threatening and adopts moderate policies. Thus instead of exerting its imperial power it will concentrate on improving its domestic economy.

Sixteen years earlier the US Congress had approved its famous 'Captive Nations Resolution', which committed the United States to a shared aspiration for the recovery by the 'captive nations of Eastern Europe of their freedom and independence.' As James Burnham was quick to point out, the new doctrine not only buried this aspiration, it proposed instead that the US should now help the Soviet Union to maintain its hegemony over the same nations. Indeed, it lamented the Soviet failure hitherto to persuade the East Europeans to accept the fact of hegemony for reasons other than force. On this point, this is what the Kissinger-Sonnenfeldt Doctrine had to say:

> The Soviet's inability to acquire loyalty in Eastern Europe is an unfortunate failure, because Eastern Europe is within their scope and area of natural interest. It is doubly tragic that in this area of vital interest and crucial importance it has not been possible for the Soviet Union to establish roots of interest that go beyond sheer power.

I offer my own comments on the new doctrine. The first is that it is an extraordinary example both of the excessive optimism and the unnecessary pessimism that have marked American and allied policy since the end of World War II. 'We are doomed to co-existence', said Kissinger-Sonnenfeldt. One would have expected students of foreign policy of the calibre of Kissinger and Sonnenfeldt to exercise greater care in the avoidance of semantic pitfalls. Were the distinguished authors of the 'doctrine' using the word 'co-existence' in its Western or its Soviet connotation? If the latter, the implication was that the West and indeed the whole Target Area were doomed to put up with Soviet subversion and could do nothing about it. Another note of pessimism was in the clear statement that the US fully recognised (where previously it had rejected) that the Russians were *entitled* to keep the non-Russian nationalities of the USSR under permanent subjection along with the peoples of Eastern Europe. By implication, the Communist governments imposed on the whole area by Soviet power were recognised as legitimate.

One particularly puzzling aspect of the Kissinger-Sonnenfeldt Doctrine was the explicit fear of a shooting war. There was no serious threat of a shooting war in that sense in 1953, when Soviet tanks crushed the East Berlin workers; nor in 1956, when the Hungarian workers were being butchered, nor again in 1968 when the Warsaw Pact powers occupied Czechoslovakia. Why, then should another world war be regarded as the only alternative to 'détente'? The only difference between the 'Cold War' and 'détente' was that the Americans and their European allies had stopped hitting back when attacked.

One aspect of the Kissinger-Sonnenfeldt Doctrine, however, deserves praise: it accurately described the realities of Soviet imperialism. But diagnosis alone is not enough, if the response to the evils diagnosed is marred by excessive pessimism.

To digress for a moment, pessimism in the conduct of foreign policy is not an American monopoly. Similarly, an eminent British diplomat, Sir William Hayter, once wrote one of the most lucid analyses of the character of the Soviet autocracy, but drew pessimistic conclusions from it:

> Ought we to do more, and not lose the Cold War, to go over to the offensive, and win it? I think not. Admittedly, there are arguments of logic in favour of this. After all, if we believe, as I do, that it is the very nature of the Soviet Union that makes peace between it and the rest of the world impossible, it would seem sensible to try and change that régime. But in fact it would only be sensible to try to do this if we saw any possibility of success, and in my view there is none. . . . It seems that we must face the fact that we are now confronted with a period of cold war of indefinite duration, a war which we cannot and should not try to win but need not lose, a war we cannot shorten because the factors prolonging it are outside our control, a war in which we are condemned to be permanently on the defensive.[1]

Sir William went on to say that Western attempts to undermine the Soviet regime would lead only to increased Soviet suspicions and to more active, and probably more effective, Soviet attempts to undermine our own regimes. The message of Sir William Hayter's analysis was therefore one of total pessimism, even though he allowed himself the illogical note of mild optimism in expressing the view that we 'need not lose' a war which by his own admission we could not win.

Pessimistic though it was, the Kissinger-Sonnenfeldt Doctrine also made some strikingly optimistic assumptions. The authors of the Doctrine cherished the delusion that a regime based on force and respecting only counter-force would allow itself to be civilised by a rival super-power. A strange notion,

1 *19th Montague Burton Lecture on International Relations*, University of Leeds, 1961, pp. 9–10.

given the fact that the said rival super-power was explicitly disposed to recognise previous Soviet conquests and acts of arbitrary violence, ready moreover to extend the credits that visibly contributed to the expansion of the already disproportionate Soviet military power. And this in the face of the evidence of the previous 59 years, and particularly of post-Khrushchev Soviet expansionism. There was a similar touching faith in the power of the persuasive example of the United States to cause the collapse of the 'evil' regime of Stalin's day in George Kennan's article in *Foreign Affairs* in 1947. Thus, nearly thirty years after the launching of 'containment' an utterly unrealistic and contradictory policy was formulated by the leading brains of the leading power of the Western Alliance.

7

Know Your Enemy (1)

The enemy is now immensely powerful. But he is not invincible, otherwise there would have been no point in writing this book. The power is there for all to see, if only from the colossal military parades on Red Square and spectacular growth of the Soviet presence on the seas and oceans of the world. And that is only the tip of the iceberg, as we shall see. But, fortunately for us in the Target Area, there are also serious sources of weakness and disunity, which we shall look at in a later chapter.

Here and now, we shall look at the *nature* of the enemy's power, and the *ways* he has of exerting it. Some of the points in this chapter have already been mentioned: this is where the threads are drawn together.

The nature of Soviet power
All powerful states exert their power in some way beyond their borders, and not necessarily by conquest. The acceptance of tributes by smaller countries reflected the power of imperial China, even if the Chinese showed relatively little interest, over long centuries, in conquering distant places. Even a comparatively benign power, the United States, has at times exerted considerable power in wars overseas and in other ways.

It is not, therefore, the fact of power as such, and of exerting it all over the world, that makes the Soviet Union different in kind from other great powers in history. At the heart of Soviet power, and of the threat it represents to all other countries, lies *ideology*. Unless the nature of Soviet ideology is understood, the nature of its power will not be grasped.

As everybody knows, the State ideology of the USSR is Marxism-Leninism, and the nature of the threat which this ideology represents for the rest of the world may be expressed in one sentence: The party that rules over the Union of Soviet Socialist Republics believes that it is entitled, in the name of History, to perpetuate its own power, and to extend it to all other countries in the world.

You will note that there are two main clauses in this sentence, and they correspond fairly neatly to the two halves of 'Marxism-Leninism'. Lenin and his little gang seized power in Russia in November 1917 in the name of Marxism, and in the name of Marxism the leaders of the Communist Party of the Soviet Union justify their perpetual hold on power. From the days of the *Communist Manifesto* of 1848, however, Marxism has transcended national boundaries; and Leninism added two main ingredients to Marxism: a successful technique for seizing power, and a range of techniques for extending the ideology of Marxism-Leninism all over the world. But note one other point: as the original home of the 'first workers' revolution', the Soviet Union itself decides, or claims the right to decide, just what constitutes Marxist-Leninist orthodoxy. In practice, therefore, it is not just the ideology that is exported, but Soviet power.

The easiest way to grasp this vitally important point is to imagine that the 'first workers' revolution' had taken place in, say, Albania. If it had, would Communism have become a world problem? I beg leave to doubt it. Having seized power from the feeble democratic regime that had overthrown the Tsars, Lenin negotiated a separate peace with Germany and consolidated his power through civil war. Churchill tried to overthrow the Bolsheviks, but failed. And today, sixty years on, Lenin's party is still in control, and the whole world is threatened by that fact. For Russia is not Albania.

If Russia, on the other hand, were a kind of gigantic Yugoslavia, ready to dilute its ideology at home and allow its people to travel freely while not attempting seriously to export revolution abroad, then compassionate tears might be shed from time to time over the victims of tyranny in Moscow, Leningrad or Irkutsk, but the rest of the world would have no need to tremble. In such circumstances, the term 'the Target Area' would have no relevance. But that is not the way things are. From the start, Lenin's gang kept his people imprisoned and kept the foreigners out. Stalin and his successors have carried on the same policy, essentially unchanged. To doubt the *legitimacy* of Marxism-Leninism would be to imperil the party's hold on power. So whatever the evidence, and however cynical its denial inevitably makes the ruling group, the basic tenets of the ideology must be constantly reaffirmed. And the ideology must be exported, not only because the export of it is part of the ideology itself, but so that the world can be made safe for Soviet communism.

Objectives and techniques

I shall not attempt a full analysis of Leninism, let alone of all the twists and turns of ideology since Lenin died in 1924. I shall instead simply pick out a few essential points which are still fully valid today, more than half a century after his death.

1 'The ultimate aim of the Communist International is to replace the world capitalist economy by a world system of Communism' (*Programme of the Communist International*, 1924.)

2 'The successful struggle of the Communist International for the dictatorship of the proletariat presupposes the existence in every country of a compact Communist Party, hardened in the struggle, disciplined, centralised and closely linked up with the masses' (*Programme*).

3 '. . . it is most important to have the strictest international discipline in the Communist ranks. This international Communist discipline must find expression in the subordination of the partial and local interests of the movement to its general and lasting interests and in the strict fulfilment, by all members, of the decisions passed by the leading bodies of the Communist International' (*Programme*).

4 'Every sacrifice must be made, the greatest obstacles must be overcome, in order to carry on agitation and propaganda systematically, stubbornly and patiently, precisely in all those institutions, societies and associations to which proletarian or semi-proletarian masses belong, however ultra-reactionary they may be. And the trade unions and workers' co-operatives (the latter, at least sometimes), are precisely the organisations in which the masses are to be found' (*Left-wing Communism: an Infantile Disorder*, Lenin, 1920).

5   '. . . revolutionaries who are unable to combine illegal
forms of struggle with every form of legal struggle are very
bad revolutionaries . . . .' (Lenin, op. cit.)
6   'To carry on a war for the overthrow of the international
bourgeoisie, and to refuse beforehand to manoeuvre, to
utilise the conflict of interests among one's enemies, to
refuse to temporise and compromise with possible allies – is
not this ridiculous in the extreme? We might have to go in
zigzags, sometimes retracing our steps, sometimes abandoning the course once selected and trying various others.'
(Quoted in *Trends in Russian Policy since WWI*, p. 65;
Legislative Reference Service, Library of Congress;
Government Printing Office, Washington, 1947.)

Let me summarise these six points in non-ideological
language:

1   Non-Communist regimes everywhere must be overthrown, and Communist regimes approved by Moscow set
up in their place.
2   The revolution will be made everywhere by disciplined
Communist Parties.
3   These parties will obey the directives of the Communist
International, that is, of Moscow.
4   Communists must penetrate democratic organisations
and use them for agitation and propaganda.
5   They must work both within and outside the law.
6   They must be prepared to change course at any time, if
necessary reaching temporary compromises.

Lenin's instrument for world revolution was of course the
Third (Communist) International, which he founded in 1919,
and which is better known as the Comintern. Although the
Comintern was formally dissolved in 1943, its work was
resumed immediately after World War II (see below). The
first three direct quotations above are from the Programme
drafted at the Fifth Congress in 1924, and adopted four years
later at the Sixth Congress. The surprising thing is that so
much of it remains in force half a century later. As recently as
1972, for instance, the Soviet Communist Party published an
officially approved book, *The International Communist Movement*,

edited by V. V. Zagladin, a deputy head of the International
Department of the CPSU's Central Committee. In it, Lenin is
quoted approvingly to the effect that the essence of inter-
nationalism is support of revolutionary struggle 'through
propaganda, sympathy or materially . . . in all countries
without exception.' The more recent articles by B.
Ponomarev, head of the International Department, quoted in
Chapter 4 of this book under the subtitle 'The World
Revolutionary Process', are pure Leninism.

All this is not to deny that Moscow has had a lot of trouble
from Communist Parties that do not want to recognise
Moscow's supreme authority. But in Moscow itself the dogma
goes on unchanged.

It is instructive in other respects to re-read the *Programme of
the Communist International*, for one of the most striking things
about it is that some of Lenin's most cherished prophetic
assumptions have been totally disproved by events. For example, in Section 4 the Programme says: 'The capitalist system
as a whole is approaching its final collapse.' It is quite clear
from the context that Lenin did not expect the abhorred
system to be alive and, in economic terms, flourishing fifty
years later. Again: 'The law of uneven development of
capitalism, which becomes intensified in the epoch of imperialism, renders firm and durable international combina-
tions of imperialist powers impossible.' Well, what about
NATO, born in 1949 and still going strong (even if it is in need
of change and renewal)?

A very important point emerges here. Even when events disprove the assumptions of Marxism-Leninism (as has been the
case in many areas), not only is the dogma not rejected, but it
is reaffirmed. The dogma, in fact, *can't* be abandoned (though
it can be and is modified from time to time) for it is the *only*
claim to legitimacy of the ruling party in the Soviet Union and
of ruling Communist Parties wherever they may be (including
countries hostile to Moscow, such as China). The pressures
for world revolution go on relentlessly, and if at any time they
appear to have abated, the abatement is purely tactical
because conditions are judged temporarily unfavourable.
Communists never give up. That is why even a Communist Party
small in numbers (as in Great Britain) remains dangerous at
all times.

One last point before we leave ideology. It was clear to Lenin himself in the last two or three years of his life and after revolutionary attempts in Germany, Hungary and elsewhere had failed, that world revolution was *not* (despite the Comintern's Programme) just around the corner. Without abandoning his dogma that war between the two camps (capitalist and Communist) was inevitable, he settled down in practice to what was going to be a fairly prolonged interim period, during which it might be necessary to conclude treaties with the capitalist powers and trade with them to the advantage of the revolutionary homeland. It was his Commissar for Foreign Affairs, G. V. Chicherin, who coined the useful label for this period, the duration of which was left undefined to avoid the embarrassment of a further unfulfilled prophecy. It was to be called 'peaceful co-existence'. In Lenin's mind, 'peaceful co-existence' would inevitably end one day in general war and world revolution. So 'peaceful co-existence', however long it lasted, could not be more than a temporary situation, for the convenience of the revolutionaries.

Human nature being what it is, the countries of the Target Area have gone on hoping that the temporary could be made permanent, that the Marxist-Leninists would give up Marxism-Leninism, that the two systems would 'converge', that the cow would jump over the moon and that other improbable things would happen.

The advent of nuclear weapons shook the ideologists of revolution, especially in Moscow, and particularly when America had a monopoly of these world-destroying devices. Would the dogma of inevitable war have to go? Well, yes, it would, and it did when Khrushchev told the 20th Congress of the CPSU in 1956 that 'there is no fatal inevitability of war'. Here was a situation unprecedented in history and quite unforeseen by the great prophet Lenin. So 'revolutionary', in another sense, was this new dogma that the party hacks in Moscow had to be given time to get used to it. Finally, the new dogma was spelt out and worked into Chapter VIII of the new Party Programme adopted by the 22nd Congress on 31 October 1961.

So 'peaceful co-existence' subtly changed its meaning. It was still a *temporary* phase until the capitalist system should collapse and yield to Communism, but it was now argued that this could happen without general war. The world, however, would go on being divided into two irreconcilable 'camps', and there could never be any ideological co-existence between them. Indeed, to mark the point, the world Communist conference at the end of 1960 (the last major gathering of Communist Parties at which the Chinese party had been present) ruled that peaceful co-existence implied the intensification of the international class struggle (that is, of what we in the West would call the cold war). These helpful sentiments are reiterated several times a year by Soviet leaders or commentators, and in party pronouncements. After all, they know, even if we choose to ignore, that there is a Third World War on. And we cannot say we have not been warned.

Machinery and techniques

Everybody has heard of the KGB, but very few people would know that the initials RIS stand for Russian Intelligence Service. Of course there is no such organisation, nor do the Russians use the term, which is a creation of Western Intelligence services to represent the permanent reality behind the KGB (Committee of State Security), which is only the latest in a long series of sinister initials, the best known of which are CHEKA, OGPU, NKVD and MVD. Now that the crimes committed in the Soviet Union are common knowledge, Communists everywhere cultivate the habit of blaming it all on Stalin. Yet it was Lenin who set up the CHEKA (from two initial letters in its long name: All-Russian Extraordinary Commission for the Struggle against Counter-Revolution and Sabotage) as early as 19 December 1917, only a few weeks after the Bolshevik Revolution.

Despite the accusations hurled at the American CIA (some of them true, as I have said), there is no organisation like the KGB in the Western world. Vishinsky, the Public Prosecutor of Stalin's purge trials, used to call it, 'the naked sword of the revolution'. Even Hitler's Gestapo lacked the sweeping powers of the KGB. At home, it is the all-powerful instrument of repression of the Soviet State and party, with its own courts and operating outside the Constitution. It runs prisons, labour camps and psychiatric wards. It has its own private army (the Border Guards) and special units within the armed forces: indeed, it has a spying organisation within the armed forces to

detect and suppress the slightest sign of opposition to the
regime.

Outside, it is a gigantic spying organisation, probably
bigger than the CIA and all Western intelligence services put
together. And it stops at nothing, recruiting by terror, bribery
or blackmail, murdering enemies and eliminating defectors.
But again, it is more, much more, than an intelligence system.
A special Disinformation Department of the KGB spends its
time spreading untrue rumours, about itself, about other intelligence services, about Soviet policy or about the policy of a
given Western government, forcing rival services to divert time
and effort to chasing red herrings; smearing opponents and
above all influencing public opinion in Western countries in
directions helpful to the Soviet leadership in their conduct of
World War III.

Of all the functions of the KGB, this last one is the one that
the Western public has most trouble in understanding. Of all
fronts in the Third World War, this is the one most blatantly
loaded against the Target Area, and especially against the
Western democracies. For all practical purposes, it is impossible for, say, the CIA or British Intelligence to plant agents in
the USSR who will propagate Western ideas or undermine
Soviet policies. Because of the all-pervasive secret police, such
people would almost instantly be found out. Not so in the
'goldfish bowl' societies of the West, which are wide open to
the work of Soviet 'agents of influence'. Indeed in Third World
War terms, the agent of influence is at least as important as
the old-fashioned spy. By definition, pluralist societies are
tolerant of all, or most, political views. And no doubt one
reason why they are now so tolerant of people expressing
views that further Soviet intrests is that agents of influence
have done their work so thoroughly over the years.

What, then, is an agent of influence? In the strictest sense,
he or she is somebody recruited by the KGB and consciously
prepared to spread views in line with Soviet requirements, in
their capacity as journalists, deputies or MPs, high officials or
even Ministers. But for one *conscious* agent of influence, there
must be a dozen unconscious ones – people in various walks of
life who repeat what the real agents of influence have fed
them, or who attend Soviet embassy parties and absorb pro-
Soviet views, businessmen anxious to trade in Russia, etc. In

Britain and some other Western countries, incidentally, *it is not a punishable offence to be a Soviet agent of influence, even a conscious and paid one.* Needless to say, this anomaly plays into the hands of the KGB.

The agent of influence is very hard to detect. In his book on the KGB, John Barron gives an extraordinary example of a very senior French diplomat who was recruited as an agent of influence, but detected before he could do any harm through the confession of a Soviet defector. If the story were not true, it would be hard to credit. The senior diplomat was M. Maurice Dejean, who was recruited in the nastiest possible way while serving as France's ambassador in Moscow. The poor man fell straight into a KGB sex trap, seduced by a planted woman agent, photographed in a compromising situation and even being beaten up by the woman's 'husband' (another KGB agent). He was to return to Paris and influence General de Gaulle in a pro-Soviet direction. The General, however, was alerted and fired him in 1964. It is unfortunately very likely (as mentioned in an earlier chapter) that the KGB did later succeed in planting an agent in the Elysée Palace. This story, and others like it, make one wonder just how many Soviet agents of influence operate in high positions in Western governments.

In recent years, the KGB and its military counterpart, the GRU, have increasingly turned their attention to industrial espionage, in search of the secrets of Western technology and know-how. Given the readiness, and even the eagerness, of Western governments to give away their technology, or sell it on easy terms, to the USSR, one would have thought that the incentive of industrial espionage would be much reduced. But no: the appetite of the enemy is insatiable. What is not freely available must be stolen or bribed into Soviet possession.

It would be an exaggeration to say that in the face of such admirable persistence the governments of the West simply turn the other way, but only a slight one. Every now and again a spy or two will be deported after being caught red-handed in some act of espionage. There will be a brief flurry in the press, and usually, a few days later, the Russians will very ostentatiously declare *non grata* exactly the same number of diplomats from the embassy of the country concerned. Very rarely, a Western government will react more spectacularly.

There has still been nothing to compare with the decision of the Heath Government in September 1971 to send 105 KGB or GRU men packing. In general, the public applauded this unprecedented boldness, made possible by the fact that bold people happened to be in the right positions at that time, not least the Foreign and Commonwealth Office, where Sir Alec Douglas-Home was the Secretary of State. On the Labour benches, of course, some nervous spirits (and perhaps some supporters of the other side) tut-tutted. Fears were expressed that diplomatic relations would be broken off, that war even might be declared. And yet, not to the surprise of students of Soviet behaviour, Moscow's reaction was remarkably feeble. In numerical terms, strict reciprocity was impossible anyway, for the personnel of the British Embassy in Moscow numbered 35 at that time. Before the expulsions, there were no fewer than 550 Soviet officials in Britain – more than in any other Western country, including the United States. Not all of them, of course, were 'diplomats'; others were members of trade or scientific missions and the like. It was officially believed at the time that no fewer than 75 per cent of the actual embassy staff in London consisted of intelligence officers under diplomatic cover.

In this situation, what could the Russians do? They did expel some British diplomats, and they drew up a list of British citizens in various walks of life who, they said, would henceforth be barred from visiting the Soviet Union. A number of these had not been near the place for years, and had no intention of returning anyway. The 'strain' in Anglo-Soviet relations that followed, and lasted until the return of the Wilson Government in 1974, simply reflected a real situation.

The staggering increase in Soviet representation of all kinds had become a major problem to Western governments in the early 1970s. Most of them did precious little about it. According to figures released in 1972, the overall total for Western Europe had risen to 2,146, from 1,485 ten years earlier – an increase of about 50 per cent. It was not difficult to show that the Russians did infinitely more spying on the West than the West could possibly have been doing in the Soviet Union. There were about six times as many Soviet officials in West European countries than West European ones in Moscow.

At the absolute minimum, more than a third of the Soviet officials of all kinds were working for the KGB and GRU. For embassy staffs – as mentioned – the figure was about 75 per cent. What this meant was that in NATO countries, of every four Soviet officials accredited as diplomats, three were spies of one kind or another. And the trend was upward. By 1976, about 150 Soviet spies had been identified in France, compared with 118 in 1972. In West Germany the figure had risen from 82 to 95, but there was a considerably increased espionage presence from East Germany or from the new Soviet Consulate-General in West Berlin. Between 2,000 and 3,000 East German agents were operating in the Federal Republic. Even in neutral Switzerland the figure for identified Soviet spies had risen from 87 to more than 100. In the United Kingdom, the situation was unclear, but was certainly healthier than anywhere else as a result of the expulsion of the 105. However, 'industrial inspectors' had been arriving from the Soviet Union in connection with trade contracts, and it would have been surprising if they had not included the usual proportion of KGB and GRU personnel.

The situation in the Irish Republic is of special interest. Unlike other Western countries, the Irish did not recognise the Soviet Union until September 1973, when embassies were opened in Dublin and Moscow. The Irish embassy in Moscow was . . . just an embassy, for what chance did the small Irish Republic have of spying on the great USSR? The Soviet embassy in Dublin, on the other hand, was immediately used for espionage purposes, and in December 1975 the Dublin correspondent of the Soviet news agency, Vladimir Kozlov, was identified as a member of Department V of the KGB – responsible for assassination and sabotage. About nine other KGB operatives, working under diplomatic cover, were uncovered as well.

One might reasonably conclude from these figures that the situation in Western Europe was pretty bad. But it was much, much worse in the United States. There, the KGB and GRU enjoyed privileges and facilities beyond the dreams of the most sanguine intelligence organisation. An enormous amount of material was publicly available anyway, requiring only the time, patience and organisation to deal with it. But the biggest anomaly of all was the fact that the United Nations had its

headquarters in New York. This single fact made nonsense of
the restrictions imposed by the State Department on the
movement of Soviet diplomats in the embassy in Washington
– in return for similar restrictions on the movements of
American diplomats in Moscow. For once a Soviet official was
accredited to the UN, he became an international civil servant
and could roam the length and breadth of the USA without let
or hindrance. About half of the 1,000 or so Soviet officials in
the United States were based in New York – most of them in
the UN. This made New York the biggest Soviet spy centre in
the world.

The Report of the Rockefeller Commission in 1975 estimated that about 40 per cent of all Communist government
officials in the USA were intelligence officers. In the case of the
Soviets, this meant at the time that there were about 370 KGB
or GRU operatives in the United States. Nor was this all: not
only did the Americans make things easy for their Soviet spies,
they also made it as difficult as possible for their own counter-
espionage agencies to do their work. The CIA had been
reduced to impotence by the extraordinary spate of 'revelations' or 'exposures' by the press and media, and by a number
of official enquiries. but the FBI, too, was handicapped. The
UN premises, for example, were out of bounds to the FBI,
leaving the field wide open to the KGB.

For years, one of the top KGB men, Viktor M. Lessiovsky,
operated from UN headquarters. The late U Thant, on
becoming UN Secretary-General in 1961, had appointed
Lessiovsky his Personal Assistant, having known him earlier
when the Russian was serving in Burma. Doubtless U Thant
was unaware that Lessiovsky was a high-ranking KGB officer.
When Lessiovsky left the UN in 1973, he was succeeded as
Special Assistant to the Secretary-General by Valery
Krepkogorsky, himself a KGB General.

Another natural target for the KGB was the US Congress –
and here again its work was made easy by the extraordinary
growth of Congressional staffs, many of them young men of
left-wing views who had flocked there in the wake of their successful opposition to the Vietnam War. On 17 June 1975,
Senator Henry Jackson declared: 'There is no doubt in my
mind that the KGB is showing closer interest in Congress than
ever before and has established a spy network on Capitol Hill.'

Another quote. In February 1975, Mr Clarence Kelley of the FBI stated: 'Soviet bloc official representation in this country has tripled during the last fifteen years while their intelligence agents have increased fourfold.'

The reference to the 'Soviet bloc' is significant. It should never be forgotten that the work of the KGB is supplemented – often very effectively – by the intelligence services of the East European satellites, especially the Czechs, the East Germans, the Hungarians and the Poles. The Czech defector, Josef Frolik, revealed in his book, *The Frolik Defection*, that he had built up a network of contacts among British trade unionists and Labour MPs.

It was largely through the skilled and careful de-briefing of defectors that Western security and intelligence services patiently, over the years, built up a reliable, though necessarily incomplete, picture of Soviet and East European espionage activities. Josef Frolik, mentioned above, was on such source. Another one, in recent times, was the young Soviet KGB man, Aleksei Myagkov (mentioned in Chapter 6), whose distinctive value was that he was the first defector from the Third Chief Directorate of the KGB, which operates within the armed forces. His revelations may be read in his short book, *Inside the KGB*, published in various languages in 1977.

Collating such revelations is uphill work, for the KGB has no public relations department, and the Soviet Union is a closed society. The fullest and most authentic publicly available account of the Soviet secret political police and intelligence organisations is in John Barron's book, *KGB*. With the vast resources of the *Reader's Digest* empire behind him, Barron travelled the world, meeting defectors and prising secrets out of friendly security and intelligence services. The picture that emerges of this huge and ruthless organisation makes chilling reading. It is now known, however, that powerful though it is the KGB does not give the orders when it comes to subversion all over the world as laid down by Lenin in the early days of the Comintern.

What happened was this: Stalin's dissolution of the Comintern in 1943 was purely cosmetic. The Allies may have been reassured, but the international subversive apparatus of the Soviet Union remained fully operative. It was reorganised and expanded as soon as possible after World War II – to be precise, in 1946. By that time World War III was getting into its stride, and the most sophisticated methods of subversion were going to be needed. Stalin, flushed with victory, was more than ever in control – not only in the USSR itself but in all countries in which there was a Communist party. It was at this time that ingenious methods of syphoning off funds from commercial transactions throughout the world were devised, for the use of agencies of the Soviet Union and for the future use of other Communist governments – most of which, in Eastern Europe, were established after that date under Operation Satellite 1.

The main recipients were – and still are – the Western Communist Parties. Indeed, contrary to the popular belief, ever since World War III began most non-ruling Parties have been heavily dependent upon secret Soviet subsidies. In some cases, up to two-thirds of their income has come from Moscow. Apart from direct cash grants, the methods include:

Payment of inflated commissions or prices to firms controlled by non-ruling Communist Parties.

The provision of goods free or at low cost for sale by Communist Parties. The European Common Market's 'butter mountain' has benefited the French Communist Party from time to time in this way in deals by Communist businessmen involving sales (at dumping prices) to the Soviet Union, yielding 'commissions' that are ploughed back into party funds.

Direct gifts of various goods, including capital equipment, for use by the West European Parties. These include cars and lorries; printing plant and newsprint, propaganda material, Marxist-Leninist training manuals, books and articles for distribution.

In addition to printing equipment and paper, Party newspapers and journals in the Western countries receive direct cash subsidies and large orders for apparently commercial purposes, such as display advertisements, job printing costs, and not least, standing orders for large numbers of Party publications.

This background of secret subsidies from Moscow should oe borne in mind as a corrective to all the current and facile talk about 'Eurocommunism' (implying independence from Moscow). Europe's biggest and most loudly 'Eurocommunist' Party, the Italian PCI, remains heavily dependent on Soviet aid. The PCI was naturally the main beneficiary of the new financing arrangements set up after World War II. In the 1950s, millions of dollars in American banknotes reached the Party from Moscow after being channelled through individuals. One of these was said to be the late Giangiacomo Feltrinelli, the left-wing publisher who later committed suicide.

Today, the Italian Party controls profitable companies, such as Restital of Milan and its subsidiary Sorimpex, which act as middlemen to Italian businessmen wishing to deal with the Soviet bloc and which take a cut for their services. Moreover, Sorimpex in particular deals in gold, copper, diamonds and other precious stones – one of the secret funding devices perfected in 1946. According to some sources, secret subsidies from Moscow to the PCI amount to between 25 and 35 per cent of its budget. According to another estimate, the actual amount received is now about $5 million a year (considerably less than twenty years ago, but still a substantial sum).

In this context, the case of Britain's *Morning Star* is worth looking at. Between one-quarter and one-third of the paper's daily circulation is taken by the Soviet Union. At the very least, the daily purchase is of 12,000 copies, representing about £220,000 a year at 6p each. This far exceeds the monthly collection of £5,000 to £6,000 in donations from supporters. At times this hidden subsidy may have reached a daily purchase of 20,000 copies by the USSR. This, too, must colour one's view of the 'independence' of Britain's Communist Party.

The chart illustrated here shows at a glance the principal ramifications of Moscow's enormous subversive apparatus. Officially, Ponomarev's International Department is charged simply with relations with non-Communist Parties. But its hidden functions are much wider. Where subversion (as distinct from espionage and repression at home) is concerned, the KGB gets its instructions from the International Depart-

The subversive apparatus of the Soviet Union

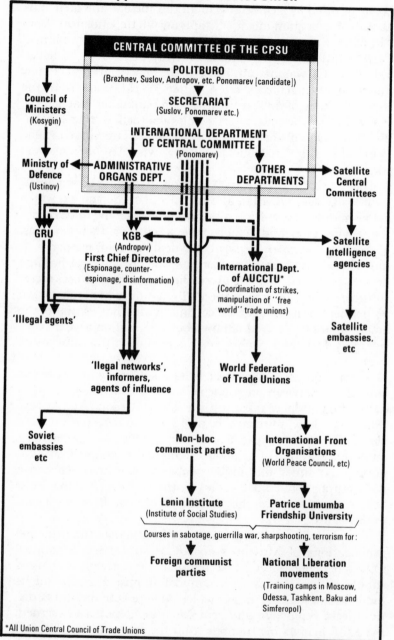

CENTRAL COMMITTEE OF THE CPSU

POLITBURO
(Brezhnev, Suslov, Andropov, etc. Ponomarev [candidate])

SECRETARIAT
(Suslov, Ponomarev etc.)

INTERNATIONAL DEPARTMENT
OF CENTRAL COMMITTEE
(Ponomarev)

Council of
Ministers
(Kosygin)

Ministry of
Defence
(Ustinov)

ADMINISTRATIVE
ORGANS DEPT.

OTHER
DEPARTMENTS

Satellite
Central
Committees

GRU

KGB
(Andropov)
First Chief Directorate
(Espionage, counter-
espionage, disinformation)

International Dept.
of AUCCTU*
(Coordination of strikes,
manipulation of "free
world" trade unions)

Satellite
Intelligence
agencies

'Illegal agents'

Satellite
embassies.
etc

'Illegal networks',
informers,
agents of influence

World Federation
of Trade Unions

Soviet
embassies
etc

Non-bloc
communist parties

International Front
Organisations
(World Peace Council, etc)

Lenin Institute
(Institute of Social Studies)

Patrice Lumumba
Friendship University

Courses in sabotage, guerrilla war, sharpshooting, terrorism for:

Foreign communist
parties

National Liberation
movements
(Training camps in Moscow,
Odessa, Tashkent, Baku and
Simferopol)

*All Union Central Council of Trade Unions

ment. So does the GRU. Through the International Department, the Central Committee controls the Central Committees of satellite Communist Parties and through them the satellite intelligence services and embassies.

Confusingly, there is another 'International Department' – whose functions are distinct from Ponomarev's. This is the International Department of the Soviet 'Trade Union' Federation, known as the All-Union Central Council of Trade Unions (AUCCTU). This other International Department specialises in industrial subversion. It runs a very large and well-equipped research section, with about a hundred researchers for Western Europe alone (10 or 12 for each major country). The Department is constantly on the look out for recruitable trade union leaders in the West European countries – that is, those who will co-operate with the Soviet Central Committee in return for money or for fear of blackmail. It is in receipt of precise reports on individual industrial disputes in Britain, France, Italy and other countries prepared by the local Communist Parties. With this information, it is able to decide when and where to launch an internationally-co-ordinated strike, for instance the simultaneous car workers' strikes in Britain, France, Germany and Italy in April 1975. Ideally, the Russians would like to bring the West European trade union organisations under their direct control. This would mean a return to the situation that briefly prevailed during earlier years in World War III. In February 1945 – before the end of World War II – the British Trades Union Congress took the initiative by calling a preparatory conference in London to set up a World Federation of Trade Unions (WFTU). The first President was Sir Walter Citrine – who of course was no Communist, but didn't know what was about to happen. A well-known French Communist, Louis Saillant, was appointed Secretary-General of the WFTU and soon packed his Secretariat with fellow-Communists. The British, American and Dutch trade unionists fought hard against Communist control, but it was a losing battle.

In January 1949, the British TUC, the American CIO and the Dutch MVV pulled out of the WFTU and later set up a non-Communist international body called the International Confederation of Free Trade Unions (ICFTU). Originally the WFTU had made its headquarters in Paris, but in 1951 the

French Government expelled it for subversive activities. It moved over to the Soviet sector of Vienna, then under four-power occupation. But after Austria had regained its independence, the government ordered the expulsion of the WFTU for endangering Austrian neutrality. Since then the WFTU's headquarters have been in Prague – along with a number of other international Communist 'front organisations', all more or less controlled from Moscow.

It is important to put 'trade unions' in quotation marks where referring to the Soviet labour organisations. In the Western sense, they are not trade unions at all but coercive organs of the State at the disposal of the ruling party. Their mission is to keep the workers in line, make sure they fulfil the norms laid down by the planning bureaucrats and force acceptance of the party line. There is no free collective bargaining and strikes are not so much forbidden as simply unthinkable: in theory, the Soviet workers own the means of production. It is therefore argued that they cannot strike against themselves.

Their 'ownership' of factories and machines is, of course, purely notional, and the notion is easily dispelled if one asks the simple question: 'Can they sell the factories and machines?' It is enough to ask it to demonstrate the absurdity of the proposition. In fact, however, there *are* strikes from time to time, as we occasionally learn long after the event from the smuggled typewritten documents of Soviet dissidents. One workers' riot, in 1972, was crushed with heavy loss of life by the Soviet military.

Appropriately, the Soviet 'trade union' organisation was for some years under the direction of a former head of the KGB, Aleksander Shelepin. (It is rather as though an ex-head of the American FBI, the late J. Edgar Hoover, let us say, was appointed head of the AFL/CIO.) An energetic man, Shelepin sought to restore the links with Western trade unions that had been severed in 1949. He began making speeches about the need to set up an all-European trade union body encompassing both Communist and non-Communist countries. Operation détente gave a big boost to his plans. Vic Feather (later Lord Feather), the anti-Communist General Secretary of the British TUC, was misguided enough to visit Moscow as Shelepin's guest in December 1972. A few weeks later, Heinz

O. Vetter, chairman of the West German DGB (the trade union organisation), did likewise.

Shelepin was doing very well, and he did even better in January 1974, when he attended the first East-West trade union meeting since 1949, held in Geneva. In December that year, Soviet and East German 'trade unionists' came to London for a conference of car workers which, despite British press reports to the contrary, was 'sponsored by Soviet metal industry workers' (as Warsaw Radio put it with obliging frankness). At the end of February 1975, a second East-West trade union conference took place in Geneva.

The high point of Shelepin's campaign was to have been his visit to Britain in April 1975, which, however, turned sour. The fact that a man like Shelepin could have been invited to Britain by the TUC in itself reflected the pace of the Soviet victories in the Third World War. Not only had Shelepin been head of the KGB, he was personally implicated in murder in Germany. He knew nothing from experience about labour organisations when appointed head of the spurious Soviet 'trade unions'. On several occasions, he had had the effrontery to hand money to British trade unionists on strike: to give one example, on 11 August 1972, Jimmy Reid, at that time the Communist secretary of the Scottish Dock Workers' Union (he has since left the Communist Party), was quoted by Moscow Radio as thanking the Soviet authorities for a grant of £17,000 to his union for strike action. (Try 'substitution' and imagine the TUC attempting to grant the equivalent sum in roubles to striking workers in the Leningrad shipyards.) But now, in the words of Len Murray, the new General Secretary of the TUC, the time had come for 'the normalisation of relations' between the Western trade unions and the Eastern 'trade unions' (my quotation marks, not Murray's).

As it happened, enough people were indignant about the Shelepin visit to spoil the operation. Hostile demonstrations forced him to enter TUC headquarters by the back door, and cut his stay short to fly home. And he was scarcely back in Moscow than he was sacked from his 'trade union' job. I wish I could add that this was the end of the Soviet attempt to woo Britain's trade unions, but it was not. Instead, visits by British trade union delegations to their East European or Soviet 'counterparts' became a regular routine.

Front organisations have always played an important part in the subversive aspects of World War III. What is a front organisation? Lenin used to call them 'transmission belts' to the masses. Essentially, a front organisation is something other than it appears to be, an organisation including non-Communists as well as Communists and manipulated behind the scenes by Communists. You can have local fronts, national ones and international ones. Apart from the WFTU, in which the Soviet AUCCTU has a direct interest, the best known is probably the World Peace Council, which is controlled by Ponomarev's International Department. Over the years, the WPC has sponsored many conferences and resolutions, mostly designed to show the Soviet Union as 'peace-loving' and the 'imperialist' USA as 'warmongering'. Many respectable but naive public figures, such as Bertrand Russell, have lent their names or signatures to such exercises. A small example of a WPC subversive operation was the 'Anti-Imperialist Festival' held in Dublin and Belfast in August 1974. Ostensibly, the 'Festival' was sponsored by the official Sinn Fein, political wing of the Irish Republican Army (IRA), but the real conveners were the WPC and all the publicity material was paid for by the Russians.

If you look at the lower end of the chart in this chapter, you will notice parallel lines leading to two so-called educational establishments: the Lenin Institute and the Patrice Lumumba Friendship University, both in Moscow. As defectors and non-Communist trainees have revealed, both organisations provide cover for intensive courses in terrorism, guerrilla war, street fighting, assassination, sabotage, sharpshooting, bomb-making and explosives, and the rest of the sinister paraphernalia of the politics of violence.

We have already looked at Operation Terrorism (Chapter 4), but I now add some organisational details. Systematic courses in the techniques of violent revolution have been on offer in the Soviet Union to selected Communists since 1967, but the fact has only been known since 1973. The courses are run by the Lenin Institute, which has a string of alternative names: the Institute of Social Sciences, the Institute of Social Studies, and the International School of Marxism-Leninism – all interchangeable and all referring to an organisation under the direct control of the Soviet Communist Party's Central Committee. The Rector of the Institute is F. D. Ryshenko. The teaching staff consists entirely of members of the party or the Komsomol youth organisation.

Each course lasts six months and at any given time between 300 and 600 men, and some women, are enrolled. They come from Latin America, the Arab world, Western and southern Europe, Asia and Africa. Although the students are kept under constant KGB surveillance, they enjoy élite privileges, such as the right to go to the top of the queue at 'full' Moscow restaurants. If a student tangles with the police, he shows his card and is immediately released. He may later, however, be punished within the closed world of the Lenin Institute.

Non-Communist terrorist trainees are processed through the Patrice Lumumba University, and sent to camps in Moscow, and at Tashkent, Simferopol, Baku and Odessa. Many, however, go as far afield as North Korea, which has trained several thousand terrorists on behalf of the Soviet Union. That way, 'National Liberation' gets a special Marxist twist. In the long-term such tactics have provided Moscow with a strategic payoff, most notably in the ex-Portuguese territories of Angola, Mozambique and Guinea-Bissau, where terrorists trained in Russia are now in power.

These, then, are the hidden dimensions of the colossal Soviet war effort in World War III, powerfully supplementing the psychological and military threat visibly represented by the armed forces, nuclear panoply and expanding sea power. The threat is ubiquitous and many-sided. If it is thought of in military terms alone, the most effective dimensions are left out of Western calculations.

8

What Are We Defending?

On 3 September 1939, Britain and France declared war on
Germany. Yet each of the two at that time had a government
that was the opposite of bellicose. Why, then, did they declare
war?

It was a complex situation, which I do not propose to
analyse in detail, but some of the relevant facts were these.
France was weak and divided, and led by men who were still
obsessed by the dreadful losses of World War I and had no
stomach for the fight. The army was large, but under the command of men who systematically rejected the technological
challenge of modern war. The Prime Minister, Edouard
Daladier, had signed the Munich agreement with Neville
Chamberlain, appeasing Hitler at the expense of
Czechoslovakia.

In Britain, Chamberlain himself clung very late to the illusion that war could be prevented; which is another way of saying that he went on hoping, long after the evidence to the contrary had reached mountainous heights, that Hitler was other
than he was. As for Hitler, having remilitarised the
Rhineland, he had grabbed Austria and Czechoslovakia. Was
he now about to attack Poland?

The unbellicose governments in London and Paris had
pledged themselves to defend Poland against aggression. The
French pledge was indeed of long standing. As far back as
1921, the Franco-Polish Treaty provided for mutual assistance
in case of attack. In 1925, the Locarno Conference had yielded
a number of pacts including Franco-Polish and Franco-
Czechoslovak treaties of mutual assistance in case of attack by
Germany. All this, of course, had happened years before
Hitler had come to power. Now, however, on 19 May 1939,
France made a precise commitment of military assistance to

Poland in the event of a German attack. Some weeks earlier, on 31 March, Chamberlain had told Parliament that his government would defend Polish independence.

Between those two dates – on 7 April – Mussolini had invaded Albania, providing a brief diversion from the fascination exerted by Hitler. He had timed his mini-aggression with exquisite cynicism, for (as Churchill pointed out in a splendid speech in the House of Commons) 7 April was Good Friday, and the Fascist dictator knew all about Britain's regard for the long Easter week-end, and was equally aware that the British Navy was otherwise engaged in routine manoeuvres long announced. On the 27th, however, stung perhaps by Churchill's constant prodding, and also by his able Secretary of State for War, Hore-Belisha, the Prime Minister announced conscription, in the face of pacifist demurrings from Labour and the Liberal party.

Now let us be quite clear why Chamberlain had guaranteed to defend Poland, and why Daladier had given a precise form to his country's existing pledges. The Anglo-French guarantees did not mean that these peace-minded politicians had suddenly become warmongers. They meant instead that they hoped, even at this late hour, to bring Hitler to his senses. This was also the meaning of conscription in Britain. Chamberlain and Daladier were serving notice on Hitler that if he invaded Poland he would face general war. But Hitler had no reason to believe in Chamberlain's resolution (which Churchill also doubted). Secured to the East by his sensational pact with Stalin, he sent his forces across the Polish border on 1 September 1939. The British and French governments had no option but to respond, and declared war two days later.

In a formal sense, then, war was declared because of the guarantees to Poland. But the true reasons went much deeper. The British and French people had watched helplessly while Hitler rode roughshod over neighbouring peoples, tearing up treaties and agreements whenever he felt like it. More, they had seen his behaviour within Germany, his contempt for the democratic processes that had brought him to power, his racist policies towards the Jews and other 'lesser breeds', his demented nationalism with its cult of the master race. They didn't like what they saw and felt instinctively – especially after Munich – that unless Hitler were stopped (which could only be by war) the whole of Europe would come under his totalitarian sway, and that sooner or later Britain, too, would be engulfed in the dictatorial tide. In declaring war, Chamberlain was responding to this public feeling, after trying as long as he could to stave off the inevitable. It is not a fantasy to say that Britain went to war to preserve a way of life that was threatened with destruction. The foregoing may appear to be a digression, but it is directly relevant to our theme. For in the last analysis, national security transcends the traditional concerns with *territorial integrity* and *national sovereignty*. These concerns remain, and will last as long as the nation-state does. But there is something else: *the defence of a way of life.*

Nor is this concern new in historical terms, although it has been obscured in the history of recent centuries. The Arabs spread Islam by the sword; and the Christians took up arms, in Spain and France, to defend the Christian way of life (or at any rate, their concept of it). Charles Martel's victory over the Saracens at Poitiers in AD 732 is traditionally credited with having saved Christianity. The Wars of Religion were in a similar category. And so is the Third World War, which is a war of aggression by an ideological counter-church for the spread of the system on which it rests. The difference is that the West, so far, has failed to throw up its Charles Martel – perhaps because so few people in the West, and almost none in political office, have understood what was happening, but more likely, because courage is indeed rarer than intelligence, although neither quality is in plentiful supply.

When I refer to the 'strategy of survival' – the title to this book and of its last chapter – what I mean fundamentally is a strategy for the defence of a threatened way of life.

The point is important enough to merit further discussion. Although territorial integrity and national sovereignty have not ceased to be important, they are perhaps *relatively* less important than they were once held to be – relatively, that is, to the preservation of a way of life. When the nine original States of America decided to unite in 1788, their way of life went on unchanged. Should the nation-States of the European Economic Community decide to shed their individual sovereignties in the interests of a wider federal structure, their way of life will continue undisturbed (unless, as components of the Target Area, one or more of them should come under enemy control).

In other words, the way of life is not necessarily affected by a loss or diminution of sovereignty. Leaving aside for a moment the emotive associations of such words as 'colonialism' and 'imperialism', neither the British conquest of India nor the French conquest of Indochina could be said to have destroyed the existing way of life in those countries. True, the British Raj prohibited *suttee* (the self-immolation of widows), but the sacred cows continued to roam unslaughtered, the Hindus went on worshipping their pantheon of gods, and the Muslims went on using their mosques for prayer. In Laos and Cambodia, the Buddhist bronzes went on wearing saffron, and the conversions of many Vietnamese to Roman Catholicism did not mean the end of the Confucian way of life for those who wished to preserve their additional rituals and code of behaviour.

Not so in Russia, or in China or wherever the ideological counter-church installed itself. In the Soviet Union today, the Bible is regarded as a subversive publication, many churches have been turned into museums, and thousands are persecuted for trying to practise their religion. Yet the Bolsheviks, who did these things and many more to the way of life of mother Russia, were not *alien* conquerors. Russia remained sovereign and the territorial concessions of Brest-Litovsk were made good in the course of time. It was the way of life that changed and it was changed by Russian nationals. It was a take-over from within by an *internal* enemy.

That is why the Soviet conquests have been so much more destructive of the local way of life than the conquests of the Western imperial powers. Take Czechoslovakia in 1948 – a particularly illuminating example. In theory and in the eyes of the international community, Czechoslovakia's sovereignty was left intact when the Communists took over from within. The way of life, however, was radically altered. And the events of 1968, twenty years later, showed that the Czechs had lost their *de facto* (though not *de jure*) sovereignty as well, as a result of the ideological change of 1948.

An important conclusion follows, although no Western government has yet had the nerve to face up to it. *The security of a country must be defended against its internal as well as its external enemies*. The Preamble to the North Atlantic Treaty showed awareness of the relationship between the external and internal threats in the passage recording a common determination 'to safeguard the freedom, common heritage and civilisation of their peoples, founded on the principles of democracy, individual liberty, and the rule of law'. But neither the Preamble nor the Treaty as a whole pressed the issue to the point of providing for co-ordinated measures to deal with the internal threat. It is fair to add that at the time, the *military* threat from the Soviet Union seemed of overriding importance.

Facing up to new techniques
As regards external defence, there are 'old' threats as well as new. One of the old threats is that of territorial conquest. It is by no means obsolete, as the conquest of South Vietnam by North Vietnam demonstrated as recently as 1975. By the criteria of this book, even nuclear annihilation is an 'old' threat. This may sound paradoxical, but is easily explained. The nuclear balance (so long as it lasts) apparently immunises nations in possession of nuclear means of retaliation (the so-called 'second strike' capability); the enemy therefore turns increasingly to other methods, which are 'new' in this context. The immunisation may, of course, be at risk should the nuclear balance be disturbed by Soviet progress and preparations for a first strike. As we saw in Chapter 5, some specialists believed this to be happening when this book was being written. However, any miscalculation would bring catastrophic consequences for the aggressor in a first strike. It can surely be taken for granted that no country, not even the Soviet Union, could risk a first strike unless certain beyond doubt that it could destroy its opponent's capacity for nuclear retaliation totally in a first strike (although recent Soviet military writings tend to undermine comfortable assumptions).

While the nuclear balance lasts, however, territorial conquest applies particularly to countries beyond the protection of a nuclear umbrella. The conquest of South Vietnam (and of Laos and Cambodia) is a clear example already mentioned. Nevertheless, the conquest of even a nuclear power by surrounding non-nuclear powers is not inconceivable. Take Israel. It was widely believed, when this book was written, that Israel already had a nuclear weapon. A tiny country, however, is extremely vulnerable to nuclear attack, which could utterly destroy it, and may therefore hesitate to use it, even *in extremis*. I do not find it difficult to imagine circumstances, perhaps in some fifth or sixth Arab-Israeli war, in which a nuclear Israel could be overrun by hostile, though non-nuclear Arab States.

What, then, are the *new* threats to security? Some of them have been mentioned here and there. They consist of: subversion, terrorism, psychological war and the denial of access to sources of energy and strategic raw materials. Let me define or explain these terms.

Subversion is *a systematic attempt to undermine a society*. The ultimate objectives are to provoke a total collapse of the State and of the society it serves.

Terrorism is *motivated violence for political ends*. Apparently motiveless vandalism, for example by football crowds, is not terrorism. Nor is excessive use of force by the State against its enemies, which I prefer to call *terror*. Terrorism may be considered in some cases as an end in itself, as it apparently became for the Baader-Meinhof gang in Germany – the sons and daughters of affluent middle-class parents, who may have started detonating bombs, holding up banks and killing people for supposed 'revolutionary' aims, then found they rather liked living that way: it was so much more exciting than the humdrum business of gainful employment. But terrorism can also be just a phase in the subversive cycle (in which case it may lead on to guerrilla war, either in the towns or in the villages and mountains, and to full-scale war: this is what happened in Vietnam). Either way, the consequences of unchecked terrorism are appalling: freedoms are eroded, people feel and are unsafe. And if the official reaction to terrorism is inadequate (as it has been in Northern Ireland), there is a gradual loss of confidence in the police, the armed forces and the government.

In recent times, subversion within and against the armed forces of the Western Powers has played an increasingly important part. The full propaganda and agitation resources of the Soviet subversion machine are mobilised to discourage or intimidate conscripts. Many Trotskyist or Maoist groups join in the fun. *De facto*, these groups are allies of the KGB and of

Ponomarev's International Department. The arguments used are always the same: that the armed forces are instruments of repression of the 'capitalist' State, and that they are in any case futile as the cause of 'capitalism' (that is, of the democracies) is lost in advance. This is what I mean by psychological war. At one end, the troops (particularly conscripts where there is military service) are told that it is wrong to allow themselves to be conscripted, and anyway useless. At the other end, talk of 'détente' discourages high military budgets by fostering the illusion that they are unnecessary because the Russians are not going to start a war; while the fact that the Soviet military machine keeps on expanding fosters defeatism – the feeling that there's no point in trying to stand up to the Russians since they're too strong already.

It is in the spheres of subversion and terrorism, above all, that the unity of the external and internal threats is apparent. It is no good standing up to the external enemy if the internal one is neglected or overlooked. Both subversion and terrorism may be home-grown. But both may be exploited or exacerbated from abroad. As we have seen in earlier chapters, the Soviet Union has long been heavily involved in subversion beyond its borders. What is less well-known is that, as also mentioned, it provides extensive training courses for foreign terrorists, and supports terrorism in other ways – through money, arms and propaganda.

Finally, sources of energy may be threatened, either by actions of the oil-producing countries (as with the 'oil weapon' during the 1973 Arab-Israeli war), or by sabotage or terrorism. The denial of strategic minerals could be the threatening outcome of victories by the ideological counterchurch in certain countries, especially in Southern Africa. The point is that the new techniques of revolution and of diplomacy have amply demonstrated one thing: *that it is no longer necessary to conquer a territory by force of arms to impose irreversible change.*

We shall come back to the requirements of a policy of national and international security in the final chapter. At this stage, let me summarise the thesis as follows:

1   The security of a nation-State or of an alliance is concerned with territorial integrity, national sovereignty and the defence of a way of life.

2   Security in this wider sense may be threatened *either* by
an external or an internal enemy, or by a hostile ideology.
3   The proper concerns of any valid study of security are:
the identification and analysis of the threats, and where
necessary and possible, prescriptions for dealing with them.
4   Such prescriptions necessarily involve the formulation
of strategic objectives, the choice of a strategy and, in
suitable cases, the selection of tactics.

It is not enough to know and understand: it is also
necessary to act. In a world war fought largely by means other
than military, the search for security cannot be confined to an
analysis of military and weapons capabilities, useful though
these may be in themselves. Nor is a purely defensive posture
enough. Containment has brought us to the brink of defeat in
World War Three. A more active policy is required if we are to
survive.

9
Know Your Enemy (2)

The enemy, I said in Chapter 7, is not invincible. As it stands, this sentence may appear to have horrendous implications, but only in the hypothetical terms of World War IV. Should there ever be a World War IV – the nuclear holocaust – one must assume that there would be only losers. The dead would have lost, and the survivors also. I am not talking about this hypothetical war, however, but about the real and current war, World War III.

In the three and a half decades of the Third World War to date, the aggressive counter-church has had many setbacks (the most important of which are listed in an Appendix). Always it has resumed its forward march, nibbling away at the Target Area, occasionally chancing its arm for a spectacular advance, or, as sometimes happens, a bloody nose. But the point is that at no time (except in the military terms of NATO and other such pacts) has the aggressor faced a determined and common counter-strategy. The resistance has been piecemeal and haphazard, and quite often non-existent.

How different the outlook would be if the countries of the Target Area, and especially the most like-minded among them, concerted their efforts against the main techniques of World War III, against subversion, terrorism, disinformation, psychological war and the denial of essential supplies. And how much better still if this counter-strategy had as its objective, not the static defence of 'containment' but the positive goal of victory.

The strategy of survival must rest on the premise that victory is attainable, for as I think I have shown, the enemy will not, because he cannot, abandon his forward drive if *he* is allowed to survive. I use the word 'survive', of course, still in the World War III context, that is, in the figurative sense. I am not suggesting that vast numbers of Russians need to be killed, merely that the regime which oppresses them and so many other peoples should be helped to collapse.

Despite the enormous military and police power at its disposal, the Soviet regime is inherently weak. If it were not, it would not be, as it patently is, utterly dependent on naked force (on this point of diagnosis, I agree with the Kissinger-Sonnenfeldt doctrine). Yugoslavs can travel freely and export their unemployment problem; why not Soviet citizens?

Here is a brief but fairly comprehensive list of the weaknesses of the Soviet Autocracy and empire which must be exploited in any strategy of victory:

The gap between promise and fulfilment.
The waning of doctrine.
Vulnerability to the truth.
Dissidence.
Non-Russian nationalities in the USSR.
Eastern Europe.
'Eurocommunism' and polycentrism.
The Sino-Soviet split.

There is a connecting link between these eight items, or rather there are three connecting links: *credibility, authority* and *force*. At home, and even in the early days of revolutionary fervour in Lenin's day, the Soviet regime has always relied on force. Abroad – that is, in the International Communist Movement, and among its many dupes – the credibility of the doctrine proved extraordinarily resilient in the face of successive shock-waves engendered by the Russo-Finnish war, the Hitler-Stalin pact and the great show trials of the 1930s. Those who wanted to believe went on believing: the Soviet system was credible to the credulous. Then came the 20th Party Congress speech, and the shock of Khrushchev's 'secret' speech with its devastating revelations on Stalin's crimes. These ghastly happenings had been dismissed as hostile propaganda so long as the disclosures came from 'bourgeois' sources, but the faithful could no longer ignore the truth when it came from the mouth of the Secretary-General of the Communist Party of the Soviet Union, by definition the repository of the ultimate truth of Marxism-Leninism.

Not only had Khrushchev mentioned the unmentionable,

he had also abandoned Leninist dogma on two important points: the inevitability of war and the necessity for violence on the way to power. The Italian comrades were the first to draw the logical inference from all this: henceforth all Communist Parties could go their own way. He called this 'polycentrism'.

Today, after twenty-one years of polycentrism and about seventeen of the Sino-Soviet rift, the international credibility of the original workers' regime has gone, and with it the authority. Only force is left – in the broadest sense of means of pressure, money and training facilities, as well as sheer military muscle. In this broader sense, force is now the only cement binding together the World Communist Enterprise, and even here fissures, cracks and gaps have developed.

It is at home in the USSR, clearly, that maximum force is exerted – on the population as a whole, on the non-Russian nationalities, on the intellectual dissidents, and on any members or groups within the establishment, including the armed forces, that might at any time have doubts, and especially if heard to express them.

Force is also at hand, in the most direct military sense, for use within the East European empire. Twenty-five years after the brief rising of the workers of East Berlin in 1953, the Soviet Union still maintains an occupation army of 20 divisions in the 'German Democratic Republic'. Twenty-two years after the Hungarian revolution of 1956, there are four Soviet divisions stationed on Hungarian soil. Ten years after the invasion of Czechoslovakia in 1968, five Soviet divisions are present to intimidate the brave and the rash. In Poland, twenty-two years after the disturbances that brought Gomulka to power in 1956, two Soviet divisions keep watch.

Nor can the fiction be sustained that the Soviet forces are where they are to fulfil defence commitments under the Warsaw Pact, as British and American forces are present in West Germany under NATO obligations. For the only occasions on which the Soviet forces have been in action were when they suppressed local populations, as in 1953, 1956 and 1968. Indeed, these are the only times the Soviet armed forces, in bulk, have been committed at all since the Third World War began. If the Soviet armies of occupation were removed, the peoples of Eastern Europe would break free.

Force is also available against the greatest dissident area within the World Communist Enterprise: the Chinese People's Republic. But for all the dire prophecies of a Sino-Soviet war, it is relevant to note that the Russians station only 43 divisions along the Chinese border – a relatively low density in view of the fact that this is the longest international frontier in the world, nearly 6,000 miles. In contrast, there are 62 Soviet divisions in Eastern Europe facing West, with a further 64 divisions in the European USSR.

In fact, apart from the inevitable skirmishes, the Soviet Far Eastern army was always unlikely to invade China while Mao Tse-tung was alive. True, Mao was the symbol of resistance to Moscow and the leader of the main schismatic counter-church. But it was always in Moscow's evident self-interest to await his death, and he duly died. It remained to be seen whether China's new and more pragmatic leadership would mend its fences with the Soviet . If they do not, it will be a tribute to America's policy of rapprochement with Peking. Of course this situation could change if America retreated into absolute isolationism in the Third World War, and if Western Europe were effectively discouraged and neutralised.

Against the Communist Parties outside the Soviet Bloc, the CPSU can at present use only means of pressure short of physical force. They can cut subsidies to West European parties (as they did when the British party criticised them over Czechoslovakia in 1968 by slashing their orders for the *Morning Star*). But there is a limit to the effectiveness of such sanctions, a kind of ideological law of diminishing returns. At a time when the West European Communist Parties are trying to assert claims of independence from Moscow, a reduction in Soviet subsidies would enhance their electoral appeal but limit their resources and therefore their capacity for action. Gone was the time when a mere word from Moscow would bring the distant faithful to heel. The counter-church has lost its aura of infallibility.

To say this is not for a moment to accept the more extravagant claims of, and on behalf of 'Eurocommunism'. During the run-up to the Italian elections of June 1976, the British Labour Party accepted the claims of the Italian Communist Party (PCI) to have become just another democratic party, playing by the accepted rules. The Socialist International decided to regard the PCI as in effect a social-democratic party. It is hard to understand such suicidal disregard for the lessons of history, and of the history of the PCI in particular.

Palmiro Togliatti, the former party leader, may have coined the expression 'polycentrism', but it cannot be ruled out that he did it in collusion with Khrushchev. Indeed the issue was discussed behind the scenes at the 20th CPSU Congress in 1956, and it was not Togliatti who first raised it. From 1926, Togliatti was an important member of the Comintern, and a year later he settled in Moscow with his family and became a Soviet citizen. Although he sometimes took issue with his superiors over Comintern directives, he always gave in in the end, switching from attacks on social democrats to united front tactics, then to revolutionary action, as ordered. During Stalin's great terror he stood by and watched his comrades being executed. For already in August 1936, when some of the original Bolsheviks, including Zinoviev, were tried and sentenced to death, Togliatti had described the trial as 'an act in defence of democracy, peace, socialism and the revolution'. As a close associate of his put it in my hearing, 'He had lost his faith but kept his zeal.'

Yet we are asked to believe that Enrico Berlinguer, the heir to this history of abject toadying and duplicity, has become a good democrat, content forever to play by the rules of a bourgeoisie the PCI is pledged to destroy. It almost passes understanding.

We shall return to 'Eurocommunism' in the next chapter. The point relevant to this one is that although the self-styled Eurocommunists remain enemies in the Third World War, their heresies and assertions of independence are distasteful and even dangerous to Moscow. Whether such things are or are not to Moscow's taste is, of course, immaterial. But the dangerous aspect is of interest. Eurocommunism weakens Moscow because it challenges Moscow's authority. It is particularly dangerous in terms of Eastern Europe. In Poland and Hungary, especially, the national Communist Parties, however dependent on Moscow, are undoubtedly tempted by Eurocommunism, on the analogy: 'If they can do it, why not us?' In that sense, Eurocommunism is an exploitable weakness in a strategy of survival.

Another weakness, of quite a different kind, is what I call

the gap between promise and fulfilment, and the waning of doctrine. The second is the natural consequence of the first. If the system fails to deliver the goods, then the doctrine which says it is going to is called in question. In Russia, as elsewhere, 'communism' in the sense of abundance for all is a Utopian mirage, receding as one moves forward. In 1961, Khrushchev presented the Programme of the 22nd Soviet Party Congress. It is an extraordinary document, quaint now from premature ageing, which deserves to be re-read by those who took it seriously at the time. It claimed that the 'threshold of Communism' would be substantially reached by 1980. Full Communism (that is, the age of plenty, under the slogan, 'From each according to his ability to each according to his needs') was to be completed in a 'subsequent period', the duration of which remained sensibly undefined.

The dogma that the Soviet State was destined to wither away was repeated, but the means left unstated. There were some staggeringly confident and concrete claims, however, in the economic section of the Programme. By 1970, Soviet industrial production would surpass the American figure for 1961. Another and vastly more ambitious claim was that by 1970 the Soviet Union would surpass the American figure for the same year (1970) of industrial production *per head of the population.*

Well, 1970 came and went and the Soviet press and leadership took care not to recall the promises of the 22nd Congress Programme, so far was the reality from the prophecy. As for the 'threshold of Communism', the USSR, by the evidence of its own sources, is a million light-years away from 'Communism' as Communists define it.

One or two stories from everyday life may make the point clear. In a centrally planned system, the Plan is all. If the Plan calls for the completion of a certain project by a stated date, then it must *appear* to be completed on the appointed day, even if in reality completion is a long way off. In his interesting book, *The Russians*, Hedrick Smith, a former *New York Times* correspondent in Moscow, gives many examples of everyday life in the Soviet Union, from which I cull the following, itself drawn from the Soviet trade union newspaper, *Trud*, of 14 June 1973. It was about a new Siberian power generator at Nazarovo, which was solemnly declared open in December

1968, to the accompaniment of much praise in the Soviet press as 'the beginning of a technological revolution'. There was only one thing wrong: the 500,000-kilowatt steam turbine generator had burnt out on the factory floor during testing. At the time of the ceremony, and while the Soviet newspapers described the new power surging into the Siberian grid system, no working generator had been supplied and the needles on the instruments were immobile. There were bands and speeches, but no power. What is more, nearly five years later, the generator was still not in operation.

Nowhere is the gap between promise and fulfilment more stark than in the remoter areas of the 'socialist sixth of the world'. One of the promises made at the 25th Party Congress in February 1976 was to improve conditions in the small towns. The case of Otradny, an oil town in Kuibyshev province, seems typical. About twenty years before the 25th Congress, State prospecting teams struck oil there and over the twenty years local oilmen produced more than 250 million tons of the stuff. Then the oil started drying up, and the oilmen started migrating to Siberia. But it was not only the oil that dried up: the money for local housing and other amenities also did. According to the Soviet publication, *Sotsialisticheskaya Industriya*, of 25 March 1976, not one rouble was allocated after 1970 for health service buildings in this town of more than 40,000 inhabitants. One 'polyclinic' served all local needs and there was no children's hospital; nor was specialised medical treatment available.

Let us be fair to Soviet Communism. The kind of thing just described can be found outside the Soviet Union. The difference, despite occasional revelations in the Soviet press, lies in the general official pretence that the Soviet system is better than the 'capitalist' systems, when manifestly it is grossly inferior.

The more patent the failures of Soviet Communism are, the harder it is to justify the dogmas that constitute (let me say this again) the *only* source of legitimacy of the Soviet autocracy. Indeed, if the system were really superior to 'capitalism', why would the Soviet regime need to turn to the capitalists for technology and credits? And if it really enjoyed the overwhelming support of the Soviet people, why would the regime feel the need to persecute dissidents?

Although the Communist press in the West continues (such perhaps is the force of habit) to print glowing accounts of 'socialist achievements' in the USSR and the East European paradises, they can see for themselves that things are not what they are claimed to be. They can see, above all, that no Western party professing uncritical admiration of all things Soviet and unwavering acceptance of the Moscow line would have the slightest electoral appeal in countries like France and Italy (although the persistence of 'Stalinism' in the French Communist Party, long after the PCI had abandoned it, was a strange thing to behold). Hence 'Eurocommunism'. Hence also the 'crisis of Communism'.

This crisis is at least as real as the 'general crisis of capitalism' which fills the theoretical journals of the world's Communist press. It is a crisis of performance and a crisis of authority. Unsold goods began to accumulate in the USSR in the 1960s. A decade later they were still piling up, apparently for the simple reason that the average Soviet buyer doesn't particularly wish to buy what the system offers him. Big price cuts for unsold goods were announced in April 1975, but by October the total value of such stocks was estimated at 4,500 million roubles, equal to about 2 per cent of the total retail trade for 1974. At about the same time, there was a dramatic increase in private savings accounts. In a four-year period (1971–4), the increase alone in private savings came to nearly 70 per cent of the total value of accumulated savings. Soviet citizens had the money, but they didn't want to use it.

By the end of June 1976, the Soviet trade deficit with the West, which had been rising sharply, reached $3,000 million, compared with $2,000 million the previous year. These figures reflected the increasing dependence of the Soviet economy on Western supplies. Perhaps the most striking single indication of the failure of the system, after sixty years of Communism, was the Soviet-American long-term grain deal of October 1975, under which the Russians committed themselves to buying at least 6 million metric tons of American grain a year between 1 October 1976 and 30 September 1981. Thus the Soviet leaders were tacitly admitting, years in advance, that by 1981 – when according to the 22nd Congress Programme the USSR should have been comfortably across the 'threshold of Communism' – they would still not be capable of feeding their people and would still be turning to capitalist America for food.

The crisis of authority was one of the natural consequences of this developing crisis of performance. Here is an example: on 21 October 1976, the leader of the French Communist Party, Georges Marchais, attended a Paris rally on human rights for political prisoners. He associated himself with a protest against the imprisonment of Vladimir Bukovsky and other Soviet dissidents. (Shortly afterwards, Bukovsky was released and expelled from the Soviet Union.) The following day the French Communists were castigated in a commentary issued by Tass, the Soviet news agency. Marchais was not mentioned by name, but the fact that unnamed members of the French party had attended the rally was singled out for attack. What riled Tass was that these Communists had put the Soviet regime on the same level as Latin American dictatorships such as Uruguay, which were also at the receiving end of protests made at the Paris rally. 'A provocative attempt has been made,' said the Tass commentator, 'to put genuine fighters for freedom and social progress who are languishing in fascist prisons on the same level as malicious anti-Soviet men who campaign against the socialist system.' In the days of Soviet authority (as distinct from brute force), no French Communists (or any other Communists) would have associated themselves with an anti-Soviet protest of any kind.

It took the CPSU two years of hard bargaining with the leaders of other Communist Parties to bring the parties of Europe, East and West, to a conference, which in the end took place in East Berlin in late June 1976. The problem was to produce a draft 'final document', for unless Communists agree in advance on the conclusions of a meeting, there is no point in holding it. Draft after draft was made and turned down by one party or another. In the end, the Final Document of the East Berlin meeting was unsatisfactory to the Soviet party in various respects. But all the Soviets could do about it was omit all the points they didn't like from their press reports of critical speeches at the conference. And there were plenty of critical points – from the Yugoslavs, the Italians, the French and the Spaniards among others. One omitted passage from a speech by the Spanish Communist leader, Santiago Carrillo, was particularly revealing. He said: 'Moscow, where our dreams first began to come true, was for a long time a kind of Rome for us. We spoke of the Great October Revolution as if it were our Christmas. This was our childhood. Today we have grown up.'

This is not the kind of language the Soviet leaders want their people to hear.

Another major weakness on the enemy side lies in the restlessness of the non-Russian nationalities in the USSR. The Treaty of Union of the USSR was signed on 30 December 1922, after Lenin's Red Army had reconquered Azerbaijan, Ukraine, Byelorussia and other nations of the Tsarist empire that had proclaimed independence when it collapsed. The first Constitution of the USSR was ratified on 31 January 1924, ten days after Lenin's death. It provided for the free secession of constituent Republics; so did the 1936 Constitution, which bears Stalin's name and is still in force today. Although many attempts to assert this guaranteed right have been made, they have always been ruthlessly suppressed by the Soviet government. Between 1958 and 1965 there was a wave of arrests and trials in the Ukraine, which the KGB successfully kept from the world until the second of these years.

From time to time, smuggled *samizdat* (privately typed and circulated news-sheets) reaching the West show that unrest continues in various republics. One such is the *Chronicle of the Lithuanian Catholic Church*, copies of which reached Western capitals in 1976, describing trials that were a mockery of justice in the normal sense. About the same time came news of a sweeping purge in Armenia. In these and the other Soviet Republics, the Constitution is a dead letter and central rule is by force, not authority.

I have left the greatest enemy weakness of all until the end: the vulnerability of the Soviet regime to the truth. It is because this is the weakness of all weaknesses that all the other weaknesses can be exploited. The Soviet leaders have shown time and again that if there is one thing they fear it is the truth. That is why they fought every inch of the way at Geneva and Helsinki to refuse all but minimal or notional concessions on the free flow of ideas and information. They know, better than any outsiders can, that if they drew back the curtain of silence that has enveloped their country for decades, the regime could not survive. That is why Soviet citizens can travel abroad only in groups tightly supervised by the KGB. That is why contact with foreigners visiting the USSR is dangerous for Soviet citizens. That is why broadcasts beamed at Soviet listeners are systematically jammed (except for brief periods when they wish to convince the West that they have become more liberal).

Knowing this, it is quite astonishing that a strong sector of the American Congress and of the media made a determined attempt some years ago to cut off all subsidies to the American-financed Radio Liberty and Radio Free Europe. Radio Liberty, beamed at the USSR, is for many Soviet citizens the only reliable source of information in a country where all indigenous sources of information are under totalitarian control. The post-Watergate orgy of revelations had provided proof of a dreadful truth long suspected: that the CIA had secretly funded these admirable instruments of the truth. Suddenly truth itself became tainted and instruments of the truth became candidates for abolition.

Senator Mansfield, Democratic leader of the US Senate, led the campaign to end the subsidies to the two radio stations. In the end, the State Department took over the commitment, but at a much reduced level. It was hard to see what was gained by this administrative juggling. It was still the American tax-payer who paid, and not enough Americans realised that their financial outlay – at $70 million about 0.07 per cent of the military budget – was paying for an infinitely potent weapon in the Third World War. Although the two radio stations were saved, albeit with many staff redundancies, the content was considerably toned down as part of America's contribution to 'détente'. Needless to say, the Soviet media's coverage of things American and Western continued on a note of un-diminished hostility, and the American gesture was thus yet another instance of unnecessary appeasement.

The weaknesses, then, are there for all to see. The only problem is to get the defeatist governments of the West to un-derstand that the enemy's weak points must be exploited if we are to survive the Third World War and preserve a threatened way of life.

10

The Sickness of the West

In the 1970s, the West was bleeding from its self-inflicted wounds. Such injuries arouse much self-pity, and even if they deserve less sympathy than damage caused by an enemy, they hurt no less and provide openings for an enemy to exploit.

I do not propose, in this chapter, to draw up a catalogue of errors and failures, whether of will or of execution. Instead, I shall try to single out the kind of thing that plays into the hands of the main enemy in World War III, drawing examples from the five main countries of the Western Alliance – the US, Britain, France, Germany and Italy.

One point needs to be made at the outset. The observations I shall make may well be dubbed 'right-wing' by those who disagree with them, or are consciously on the enemy's side, or are afraid of seeing things as they really are. But what I have to say is not aptly described as 'right-wing': indeed, in most of the points to be made about Britain my views are indistinguishable from those of the Social Democratic Alliance – a body founded by Gaitskellite members of the Labour Party, whose publications I shall quote.

It is unfortunately a measure of the successes of the main enemy's disinformation apparatus and world-wide propaganda resources that to criticise the extreme Left (Communists and Trotskyists) is widely taken as proof of extreme right-wing views. For my part, I have nothing in common with the extreme Right (fascists, neo-fascists, National Front and so forth). To point to the dangers inherent in the ideas, tactics and strategy of the totalitarian Left is merely to serve the cause of the pluralist and representative society under attack. It is not a particularly or a necessarily right-wing thing to do.

America

It is common ground that the people of the United States have been through traumatic experiences during the past few years, with the tragic, and in the end abortive, involvement in Vietnam, with the Watergate scandal, and the enforced resignation of a president elected with the biggest plurality in the history of his country. America has the most open society in the world. Understandably, a mood of self-questioning and self-criticism emerged out of the above events. There had been errors, and even crimes or misdemeanours, in high places. It was felt that everything had to be brought into the open. Perhaps in the end, this will turn out to have been a healthy thing; perhaps in the end the great Republic will emerge strengthened and regenerated from all the self-probing. What seems to me to be undeniable, meanwhile, is that the self-confidence of the natural leader of the Western world has been gravely shaken, and that its capacity to conduct a coherent foreign and defence policy has been gravely impaired.

In particular, two of the most important organs of the State, indispensable for its security, have been seriously damaged. I refer, of course, to the CIA and the FBI – the first responsible for the collection and collation of foreign intelligence and for certain categories of covert action; and the second for counter-espionage and internal security. The British equivalents, respectively, are the Secret Intelligence Service (SIS, also known as MI6) and the Security Service (also known as MI5); all major countries have similar organisations, the necessity for which is not seriously contested anywhere, except by the extreme Left – whose views cannot be accorded much credence, bearing in mind the quite disproportionate power wielded by the Soviet KGB and indeed for similar secret police organisations in all countries under 'socialist' (that is, Communist) rule.

It is no part of my purpose to defend either the FBI or the CIA for the errors and excesses of which both organisations were doubtless guilty. During his extraordinarily long reign as head of the FBI, the late J. Edgar Hoover appears (in addition to his many legitimate achievements) to have conducted personal vendettas and to have overstepped the mark in the compilation of damaging personal files (for example on the late civil rights leader, Martin Luther King) for no very good security motives.

The CIA, on its side, although the charges against it were grossly exaggerated, was certainly guilty of excesses, such as assassination plots and illegal practices, including break-and-enter operations and mail intercepts – both the latter on a small scale, incidentally, but nonetheless illegal. The mail intercepts should properly have been done by the FBI, but co-operation between the two agencies was minimal at that time. Ray S. Cline, formerly Deputy Director of the CIA and one of the best minds thrown up by that organisation, has given chapter and verse in a soberly written book which is both a personal memoir and an incomplete history of the agency: *Secrets, Spies and Scholars – Blueprint of the Essential CIA* (Washington, 1976), which is recommended reading for those whose information has derived from the biased investigations of the *New York Times*, the *Washington Post*, *Penthouse* magazine or the 'revelations' of CIA defectors.

But when all is said and done, the CIA is an essential arm of the foreign policy of the United States, and the FBI is indispensable to its internal security. Both organisations are key elements in the security of the US in the wider sense, and therefore of the Atlantic Alliance. No good purpose is served by attempting to equate them with the KGB, which is an organ for total repression at home and subversion and terrorism abroad. Even if the FBI and the CIA are lumped together, by no stretch of the imagination can they be compared with the KGB. Moreover, the KGB is an *enemy* organisation; the FBI and CIA are friendly ones. It is right that such organisations should put their houses in order and be seen to be accountable for their actions. It is inadmissible that they should be reduced to near-impotence, which has been the consequence of excessive public exposure and a proliferation of watchdog committees, some members of which have proved themselves ready and eager to leak national secrets to the press (and therefore to the enemy). We shall return to this issue in the final chapter of this book.

The current near-impotence of the American security agencies therefore counts as a 'self-inflicted wound'. In both cases, the two houses of Congress played a leading part. Nor was the damage limited to the organisations I have named. For example, the US Congress condemned the South Vietnamese – friends, clients and protégés of the United States – to torture, death and oppression at the hands of the common enemy, by denying them even the weapons to fight on that had been guaranteed under the Paris Agreements of January 1973. And then, to compound their destruction of America's credibility as an ally and protector, they denied support to the non-Marxist guerrillas in Angola in the face of a Marxist enemy heavily armed and supported by the Soviet Union and its Cuban surrogates.

Britain

In common with a number of other Western countries, Britain has been singularly ill governed in recent times, both by Conservative and by Labour admininstrations. There is no need to go into details: *any* country is ill governed which allows crime to proliferate and fails to protect the value of its citizens' money. On the first score, America is worse governed than Britain; on the second, Britain worse than America. On one score or the other all five of the major Western countries have been suffering from bad government, though in varying degrees.

The great British inflation (a poor thing, to be sure, by the standards of Weimar and Nationalist China, but Britain's very own) was triggered off when a Conservative Chancellor of the Exchequer, Anthony Barber, began to print money in large quantities. (The ex-Chancellor now sits in the House of Lords.)

Item. The Labour Party, while in opposition in 1973, opened the floodgates by lifting the long-standing ban on dual membership of the party and 'proscribed organisations', most of them Communist or Trotskyist. Thereby it invited the destruction of the Social Democratic party of Clement Attlee and Hugh Gaitskell: and advertised indifference to the eventual take-over of Great Britain. For those who understand what the Third World War is about, a fair equivalent would be Wellington inviting Napoleon to re-enter Paris, instead of barring his way at Waterloo; Montgomery inviting Rommel to help himself to Cairo, instead of standing up and fighting at El Alamein.

Item. There are two very efficient ways of causing or maintaining inflation (the great corroder of the democratic society). The Tories chose to print money, which produced growth of a kind, for example the escalation of property values as speculative skyscrapers sprouted to the disfigurement of the capital, remaining empty but changing hands to the profit of each departing owner. Labour, inheriting the great inflation, chose foreign borrowing on a massive scale, reassuring the bankers of Wall Street and Zurich by a gimmick known as the 'social contract' (unwritten and unenforceable), whereby some trade unions promised they would keep their wage claims within stipulated limits. When the great inflation went on, the Prime Minister, James Callaghan, threatened the country's creditors that Britain might have to cut its contribution to NATO if they didn't keep footing our bills. Some wit aptly called this 'borrowing with menaces'. This infinite readiness to borrow – leading in 1977 to an astronomical foreign debt of £12,000 million – did not preclude an eagerness to help others evidently judged even less fortunate than the British, such as the Soviet Union and, in a minor way, the new Marxist government in Mozambique. How many people, incidentally, have pondered the curious circumstance that the Russians expect aid from a 'capitalist' system whose inevitable collapse they wish to hasten? The Americans do not go cap in hand to the Russians except in search of imaginary concessions on 'détente' and arms control; nor do the British or Italians, when in financial difficulties, turn to Moscow for help. One of the West's unseen exports to the USSR is that of a continuing supply of material for cynical fun at the expense of the Western democracies).

Of the items listed above, perhaps the gravest, in terms of World War III, is the opening of the floodgates to the avowed enemies of social democracy (and of democracy *per se*). The disastrous consequences of this conciliatory gesture continue to gather momentum. In June 1966, Harold Wilson, at grips with a seamen's strike following a Communist capture of that union's leadership, could complain in Parliament of the 'tightly-knit group of politically motivated men' who had forced his government off course and precipitated the devaluation of sterling. He could, and did, name the British Communist Party as the group behind 'this accelerating development of peacetime fifth column activities'. In his second period of power (1974–6), he was reduced to public silence, although (and because) the grip of the Communists and other extremists had further tightened on the unions, although (and because) the National Executive Committee of the Labour Party had passed under extremist control, and although (and because) the disguised Marxist presence in the House of Commons had more than doubled, from about 35 to about 80 since he was last in power.

The outcome of the situation Wilson guardedly described (after he had shed his responsibility for allowing it to develop) was paradoxical. Although Labour 'moderates' (such as Wilson himself, and his successor, James Callaghan) far outnumbered extremists in office, it was the extremists who dictated the legislative programme, through the 1976 Manifesto of the party – a Marxist document, with its echoes of standard Soviet themes (the closing down of the American Polaris bases, the dissolution of NATO and the Warsaw Pact, heavy defence cuts, aid to 'national liberation' movements), and its demand for 'irreversible' social change.

Perhaps the most alarming symptom of the Marxist takeover of the Labour 'movement' was the now blatant cultivation of 'fraternal relations' with the totalitarian parties of the USSR and Eastern Europe. The low points of this self-destructive course were the TUC's invitation to Aleksandr Shelepin, at that time boss of the Soviet 'trade unions', and a former head of the KGB, to Britain in April 1975; and the Labour National Executive Committee's invitation to Boris Ponomarev, head of the world subversive apparatus of the Soviet Union, to visit Britain in October 1976. But in addition, visits by British trade unionists to their 'opposite numbers' in the Soviet empire became a regular routine, to the explicit indignation of the Social Democratic Alliance.

When Reginald Underhill, the Labour Party's National Organiser, compiled a report on Trotskyist infiltration in the party, the National Executive Committee ruled that it should be ignored, overruling Harold Wilson. When the National Executive appointed a young Trotskyist agitator, Andy Bevan, as National Youth Organiser, the explicit protest of Mr Callaghan – that is, of Labour's own Prime Minister – was disregarded.

Equally disquieting was the invasion of Labour constituency organisations by Trotskyists and other extreme leftists with the avowed object of disowning moderate MPs and replacing them as election candidates by men of their own persuasion.

All the developments mentioned above, and others, have been explicitly and factually denounced by the Gaitskellite Social Democratic Alliance – which I mentioned earlier and which describes itself as 'Labour's moderate grass-roots organisation'.

It was never surprising that Communists, crypto-Communists, Trotskyists and other Marxist-Leninist revolutionaries should behave as revolutionaries do. What was disquieting, in terms of the Third World War, was the abject acceptance of these defeats by 'moderate' Labour MPs, and of the situation as a whole by British businessmen. True, Wilson told the NEC that he thought the Underhill report should be published; but he let the matter rest when the party bosses overruled him. Although Callaghan had behind him a lifetime of opposition to Communism, he condoned the invitation to Ponomarev, whom he actually received at 10 Downing Street.

The standard defence of such invitations is that it is necessary to keep in touch with the Russians, if only to find out how they are thinking. Indeed it is, and the proper machinery for such contacts already exists, through the respective embassies. If, in pursuance of British state interests, the British Prime Minister should feel it necessary to invite his Soviet opposite number to London, and to 10 Downing Street, there could be no reasonable cause to object. But the issue is 'fraternal relations' between a party that still calls itself 'social democratic' and a totalitarian party that has never for long hidden its detestation of social democracy.

In the cases of Shelepin and Ponomarev, as of Trotskyists in the Labour Party, what counted in the end, for both Labour Prime Ministers, was the illusory 'unity of the Labour movement'. To oppose the enemy within would have split the party both inside and outside Parliament, and incurred the wrath of the trade union leadership. But the money and the power came from the trade unions. Ahead loomed the bleak prospect of electoral defeat and individual elimination at the polls, and of a long stay in the political wilderness. It was too much, and the Parliamentary 'moderates' either swallowed their moderation in silence, or (as in the case of perhaps the ablest Labour backbencher, Brian Walden), got out of politics.

When the Leader of the Opposition asked the Prime Minister in the House of Commons on 5 July 1977 whether he would repudiate the views expressed in the *Morning Star* by his fellow Labour MP, Sydney Bidwell, Mr Callaghan sidestepped the issue with a joke at Mrs Thatcher's expense. Mr Bidwell had declared that his views were identical with those of the Communist Party except that he would not rule out civil war in achieving his and the Communists' common aims. It was left to Douglas Eden, the organiser of the Social Democratic Alliance, in a letter to the *Daily Telegraph* on the 9th, to praise Mrs Thatcher's courage and declare his sense of unity with her on this issue. Mr Eden expressed his understanding that some members of the 'moderate' Manifesto Group in Parliament had been enraged by Bidwell's article, and his regret that (at that time) 'their privately expressed anger has not been converted into publicly effective action'. Two days earlier, in an article on the editorial page of the same newspaper, the President of the Social Democratic Alliance and long-standing member of the Labour Party, Dr Stephen Haseler, had denounced the abuses of the closed shop by the trade unions – a theme pressed vigorously some months earlier by another social democrat and former editor of the *New Statesman*, Paul Johnson, in that left-wing weekly.

Less defensible even than the attitude of the silent Labour moderates in Parliament was that of many businessmen. The facts that stuck in their heads were these: that Britain had been plagued by strikes in 1972 and 1973 and that the Tory government had been brought down by a general coalminers' strike in 1974, while the country had been remarkably strike-free since then. Never mind that the strange industrial peace of the Wilson-Callaghan era had been bought by general surrender to the trade unions, by formalisation of the 'closed shop', by massive foreign borrowing, by defence cuts, and by acceptance of a Marxist programme which, if carried to its logical conclusion, would lead to the death of what was left of the free enterprise system (the 'mixed economy') and therefore to their own extinction. Just as many businessmen cheerfully went along with their government's injunctions to aid the economy of a hostile super-power committed to their

destruction, so these same men connived at the deliberate erosion of the system that was their *raison d'être*.

At the end of 1920, Lenin wrote to his Foreign Commissar,
Chicherin, describing his chosen methods for destroying
'capitalism', and went on:

> The capitalists of the whole world and their governments
> will shut their eyes to the kind of activities on our side that I
> have referred to, and will in this manner become not only
> deaf mutes but blind as well. They will supply us with the
> materials and technology which we lack and will restore
> our military industry, which we need for our future vic-
> torious attacks upon our suppliers. In other words, they will
> work hard in order to prepare their own suicide.

Nearly sixty years later, the businessmen and governments
of Western Europe were behaving just as Lenin said they
would. The attitude of the City of London during the brief
'confidence' crisis of March 1977 illustrates the point. The
leader of the Conservative Party, Margaret Thatcher, had
challenged the Callaghan government to a vote of confidence,
which took place on Wednesday 23 March. Shares fell in temporary fear of the government's defeat, and picked up again
when the government won by 24 votes (with the help of the
Liberals). All reports, including a public opinion poll, confirmed that the City, in general, preferred a Labour government to the prospect of strife implicit in a victory for the anti-
Communist Thatcher Conservatives, although the Thatcher
Conservatives were outspoken champions of the free enterprise system. Better the peace of surrender than a victory
bought with 'blood, toil, tears and sweat'.

Italy

The mismanagement of successive governments, and their
surrenders to trendiness and more sinister pressures, had
enabled Britain to compete with Italy for the title of 'the
sickest man of Europe'. But Italy had been at it much longer,
so Britain still had some way to go. The British traditionally
expected good government (latterly in the face of all the
evidence). The Italians didn't: they expected bad government,
and got it. Yet it was not always so. Emerging from the

Second World War and nearly three decades of fascism, Italy
had the great good fortune of throwing up a man of outstanding integrity and ability, Alcide de Gasperi, who headed
the Christian Democratic party and was Prime Minister of
four successive governments from 1948 to 1953. In the 1960s,
thanks largely to de Gasperi's groundwork (but also to
Marshall Aid, the leadership of a united Roman Catholic
Church, dynamic entrepreneurs and the hard work and in-
genuity of the Italian people), came the 'Italian miracle'. Poor
though Italy was in natural resources (lacking coal and iron),
industrial development bounded ahead, increasing during the
decade at 7 or 8 per cent a year, not far behind Japan and
West Germany. By the 1970s, however, the economy was
bogged down, inflated and strike-ridden; the Christian
Democratic party, though still in office, depended on the good
will (strictly opportunistic) of the Italian Communist Party
(PCI). As an outstanding Italian political scientist, Vittorio
Pons, pointed out, in twenty-eight years, from the first post-
war elections in 1948 to the 1976 elections on 20 June, the
Christian Democrats, with 263 seats in the Chamber of
Deputies, had lost 44: and the Communists, with 227, had
gained 97. This Christian country (officially listing 99 per cent
of the population as Catholic) had brought the atheistic PCI
(that it was atheistic in itself disproved the religious claims of
the census) to the threshold of power.

How had this decline happened? Who or what had given
the PCI its apparently winning position in the Italian Target
Area?

Italy, too, had its self-inflicted wounds. The Christian
Democrats had entered a slow but accelerating decline after
the death of de Gasperi and had become faction-ridden. Too
many Italian politicians were of the kind best described in the
Italian word *politicante* – a politician for whom politics is a self-
seeking game. The industrialists, here as elsewhere in the
capitalist West, had provided nails for their own coffins. The
best-known of all, Signor Agnelli, head of the giant Fiat company, did just that when he set up factories in Russia and
Poland, to build cars for the Communist market, thus competing with his own products and giving the enemies of
capitalism a powerful lever, in a strike-free economy, to control the market (not to mention the opportunities his training

scheme for Soviet technicians gave for industrial subversion by the KGB and Ponomarev's International Department).

But in Italy's case, I would rate self-inflicted damage as relatively less important than in Britain's or America's in the recent retreats in World War III. As Vittorio Pons has shown, the Communists have achieved their victories by the patient and intelligent application of a strategy first formulated by Antonio Gramsci, founder of the PCI. Gramsci recognised the importance of the Church in Italy, but advocated winning over the Catholic workers to an anti-capitalist and anti-bourgeois programme, on the ground of alleged similarities between Christian doctrine and Marxism.

In Italy, as in France, the Communist Party emerged from World War II with the prestige of having played a leading rôle in the Resistance. Togliatti himself ('Ercole Ercoli' in the Comintern) helped to draft Italy's new Constitution in a manner that would favour the Communist strategy. He was careful to oppose any clauses that would offend the Vatican or the Catholic feelings of the masses. And he successfully resisted any laws likely to weaken the trade unions or impair the right to strike.

The PCI (its Stalinist past carefully tucked out of sight), worked steadily towards three objectives:

1 To reduce the Socialist Party to insignificance and subservience to the PCI.
2 To win over the Catholic workers, thereby keeping Catholic trade unions small and weak.
3 To sell to the middle-class the PCI's credentials as a national and European party, independent of Moscow, honest in local government and anti-bureaucratic.

It succeeded brilliantly in all these objectives. It was Togliatti who popularised the concept of 'polycentrism', or independent national roads to socialism. It was the present leader, Berlinguer, who successfully spread the notion of Eurocommunism (Communist Parties independent of Moscow, free of the Stalinist taint, and ready to respect the electoral process). In Germany and in Britain, social democrats were ready to endorse the claims of Eurocommunism, at least in respect of the PCI, which was accepted as a slightly different brand of social democracy.

This readiness to accept a party which has never repudiated Leninism as a 'democratic' party in the Western sense must be chalked up as yet another instance of suicidal self-wounding. It flies in the face of the following realities:

1 The PCI has never abandoned 'democratic centralism' – Lenin's requirement that in a Communist Party a small executive committee should hand orders down the line to the rank and file.
2 It still abides by all the other principles of Leninism, including the *duty* of destroying 'bourgeois' parties if given the chance.
3 Its differences with the Russians over foreign policy are purely tactical. For instance, the Russians maintain undiluted hostility towards the European movement; the PCI advocates penetrating the European institutions and taking them over from within. The end result is the same. Moreover, its other stated foreign policy objectives are substantially identical with Moscow's. On NATO, the PCI has deceived many European observers by supporting continued Italian membership of the Alliance, even if it should come to power – but only until NATO and the Warsaw Pact are dissolved: a primary Soviet objective designed to get the Americans out of Europe militarily.

The fact that the PCI publicly disclaims violent intentions simply reflects an intelligent appraisal of electoral appeal in a democratic country. Once in power, and given the three points listed above, it would move as swiftly as parliamentary arithmetic allowed towards laying the foundations for the totalitarian Italy of the future. As these lines were being revised in the summer of 1977, came the news that after 14 weeks of talks and 61 formal sessions, the Christian Democrats and Communists had reached an agreement giving the Communists a voice in government policy in return for guarantees of parliamentary support on specific issues. Thus inch by inch the Italian Communists were heading towards power.

France

All that I have said about the PCI is applicable in greater
degree to the French party – the PCF, whose 'conversion' to
the rules of the democratic game and to 'independence' from
Moscow is much more recent than the PCI's, and which was
indeed talked into it by the PCI. Of course even the PCF has
changed. All groups, even Communist Parties, change when
old men die and young men, who have no experience of the
past and don't want to know about it if the truth is damaging
or inconvenient, come along. I am sure the young French
Communist militants of today feel happily remote from Stalin
and the horrors of his rule, of which their elders so lately dis-
claimed any knowledge. It may indeed be embarrassing to
think that a party which has always claimed the absolute
truth now has to admit, as obliquely as possible, that perhaps
it wasn't absolutely right about the Soviet Union under Stalin.
Better by far not to think about such things, and try to
cultivate the party's new 'humane' image as a supporter of
Soviet dissidents and advocate of an ordered and 'democratic'
transition to a socialist society.

In France as elsewhere, the Communists have had more
success than they deserve in persuading average voters that
they are no longer the Stalinists they used to be, and have
become a party that can be trusted with political power. They
have been powerfully aided in that deceptive image-building
by their acceptance as partners by the revived French Socialist
Party under François Mitterrand. The assumption in the
minds of many French voters is that the new French Socialist
Party is essentially the same old staid and reassuring party
which that good Jewish bourgeois Léon Blum ran in the
1930s. But this is far from the truth. Mitterrand was the
nearest thing to a charismatic leader the French Left had. The
Communists thought they were running no risks when they
signed their Common Programme in June 1972, but they soon
discovered that it was Mitterrand and his Socialists who
pulled in the votes, not Marchais and his Communists. Instead of being the unquestioned senior partner, as they had
confidently expected, they found themselves very much in the
junior rôle. Not only did Mitterrand attract votes, he also attracted more and more followers, many of whom were Marxists of one kind or another, so that very soon the Socialist

Party had become a danger to French democracy in its own right.

The electoral figures are startling and tell their story instantly. When Mitterrand challenged Giscard d'Estaing, candidate of the centre-right, for the Presidency of the French Fifth Republic, on 10 May 1974, he polled 12,971,604 votes to Giscard's 13,314,640. In percentage terms, Giscard beat him by only about $1\frac{1}{2}$ per cent (50.7 to 49.3 per cent of those who voted). Three years later, in the municipal elections of March 1977, 55 French towns (of the 167 towns of more than 30,000 inhabitants that voted) changed hands, to the loss of the government parties and the gain of the Communists or Socialists. General elections in France are due within a few days of the publication of this book and prediction is fruitless. Suffice is to say that a victory of the left alliance would yield a government including Communist Ministers and would take France sharply in the direction of the totalitarian State.

There were those who argued that even if Mitterrand, once in power, took France along the socialist path internally, he would do nothing to weaken his country's foreign alignments. France, it was said, would remain a member of the Alliance and of the EEC, essentially in the Western camp. My own view is that a popular front government would inevitably destroy not only the free enterprise sources of France's astonishing economic spurt in recent years, but along with these the way of life that made France an essential part of the West. A major component of the Target Area would start slipping into the enemy camp, and the PCF's protestations of independence from Moscow would be seen for the sham they are.

Germany

Superficially, West Germany looked healthier than its European partners or its great American ally. Inflation, at 4 or 5 per cent, was very modest, compared with Britain's 15 per cent or more. Relatively, the West German trade unions were less penetrated by Communists or Trotskyists than the British. Nor was the new German Communist Party – the DKP, authorised in 1968 after a lengthy ban – a mass organisation on the French or Italian model. And yet, in terms of the Third World War, the Federal German Republic was more vulnerable than appeared.

For one thing, the numerical weakness of the DKP and its overt organisations was not a true reflection of its real strength. Under the German Constitution, small parties do not get a chance of cluttering up the Bundestag, for any party that polls less than 5 per cent of the total votes cast is not granted representation. At the general elections of October 1976, the DKP polled only 1.5 per cent of the votes, and therefore sent no deputies to parliament. However, of the 214 Social Democrats (SPD) elected, many – more than a third – were Marxists, avowed or not. Moreover, the SPD's youth movement, known as the Jusos (from the German for Young Socialists), were controlled by the extreme Left. These circumstances recalled the British experience of a hidden presence, in contrast to the open power of Communism in France and Italy.

The great surge of leftism in the late 1960s had given the Marxists control of two German universities (Bremen and the Free University of Berlin). Although the German Chancellor, Schmidt, was a staunch 'European' and supporter of the Alliance, his predecessor's policy – the notorious *Ostpolitik* described earlier – had seriously weakened the Federal Republic, to the advantage of the competing East German republic and of the main enemy, the Soviet Union, and greatly increased an already serious espionage problem.

Although the foregoing analyses are necessarily incomplete, the picture they paint, in terms of the Third World War, make gloomy reading. I believe, nevertheless, that unalloyed pessimism would be out of place. There were encouraging signs as well as discouraging ones. Although President Carter made the shaky start in international affairs that could have been expected from his relative inexperience, he quickly demonstrated that in the important area of human rights in the USSR (and elsewhere), he was going to speak his mind. The indignation with which Soviet spokesmen greeted his frankness, and above all his decision to write to Sakharov in Russia and receive the deported dissident Bukovsky, was an accurate measure of the pain inflicted. He had picked perhaps the most sensitive area in Russia's totalist carapace – the eye of the rhinoceros. Unless all the premises and arguments of this book are mistaken, there was no chance whatsoever that the President's welcome hardness in this area would cause a change of heart in Moscow and the emergence of a true as distinct from a spurious détente.

In Britain and France, new leaders were coming along. Mrs Thatcher had brought a new toughness and intelligence into the leadership of the Conservative Party. She had dared to speak her mind on the Soviet threat and on Communism in Britain, and had enormously gained in popularity as a result. In France, the relatively young and very dynamic ex-Premier, Jacques Chirac, had demonstrated his courage and understanding of the Marxist challenge. The political ineptitude of President Giscard had driven Chirac from office but also given him his chance of pulling off the spectacular coup (in March 1977) of plucking the job of Mayor of Paris from the President's nominee. It was too early, when these lines were written, to assess his chances of defeating the powerful Communist-Socialist alliance in a complex political equation. But the chances were that sooner or later he would get his chance of leaving a permanent mark for good on the impending history of France.

In Germany, the most able and dynamic of conservative leaders, Franz-Josef Strauss, was prevented by the very special circumstances of his country from aspiring to the Chancellorship, which he was better qualified than anybody else to justify. In his native Bavaria, he was the uncrowned king. But his wing of the Christian movement, the CSU, was strong only where he reigned, and distinctly the junior partner to the dominant CDU. In the 1976 elections, the Christian Democrats had failed, but only just, to get back to power. With 244 seats to the SPD's 213, the CDU/CSU had come out as the leading party in the Bundestag, but Chancellor Schmidt had been able to stay in office with the support of the 39 Liberal (FDP) deputies.

The way ahead, then, was blocked by the small FDP, which, in alliance with the Social Democrats, had veered more and more sharply to the left. What should be done about it? The CDU wanted to win the Liberals over and make a deal with them. The CSU wanted to destroy them, by reducing their share of the popular vote to less than the statutory 5 per cent. On this issue, and at Strauss's insistence, the coalition agreed to separate (though not, we may assume, for long). Overall, the voting trend was encouraging: it led away from the left. With a majority of only eight, the SPD's hold on power had become precarious.

In Italy alone, of the countries I have written about in this chapter, there was little to encourage confidence in the future. Elsewhere, the situation was bad to very bad, but nowhere was it desperate. The war could still be won.

11

A Strategy of Survival

Our devious journey towards a strategy has reached its close. On our way we have passed the following stopping points:

The definition of the Third World War: a war unlike previous ones, without armed hostilities between the superpowers or rival alliances, with fighting mainly in peripheral areas, such as Korea and Vietnam; a unilateral war of expansion and aggression from the Soviet land mass; an ideological war by a counter-church militant; 'fought' mainly with non-military or paramilitary techniques, such as subversion, disinformation, psychological war, espionage, diplomatic negotiations, military and economic aid programmes, terrorism, guerrilla war.

Phases of the Third World War: Operations Satellite 1, Insurgency, Indochina 1 and 2; Satellite 2, Terrorism, Détente.

The Target Area defined: the whole of the world not under Soviet control. The 'World Revolutionary Process'.

Failure of 'containment' and general inadequacy or feebleness of Western response.

Enemy strengths and weaknesses.

The meaning of security.

Sickness of the West.

A strategy of survival must take all the foregoing elements into consideration, plus one other: the tremendous economic power and growth potential of market economies and free enterprise systems; and even (though much less) of 'mixed' economies. The USSR turns to the capitalist West for aid, not the other way round. In economic terms, the West is more than strong enough to win. Winning is far more a question of will than of economic capacity. In a war in which defeat means the end of a way of life, and the advent of what I have called 'the long totalitarian night', it is not sufficient to resist, to be on the defensive. We must aim at nothing short of VICTORY.

Since no strategy is worthy of the name unless it defines clear objectives, we can now do so:

1 Long-term objective
This can be only the end of the Soviet system: the dissolution of the ideological counter-church in its original national home. Since the enemy's aim is world domination – that is, the incorporation of all other countries into the Soviet ideological empire and system – no other long-term objective would be appropriate. Remember always that we are talking about surviving the *Third* World War, not the Fourth. We are not talking about a nuclear holocaust, but of victory within the terms of the Third World War, as practised unilaterally since 1944/5 by the main enemy.

2 Medium-term objectives
Again, within the terms of World War III, the aims must be: to bring back lost countries of the Target Area within the non-Marxist system. It is, in other words, a job of *reclaiming*, much as the Dutch through the centuries have reclaimed land lost to the encroaching sea. In this context, peripheral satellites of the USSR, such as Cuba or Angola, should be primary targets. The East European satellites become penultimate targets; and the USSR itself (the long-term objective) the ultimate target.

3 Short-term objectives
The most urgent objectives in a strategy of survival are the main citadels of the Target Area, hitherto unconquered, but some of them already deeply penetrated and threatened: Western Europe, North America and Japan; Argentina, Uruguay and Chile (together constituting the South American *cono sur* or southern cone), with Brazil and other countries in the area; Rhodesia and South Africa; Australia and New Zealand; Thailand, Malaysia and Singapore, and Indonesia and the Philippines; South Korea and Taiwan; India, Pakistan, Bangladesh and Sri Lanka; Iran, Saudi Arabia and

Turkey; and others. The countries on the list are not in strict order of priority. Nor is it easy to establish priorities. My own order would run roughly on the following lines:

First: the United States, Britain, France, West Germany and Japan (because if any one of them is lost to the counter-church, the chances of survival of the rest, and of the entire Target Area, would be gravely impaired).

Second: Rhodesia and South Africa (for if the first goes, the second is more imperilled; and if the second goes, in the sense of being taken over by Marxists under ultimate Soviet control, the West will have been deprived of vital raw materials and a vital strategic base, rendering survival at the last problematical). It should be noted that the threatened countries of the Latin American *cono sur* (see above), though one of them (Argentina) was still under serious terrorist threat when these lines were written, have been fighting back vigorously, as has Brazil and as did Venezuela some years earlier. The authoritarian and military governments set up in those countries may not be to the taste of those of us nurtured in the traditions of Western democracy, but deserve the grateful thanks of other threatened countries. Instead, they have been reviled, with, of course, every assistance from the vast subversive apparatus of the main enemy. In a saner world, in which the strategic issues were understood, Chile and Uruguay, in particular, would have received maximum Western assistance, instead of abuse and boycotts. (Larger and richer, Brazil and Argentina are better able to look after themselves.)

In Rhodesia, where the overwhelming majority of the population, white or black, are non-Marxist, the effect of British and American readiness to deal with the Marxist and Soviet-protected Mugabe was that the non-Marxist majority of the population had reason to fear for the future. As for South Africa, one must clearly distinguish between private sentiments and public interest. For the record, I had never (when these lines were written) visited that country despite repeated invitations, because of my private distaste for institutionalised *apartheid*.

The public interest, however, has nothing to do with such sentiments. Objectively (as the Marxists say), South Africa has never been a threat to its neighbours. On the contrary, it has been at the receiving end of aggression, threats of all kinds, boycotts, and a general revilement far greater than suffered by the Soviet Union and other Marxist and totalitarian tyrannies.

The most striking example was surely the independence of the Transkei. By all the normal criteria of independence, the Transkei was independent: in terms of control of its own territory, freedom from interference in its internal affairs, and economic viability – far freer in the first two of these respects than, say, Czechoslovakia; and, in the third, than a wide range of poverty-stricken 'States' that are full members of the United Nations. Yet that egregious body almost unanimously (134 to 0, with the US abstaining) declined to accept the independence of the Transkei as genuine, for no other reason than that it was conferred by the hated South African regime. This kind of treatment undoubtedly contributed to the 'laager mentality', and gave Dr Vorster his excuse, in the closing months of 1977, to sweep aside the cautious moves towards greater racial equity that had been made earlier, in a wave of new repressive measures.

Third: the rest of the Target Area, not because each individual country is in any sense unworthy of being defended, but because if any of the other countries were lost the damage, however great, would not necessary be *fatal*: I am trying to establish a rational order of strategic priorities.

Having established our priorities, let us look at the principles of a counter-strategy. Bearing in mind the failure of 'containment', it is evident that what is now needed is a more active policy. Let us call it the New Forward Policy. (As always, we are speaking of the Third World War; the New Forward Policy therefore need not involve a major clash of arms between the forces of NATO and the Warsaw Pact, and must not involve nuclear weapons.) The guiding principles that follow are intended primarily for the use of all members of the Atlantic Alliance. They may be applied, however, with suitable adaptations by any country, whatever the degree of its development, that wishes to defend itself from the kind of attack characteristic of World War III. There are three guiding principles:

1 Unity of the threat
It is essential to recognise that the enemy is internal as well as

external. Any Western initiative not based on recognition of this fact is doomed to failure.

2   Informing public opinion

We in the West live in pluralist and representative systems. That is what makes us what we are, that is the way of life we are defending. Since what I am proposing is a profound policy change, and since we live in open societies, that change must be explained. The public will need to be told why it is necessary, why the threat must be met by a new and more positive approach, after decades of failure. The responsibility for explaining and persuading falls in the first instance on the political leaders. It cannot be successfully undertaken by others, although their support will be needed. It is not enough for a writer, or a lecturer or commentator or journalist, to take the initiative. The politicians must do the job, even if initially they pay a cost in popularity.

3   Internal war

This third principle follows from the first. Any war usually involves some reduction or suspension of the traditional liberty of the individual. In normal wars – such as World Wars I and II – the public usually understand the need for such restrictions, and so long as they have reasonable confidence in their leaders (as the British, for instance, had confidence in Churchill) they will accept the necessary restrictions without too much grumbling – confident in the belief that they are imposed only 'for the duration', and will be lifted when victory is attained. It is much more difficult, for obvious reasons, for the public to understand the need for similar restrictions in an internal war. The more so since political leaders, with very rare exceptions, have themselves given no sign of understanding the character of World War III. The necessity for suitable explanations is all the greater. If the character of this Third World War had been understood much earlier, or if those who understood it had had the courage to speak out, then the need for some kind of emergency measures would not have arisen. Even now, they may not be necessary for long (and in some countries at all).

Since the threat is a dual one (although the essential unity of it must be understood), the strategic requirements fall into two categories:

External policy

Having grasped the nature of the problem and taken the fundamental policy decision to go over to the New Forward Policy; and having explained the necessity for a change of course to the public and acquired its majority support, all members of the Alliance will need to take action in the following areas:

(i) The convening of an extraordinary session of NATO to consider: (a) extending the geographical area of concern to the Alliance, which, although it has already been extended beyond the original area of the North Atlantic Treaty, by no means covers all the regions of the Target Area in which Treaty members are at risk; (b) co-ordinating the Forward Policy; and (c) in line with (b) co-ordinating counter-subversion and counter-action against terrorism. The last of these points is of special importance in the context of this book. Although the Treaty members do often exchange information on subversion, it is sometimes difficult and embarrassing for them to do so (for instance, when Portugal looked as though it was 'going Communist'). Moreover, systematic exchanges in this field are hampered by professional inhibitions of the security and intelligence services in each country. What is needed is a central, computerised bank of intelligence and relevant background on enemy agents, and the 'internal enemies', with individual biographies, notes on techniques, etc.

Also needed is the creation of a Task Force to combat subversion or terrorism not only in threatened countries that are members of the Treaty, *but anywhere in the Target Area.* Specifically, any country anywhere, whether or not it is a member of a Western alliance, should be able to appeal to NATO for instant help. It could be Mexico, it could be Turkey, it could be Cyprus or Sri Lanka. These and many more have suffered from subversion and terrorism. Each member country of the Alliance should set up a similar Task Force, or preferably a 'Department of Unconventional War' (or similar suitable name) to co-ordinate the work of various departments in the fields of counter-subversion and counter-action against terrorism. The history of the years since the Second World War has repeatedly shown a depressing pattern: faced with an emergency (as in Malaya, Algeria or Ulster). the threatened authorities set up ad hoc committees bringing together the necessary skills and expertise, but only 'for the duration'. Guerrilla warfare specialists in interrogation methods, where necessary linguists and psychologists, security and intelligence officers – all these are needed. Invariably, once the danger has appeared to recede, the talents thus painfully assembled are dispersed to their respective jobs in the administrative machinery, to academia, or indeed to well-deserved retirement. The threat today has become too widespread and too permanent for such irresponsibility. The time has come to create such departments and open them to young persons in search of a career, under the guidance of specialists from the various services or departments on permanent career secondment.

The central 'Department of Unconventional War', at NATO headquarters, would be composed initially of suitable secondments from the various member-countries. This central department need not, at least initially, be large: its function is advisory and consultative. But in the event of an emergency it would need to move fast, seeking reinforcements from the capitals of member States. The Task Force would then go into action in whatever place was threatened – in the same way as an international expeditionary force was sent to help South Korea during the Korean War. The military capacity exists (although in need of improvement); the counter-subversive and counter-terrorism capacity is simply not there in a collective sense.

(ii) A massive extension and intensification of overt and covert propaganda and information, with special attention to improving or restoring the capacity of Radio Free Europe, Radio Liberty and other overseas services. Immediate attention should be given to examining the technical feasibility of direct beaming of television programmes onto Soviet and East European screens. Given the great vulnerability to the truth which we examined in a preceding chapter, no more important priority can be imagined. This exercise alone, if properly organised and financed, could have a major destabilising effect on the Soviet system – that is on the hostile ideological counter-church.

(iii) The immediate cessation of credits for and exports of technology to the USSR. The end of grain deliveries unless, for instance, the Soviet Government agrees to heavy defence budget cuts, with a greater emphasis on agriculture (with an extension of the highly-productive private plots) and on consumer goods. Any such changes would, of course, need to be subject to inspection and verification.

(iv) A careful examination of the desirability of ending all Western economic and military aid programmes for all Marxist or revolutionary governments, which should in future be told to look to the Soviet Union for such assistance. Admittedly, it is never an easy matter to decide whether a government is 'revolutionary' or 'Marxist'. There may be cases where the withholding of aid could drive a hostile but wavering government into complete dependence on the Soviet Bloc. What I am saying is that it should not automatically be assumed that a hostile regime can be made friendly. I cannot readily recall any convincing example. In any case, resources available for foreign assistance are invariably small. They should be reserved for friends and allies, rather than potential enemies. It is unfortunately true that foreign aid often engenders nothing but ingratitude. But this is not invariably true: it depends to some extent on the character of the aid given, and the kind of strings attached to its use. What is certain is that nothing angers a friendly recipient more than the realisation that unfriendly recipients are also being aided, and sometimes on a much larger scale. The Russians themselves may have learnt this lesson from their experience with China, which resented Soviet aid going to such countries as India and Egypt.

Here again, some guiding principles can be laid down: (a) greater generosity to friendly countries; (b) greater selectivity, with the emphasis on programmes designed to benefit peoples not governments; and (c) the courage of governments in the Target Area in standing up for their policies in the face of Soviet-sponsored pressures.

(v) Guerrilla training schemes. One of the most successful things the Americans have done is to run a training course for counter-guerrilla operations in the Panama Canal zone. This scheme has proved of great benefit to Latin American countries, most notably Bolivia in 1967, when the local security forces easily disposed of an admittedly pathetic attempt at insurgency directed by the late 'Che' Guevara. Similar facilities should be made available for threatened countries, in Africa, Asia, Western Europe and so forth. The Russians used Cuban proxies for the conquest of Angola. By agreement with threatened countries in Africa, guerrilla counter-forces could be trained in Africa itself, under the aegis of NATO. Nor should the possibilities of guerrilla action in Communist territories be overlooked.

(vi) 'Détente'. These lines were revised during the early stages of a conference in Belgrade to examine the application of the Helsinki Agreements of 1975. If my analysis of 'Operation Détente' in this book is accepted, the only problem to determine is whether formally to abandon Helsinki or merely allow it to pass into desuetude.

(vii) A more realistic approach to the West's financial contributions to the United Nations. This curious organisation, greeted with so much hope by so many, was based from the first on a fundamental fallacy – the assumption that the wartime allies (including, of course, the Soviet Union) could be trusted to maintain 'peace', and that the only possible threats to 'peace' came from the powers that had been utterly defeated in World War II. It has occasionally been useful (most notably in the Korean War, by the fortuitous circumstance that the Russians were boycotting the Security Council at the time) and provides certain marginal services that might be preserved. In recent years, however, it has degenerated into an increasingly noisy and irresponsible gathering, useless for its original purpose, costly and counter-productive to the Western powers, and more often than not ready to render one-sided service to the Soviet Bloc in the Third World War. Where any such services are clearly being rendered, all Western financial contributions should be reduced or suspended. My own view is that the international organisation has long outlived any usefulness it might once have had, and that all the members of the Western Alliance should withdraw from it. At the very least, a realistic discussion of the issue is overdue.

(viii) Military defence. Although placed last, this is by no means the least important consideration. I have put it where it is to give more emphasis to other items that tend to be overlooked altogether. It is part of the strategy of the main enemy to overawe the Western Alliance, and indeed the Target Area as a whole, by the display of its disproportionate military power. This display is meant to intimidate, and it does. The Western powers are not in business to compete with the Soviet Union in the exercise of striking awe. But they must at all times maintain a collective capability to deal with the common enemy. In recent years, this capability has clearly been insufficient. The British, in particular, have allowed themselves the impermissible luxury of cutting down their armed forces to well below the margin of safety. For an enemy with a powerful fleet, the long unguarded coastlines are an invitation to enter and help themselves. The Army – one of the best in the world, but seriously below strength – is heavily stretched in Ulster, and its potential as a 'fireman force' gravely reduced. By any criterion except the logic of suicide or surrender, it is a tragic absurdity that the British forces should now be weaker in numbers than those of neutral Sweden and Switzerland. In Britain's case, the successive cuts were made by Labour Governments with the unworthy objective of placating the extreme left of the party – that is, the internal enemy in World War III. The protests of the chiefs of staff have been disregarded. In France, in contrast, a decision was taken a year or so before this book was written to increase defence expenditure by 20 per cent. In the United States, however, the acceptable level of nuclear capability held to constitute a balance with Soviet capability has been reduced in relative terms, so that the Soviet Union now has at least parity with, if not superiority over, the USA. Nobody wants an arms race, which in any case is irrelevant to the Third World War, except in the important psychological sphere. But World War III could still be lost without crossing the threshold into World War IV, if the Russians were allowed to establish and maintain, and then increase, a clear nuclear superiority. Strictly speaking, there is no real answer to the question, 'How much is security worth?' (how long is a piece of string?) but defence against external enemies is, or ought to be, one of the top priorities of the State, without which the State ceases to have its full justification.

(ix) Foreign intelligence and clandestine operations. In the real war, here and now, as distinct from the hypothetical war that may never come, foreign intelligence and the capacity for clandestine operations must hold a very high priority. (It is arguable that the weaker a country is, in economic and military terms, the greater its need for efficient and reliable intelligence. This applies to Great Britain, as it applies in quite a different context to Israel.) The destruction of the operational capacity of the American CIA, through an unfortunate combination of domestic irresponsibility, misguided puritanism and subversion by the main enemy and its ideological allies, is perhaps the gravest reverse suffered by the Western Alliance since 1949. Under a new President and Administration, untainted by Watergate, the opportunity exists for restoring what has been destroyed. To say this is not to give moral approval to everything the CIA did. But then I would not give unqualified moral approval to the destruction of Hiroshima by the first atomic weapon exploded in anger. A war is never pleasant, and the war I have described has been going on for decades. By the nature of secret intelligence, only the failures are as a rule trumpeted; many of the successes never get written about. As I've exemplified elsewhere (in *The Masters of Power*), those that do prove beyond doubt that in terms of cost-effectiveness, secret intelligence operations far surpass military ones in certain circumstances.

Internal policy

As soon as we mention domestic affairs and internal policy, we find ourselves inevitably on still more controversial ground. For most of the open societies of the West protect themselves instinctively against unpleasant thoughts with the consoling notion that 'it can't happen here'. Security is concerned with the defence of a way of life, and if that way of life is open and tolerant of political dissent, doesn't the way of life itself provide its own best protection? Don't good ideas displace bad, as John Stuart Mill thought? Besides, we live in nation-States: if we have enemies, are they not, by definition, bound to be 'foreigners'? We may, of course, have traitors in our midst, but does not the concept of treason apply only in war-time, and are we not at peace?

These are precisely the misconceptions that must be dis-

posed of if the concept of internal security is to be understood
at all in contemporary terms. First, we are *not* at peace, as the
evidence assembled in this book amply demonstrates. We – all
countries of the Target Area, but none more than the Western
democracies – are at the receiving end of unilateral aggression
from the ideological counter-church and its schismatic
branches. As we have seen, it is a war fought mainly by non-
military means, and those who wage it are not necessarily
'foreigners'. Indeed this kind of war is waged to greatest effect
by nationals of the country being attacked. In their own country, they operate normally under constitutional protection
denied to aliens.

The point is perfectly illustrated by the much discussed
Agee-Hosenball case in Great Britain. Philip Agee, a former
officer of the CIA, was that agency's first ideological defector.
Turned Marxist, he started working quite openly for the
destruction of his former employers. Mark Hosenball, a young
American journalist, appeared to have similar interests and
intentions. In November 1976, both men were served with
Home Office notices of impending deportation from the United Kingdom. They took vigorous measures, partly through
the courts, to delay or frustrate the deportation orders, and
were finally expelled in June 1977.

Under British law and British procedure, the Home
Secretary has the unfettered right to deport foreign nationals
if, in his judgment, their presence is undesirable on security
grounds. Nor is he bound to spell out the grounds for deportation (in most cases, to do so would be to compromise sources
of information). The fairly large, and very vocal, lobby that
defended Agee and Hosenball argued that the two men should
have been tried on specific charges, or if not tried, told of the
charges against them so that they could defend themselves.
But this was to miss the point. There *were* no charges. They
were aliens enjoying British hospitality. In the view of the
Labour Home Secretary, they had abused that hospitality and
were no longer wanted. They were being shown the door; it
was as simple as that.

In all this, the point that is relevant to my argument is that
citizens of a country under subversive attack are better protected than aliens. Unlike aliens, British citizens cannot be
deported: they have to be charged with specific offences, or left

alone. At the time of writing, two British citizens had in fact been charged with offences under the British Official Secrets Act in the Agee-Hosenball case. But many other British associates of theirs could continue to operate with impunity, subject only to defamation writs issued by individuals in respect of articles appearing in various publications. The State could not act against them, unless it could prove they were giving or selling official secrets to a potential enemy. Indeed, the political climate was heavily weighted against any State action in matters of security. It was a measure of the weakness of the State that the Home Secretary hesitated so long before deciding to issue deportation orders, then allowed months of litigation and organised protests before implementing his own decision.

It is sufficiently clear that complacency is desperately misplaced, not only in Britain but in the US, France, Italy, Germany and other Western countries.

What about Mill, and his optimistic view of the triumph of good over evil in liberal debate? In another book (*A Theory of Conflict*, 1974, pp. 200–201) I have examined Mill's innocent optimism. In a civilised, disciplined and genuinely free debate, no doubt good ideas do drive out bad ones. But not when the upholders of good ideas are jostled out of the way, physically cowed, or mentally intimidated, by intellectual bully boys in schools, polytechnics and universities. The Marxist invasion of centres of learning in the Western world is in no sense the outcome of free debate under agreed rules: it reflects a series of victories by organised forces of the enemy counter-church and its variants. These are operations in the Third World War, and they will continue to end in defeats for the upholders of law, order and freedom – that is, of the threatened way of life – until they are seen for what they are and appropriate countermeasures are taken.

What, then, of political dissent? There must, of course, be dissent in open and pluralist societies; or they would cease to be open and pluralist. To grant freedom of speech and the printed word to those with whom you agree is the tiniest of concessions: it is the people you *disagree* with who must have and exercise these freedoms. But freedom that is absolute is self-defeating. We do not grant our fellow-citizens the right to kill, or we might ourselves be the victims. Nor should we grant the enemies of freedom the unlimited right to destroy the freedom in the name of which they claim the right to destroy it. The proposition is absurd and should be seen as such.

Put the question in another form. In general elections in Great Britain, only one trade unionist in a thousand votes for Communist candidates, and far fewer still for Trotskyists; yet about one in ten of the members of trade union executive committees is a Communist or ultra-leftist. In strict democratic terms, therefore, the totalitarian left is over-represented by 100 to 1. If the population as a whole is considered, the percentage of votes for ultra-left candidates is considerably lower.

An interesting illustration of this point occurred at the precise moment these lines were being written, with the news of the results of a Parliamentary by-election on 31 March 1977 at Stechford, a working-class constituency in Birmingham. The 'news' was that there had been a swing of 17.4 per cent from Labour to the Conservatives, as compared with the general election of October 1974, giving the Tory candidate a convincing win in a traditional Labour stronghold. But the interesting point, in the context of this chapter, was the dismal showing of the ultra-left candidates. There were two, both Trotskyists. One stood for the International Marxist Group and polled 494 votes; the other was Paul Foot, nephew of Labour's then Minister of Labour and leader of the House of Commons, Michael Foot, and he polled only 377 votes. Anybody following the career of this young agitator, with his appearances on television and his exposure in the national press as well as in a number of publications controlled by his Socialist Workers' Party (formerly the International Socialists), might have been forgiven for supposing that he had a mass following. In percentage terms his 377 votes, in a total poll of 36,240, works out at 1.04 per cent. The two Trotskyists, together, achieved 2.4 per cent of the electoral turnout. (In comparison, the fascist National Front candidate, ahead of the Liberals, attracted 2,955 votes, or 8.15 per cent of the total.)

Despite this minuscule electoral appeal, Trotskyist parties are heavily represented in the media, the teaching profession, and (by the practice of 'entryism', or joining ostensibly non-totalitarian parties) the Labour Party itself, both within and outside Parliament. Is it 'just', in the name of 'democracy', to use two terms constantly on the lips or typewriters of the ultra-left, that an ideology so patently unattractive to the voters, that is to 'the people' (another favourite term) should, for instance, have achieved a kind of stranglehold on certain faculties in institutions of learning and be so grossly over-represented in the press and television? Take a case, by no means untypical, of a major university, known to me, in which at one time nine of the thirteen members of the Department of Politics were Marxists (the proportion having since been reduced to seven out of thirteen). Let us take the lower figure: seven out of thirteen is nearly 54 per cent. Even in a stronghold of the Labour left, polling (as at Stechford) at the maximum 2.4 per cent, the Marxist over-representation in the faculty mentioned is more than 22 to 1.

Such staggering negations of the democratic process are made possible by abuses that constitute a form of subversion. If a dissenter, not content with expressing his discontent by peaceful means, combines with others to destroy the society in which their dissent flourishes; if dissenters bully or cow the unorganised majority, through strikes, intimidation, demonstrations, pressures of various kinds, in some cases falsification of voting returns, profiting from the apathy of 'moderates' to stay late at union meetings, outstaying those less politically motivated to vote 'revolutionary' resolutions; if, *a fortiori*, they are aided in such efforts by money from the main ideological counter-church; then in sum, such activities constitute subversion – a main weapon in the Third World War.

The whole question of subversion is fraught with difficulties. As a pluralist, I cannot oppose the teaching of Marxism or the availability of Marxian books. If Marxism were simply taught, in our universities, along with other philosophies, there need be no problem. It is right that students of politics and history should learn about Leninism, as well as about Nazism, about Trotsky and Stalin as well as about Hitler and Goebbels. The problem begins when Marxists (and *a fortiori* Marxist-Leninists) do the teaching. For Marxism claims scientific authority and universality and is by its nature activist; while Leninism is above all a system for seizing power and keeping it forever. In contrast, the philosophy of Mill and Locke is more passive, since no one school of thought is allocated a monopoly of wisdom. What is certain is that there is something seriously wrong when Marxists and Marxist-Leninists can dominate a faculty, a school or a university. (In Bremen, Germany, for instance, the entire university was brought under Marxist control in the late 1960s.)

As it happens, the same day – 1 April 1977 – on which the British national newspapers carried news of the Stechford by-election also brought into the open the successful campaign organised by Bernard Levin, of *The Times*, against left-wing fanatics in his branch of the National Union of Journalists. The fact that Mr Levin, in his column that day, was able to reveal what had been going on, was itself a tribute to his skill and persistence against the left-wing grab of the London Freelance branch of the NUJ. For by mobilising the apathetic majority and ousting the fanatics from all offices, he had managed to change the book of rules, which until then had favoured the totalitarians. One of the new rules allowed him to discuss branch affairs (previously forbidden, so that the left-wing coup had been engineered in statutory secrecy). Another new rule limited branch meetings to $3\frac{1}{2}$ hours, thus frustrating the favourite left-wing trick of waiting till the less hardy had gone home to pass the resolutions they had cooked up.

I have dwelt at such length on these tiny matters because they illustrated, better than theories, the facts and techniques of subversion. A society that does not defend itself is doomed. A system that remains passive in the face of attack deserves to go under. Those unwilling to defend freedom will become unfree. To stand idly by is to commit suicide.

What, then, can the free, open and vulnerable societies of the West do to defend themselves against the enemy within? Repetition can be tedious, but is sometimes necessary. Remember that we are talking about 'the war called peace'. We are at war, and the enemy is within as well as outside each of our countries; he or she may be a fellow-citizen, and is not necessarily an alien.

Think also of the consequences of passivity. In the world today (apart from such aberrations as Idi Amin's sanguinary tribal dictatorship in Uganda), there are really only variations on three options available: Western-style democracy; authoritarian rule; and totalism (as I prefer to call totalitarianism). As I have pointed out, and despite popular belief to the contrary, authoritarian and totalitarian systems are in some respects each other's opposites. Franco, a typical authoritarian ruler, wanted to abolish politics and if Spaniards kept out of politics (apart from approved channels), they could enjoy a fairly wide range of personal liberties, such as: marriage to a person of their choice; private ownership of property; travel either inside or outside Spain; changing one's job; and even religion (although the bias in favour of Roman Catholicism naturally remained strong).

In contrast, all totalitarian States, from the dead fascist dictatorships of Italy and Germany to the unfortunately live tyrannies in all the Communist countries, try to involve the entire population in politics. This is particularly true of the Chinese People's Republic, where it is impossible for ordinary people to opt out of politics. In all such States, to a greater or lesser degree, the normal freedoms are simply not available. In Russia and China, you have to have the party's permission to marry, and if you try to marry a non-Communist foreigner, you will very quickly discover the limits of freedom in this elementary matter. You cannot buy a house of your own, still less a factory; you cannot change your job without permission (and in China, university graduates will be sent to plough fields in distant areas); you cannot travel freely either in the country or abroad (in the USSR, there is an internal passport as well as the usual one for foreign travel, and Soviet citizens can normally travel abroad only in groups under secret police escort). To be fair, some Communist regimes are slightly easier in some respects than others. Both Poles and Yugoslavs can travel abroad fairly freely, and do. But the principles remain.

All this is not to say that authoritarian rule is not, in certain respects, very unpleasant, especially if you happen to be politically inclined, when you might find yourself in gaol or under torture. I still remember how grey and oppressive I found Salazar's Portugal on my first visit there in 1956; in contrast, Spain was already easing up, and ten years later was a much more relaxed country altogether. Undoubtedly, however, ordinary people are infinitely better off under authoritarian rule than under totalitarian, especially if they happen to be not particularly interested in politics.

There is another important difference. Authoritarian regimes are not necessarily permanent. Even Salazar's regime, which began in 1928, survived him only by a year or two, before being overthrown in 1974. A year after Franco's death in November 1975, Spain was well on the way to party-democracy. The Greek colonels held power for seven years, then fell. In contrast, no totalitarian regime has ever collapsed except as a result of a world war; and no Communist party, once in full national power, has yielded to democratic rule since Lenin seized power in 1917. Philosophically, there is no very good reason to suppose that they are perpetual, but within living experience nobody has yet dislodged one. So the only safe assumption, in practical terms, is that once Communists are allowed to take power, you are going to be stuck with them for the term of your natural life. It is a frightening thought.

The consequences of passivity, of doing nothing, are therefore plain, and are plainly illustrated, in microcosm, by the events in the London Free-lance branch of the NUJ. If Levin had not organised opposition to the takeover, the only voice tolerated would have been that of the Trotskyist left. As in this branch of a relatively small trade union, so in the country as a whole. The passivity of the Labour 'moderates' had enabled the enemy to dictate the terms of the 1974 Manifesto and therefore of the government's legislative programme, laying the foundations of a totalitarian State if the process were allowed to continue unchecked. The passivity of the mass membership of the trade unions had allowed the enemy to take over these powerful instruments of coercion. It would be the same in France or Italy, if the mass of voters were misguided enough to vote the 'Eurocommunists' into power.

But, of course, there was an alternative in all the threatened Target Area countries of the West – not a particularly pleasant one, but inherent in the nature of the options I have described. Somewhere on the way to the point of no return the Army might decide to step in. Again, one must question the 'it can't happen here' syndrome. Only twenty years ago, the French Army intervened in politics and brought Gen de Gaulle back to power. In Britain today, all proportions kept, there is a *malaise* in the Army that reminds me curiously of the state of mind in the French Army in 1958, with the frustration of Ulster paralleling the frustration of Algeria. I don't want to carry the comparison too far. Nothing I have seen or heard supports the view that the British Army would, in the foreseeable future, intervene to overthrow a constitutionally elected government, unless the government were guilty of illegalities so gross as to cause widespread public disorder. But the Army would probably be available to maintain a constitutionally elected government in power if an attempt were made to prevent it from governing or to bring it down, for example by a general strike.

Of course nobody would want a military regime in countries like Britain or America; and nobody would want a totalitarian police State. The proposed measures that follow are designed to prevent such unpleasant options, one of which is inevitable if the drift towards revolutionary anarchy and arbitrary government is not challenged and stopped.

Since all Western countries, whatever their similarities, have different constitutions (or none, as in Britain), and legal systems, the proposals are not intended to be adopted in their entirety by any one country. They are intended simply as guiding principles to the kind of thing that will need to be done to prevent final defeat in World War III.

1   Espionage, and the safeguarding of official secrets

Britain and some other countries are reasonably protected under existing law, although the British Official Secrets Acts have come under severe fire and a Royal Commission has proposed that one of its sections should be dropped. In the United States, the situation is absurd. A person handing classified material to, say, the KGB, can still be prosecuted under the Espionage Act. But the same person, offering the same material to, say, the *New York Times* or the *Washington Post* expects and normally gets acclaim as a kind of public hero. Since the Russians can read, the exposure of CIA or FBI secrets amounts to treason, publicly carried out and to the applause of the mindless and ill-intentioned.

A newly appointed civil servant in the Administrative Branch in the United Kingdom is required to sign the Official Secrets Acts, under which he can be criminally prosecuted should he part with classified material without permission or to unauthorised persons. A successful candidate for the CIA merely takes an oath not to part with such material and is liable only to the long, hazardous and unpredictable processes of the civil law. Thus is treason made easy, and indeed rewarded. There is widespread recognition in the US that something will have to be done about this untenable situation. Whether something *will* be done, and if so how soon, remained unclear when these lines were written.

Another point of special US interest is the dangerous anomaly that gives KGB and GRU officials unlimited access to American territory if they happen to be on secondment to the United Nations. If no way can be found to plug this glaring gap, here is yet another reason for the Americans to withdraw support from the UN, or at any rate expel it from American territory. A suitable home might be Moscow, in recognition of the Soviet Union's services to world peace.

2 Subversion

Although there are legal safeguards against true espionage in most advanced countries, there is virtually none against subversion by alien secret services. Astonishingly, as was mentioned earlier, it is not an offence under British law to be an *agent of influence* for the Soviet Union, nor even to be employed by, or receive money from, the KGB. There is an offence only when classified material changes hands, even for no monetary reward. As the KGB attaches at least as much importance to agents of influence as to spies, this is clearly a glaring loophole that needs to be plugged.

The only way to plug it is to legislate for the compulsory registration of agents of the USSR and the bloc, and possibly of carefully designated Marxist governments. Naturally, agents of influence would go underground, but the fact that in concealing their affiliation they would be breaking the law would make it that much easier to prosecute them.

The situation in America is different, but nevertheless hardly more satisfactory. An American citizen working for *any* foreign government is required to register as an agent of that government. This catch-all requirement equates working for an ally with working for an enemy. What is needed is a list of governments, to work for which in designated capacities would be an offence, the list to be reviewed from time to time.

There is a similar laxness about the unfettered imports of

propaganda material from the Soviet Union. I drew attention
in an earlier chapter to the fact that the relevant propaganda
for an 'Anti-Imperialist Festival' held in Dublin and Belfast in
August 1974 had been printed 'through the good offices of the
Soviet representatives'. On what basis was this material
allowed either into the Irish Republic or into Northern
Ireland? The reply may be that it is not the policy of the
authorities concerned to ban the import of printed material
(other than pornography) whether from the Soviet Union or
any other country. To this, my rejoinder is does the Soviet Union allow the import of corresponding material from the West?
Would leaflets advocating the overthrow of the Soviet system
be passed by the Soviet customs without detriment to the
traveller carrying them in his luggage? In this as in all other
aspects of relations with the main enemy, the minimum
guiding principle should be *reciprocity*. The principle is observed in respect of diplomatic travel in the respective countries.
There seems no good reason why it should not extend to
hostile propaganda.

3   Visitors to the Soviet Union and other Communist countries

Doubtless the great majority of such visitors are either innocent tourists or innocent businessmen. But there is obviously a
small hard core of agents or terrorists who return to do what
damage they can after undergoing training in one of the Soviet
Union's schools for saboteurs and terrorists, or in Marxist-
Leninist 'agitprop'. These people go free at the moment but
they should be exposed. The easiest way to do this is to re-
quire returning travellers to sign a declaration along the
following lines:

> Mr Bloggs has/has not undergone training in 'agitprop',
> hand-to-hand fighting, sabotage, guerrilla war, sharp-
> shooting, manufacturing of explosives, etc. (Strike out
> were inapplicable.)

Would this be regarded as an intolerable piece of
bureaucratic interference? I wonder: the inconvenience would
be a minor one, similar to the customs examination in the
USA, which also requires the signing of a declaration. The in-

nocent would have nothing to fear on signature. The guilty would live with the knowledge that they face prosecution on exposure.

4 Marxists in education and the media
It is intolerable that enemies of the open society should hide behind the protective tradition that a person's politics are his or her own business. In the election booths, yes. Not in such places as schools, universities, polytechnics, newspapers, radio and television, companies, where hidden or even avowed Marxist-Leninists can do their subversive worst with impunity. A gradual weeding-out is essential to the strategy of survival. These remarks apply to all Western countries, for all suffer in greater or lesser degree from the Marxist invasion of centres of learning and of the media. In Britain in particular, in this as in other areas, the promulgation of a written Constitution (as suggested by Lord Hailsham among others) would immensely facilitate the work of counter-subversion, in that candidates for posts in education and communication could be required to sign a declaration of loyalty to the Constitution (as with civil servants in Germany).

5 Compulsory registration of Communist front organisations
This would apply to all Western countries without exception. The list would have to be revised and brought up to date from time to time.

6 Declaration of loyalty by political parties
In time, the extension of the principle that those who intend to abide by the rules of the free society should declare their readiness to do so, should be extended to political parties. Only political parties prepared to declare unreserved allegiance and support to the system of pluralist democracy should be allowed to present candidates for election to parliaments and national assemblies. In this context, I offer a personal view on the economic foundations of the pluralist system. The debate on this issue lies at the heart of the problem of the Third World War. A fully nationalised and centrally controlled and directed economy – as in the USSR – is incompatible with the free society. Such a centralised

system concentrates all economic power in the hands of the State, and in the process of acquiring that power, whatever ruling group or party happens to control the State inevitably neutralises, removes or physically eliminates all opposition. It follows that the closer the State moves towards total control of the economy, the closer it moves to a totalist political system as well.

There are many definitions of 'socialism' and many that contradict each other. But if socialism means total control over the economy, it cannot also be compatible with democracy. The fallacy that it can is the great delusion of social democracy; and the Fabian tag, 'the inevitability of gradualness', merely postpones the shattering of the delusion to an unspecified future. The German Social Democrats recognised this contradiction and abandoned nationalisation as an instrument of policy. The British Labour Party did not, despite the intelligent leadership of the late Hugh Gaitskell, and kept the notorious Clause 4 of the Party's Constitution, calling for the 'socialisation of the means of production, distribution and exchange'. In recent years, socialist rather than democratic objectives have prevailed in the legislative programme of the Labour Party in office; and the move away from freedom and towards coercion has accelerated very sharply in consequence.

This is not to rule out the 'mixed economy' completely. It is a question of degree. Generally speaking, the State is bad and inefficient at creating wealth, and grossly inefficient in commerce, especially if it acquires a monopoly in any area. There is a danger point, which is difficult to pin-point, and which may vary from country to country. It is important that the subject be debated and that a consensus should emerge, at least among individuals, groups and parties that give top priority to the survival of free and representative institutions. It should be clearly understood, however, that a large and flourishing private sector in the economy is the *sine qua non* for the survival of a pluralist and representative system.

7   Should Communist and Fascist parties be banned?

There is an illiberal ring about even posing the question. Yet it cannot be rejected out of hand. If the point is ever reached where a democratic system, in its own defence, requires an oath of loyalty from political parties, the question may solve itself. Such a declaration would equally disqualify fascists, as well as Marxist-Leninist, parties, and indeed members of front organisations listed as under Item 5 above. It would severely test the intentions of self-styled 'Eurocommunist' parties. (Any such party which renounced Leninism might as well go out of business.) A formal ban might thus be unnecessary. In countries such as France and Italy, where the Communist Party has come within sight of power, either on its own or in coalition with Socialists, the idea of a ban was, of course, not practical politics when these lines were written. Whether it would ever become practical would depend on the success or otherwise of alerting public opinion to the dangers as a result of some of the measures proposed above.

The Spanish and German examples are of particular relevance to this argument. The Suárez government in post-Franco Spain legalised the Communist Party in time for it to take part in the country's first general elections in 41 years, after much heart-searching and partly in response to the consensus of views in the EEC which seemed to regard legalisation as a test of democratic credentials. Bear in mind, however, that *West Germany did not lift the ban on its own CP until 1968, yet its claim to be a democracy was not disputed by its allies before that time.* In logic, there is no reason why parties whose ultimate aim is the destruction of democracy should not be banned under a democratic system. The practicality of a ban is something else. The penetration of the British Labour Party by Marxist-Leninists and of the Social Democratic Party in Germany clearly shows that there is no necessary correlation between the legal existence of a Marxist-Leninist party or parties and their capacity to advance enemy aims.

It cannot be said often enough that no Communist Party (whether or not aligned with Moscow, and regardless of its formal name) or other Marxist-Leninist Party should ever be considered as 'just another party'. All are conspiratorial organisations dedicated, by definition, to the spreading of the ideology of the counter-church and its schismatic variants by fair means and foul, and to eliminating all competing ideologies. They are regiments or divisions fighting the unilateral war of aggression against all countries of the Target Area. At certain times and places it is useful that they should be legal, so that their failure to appeal to the electorate should be exposed and their activities openly observed. In time perhaps threatened countries may realise that they can no longer afford the luxury of misplaced tolerance. In military terms, the equivalent would be to invite enemy formations, at the height of the battle, to operate behind one's lines. The absurdity of tolerating totalist parties in free societies is not perceived only because the nature of the Third World War, and even its existence, are not widely understood.

8   Industrial subversion

In Britain, where tiny votes often bring political extremists to trade union executive office, and in other countries, the remedy is compulsory and secret postal elections for all executive posts. If the Heath government had gone for this single measure instead of the catch-all Industrial Relations Act which brought the Tories down, the problem of trade union extremism could have been solved in peace. It is not too late to make amends.

But more than this is needed to end the subversive use of trade unions in the Third World War. Appropriate legislation is needed, in several Western countries, to make it a criminal offence for a trade union to receive financial help from the Soviet Union, or indeed from all foreign countries (since the possibilities of covert financing are almost infinite), and from all Marxist-Leninist sources. Also needed are the following supplementary measures:

(i)   Political strikes should be outlawed. In general, workers should have the right to withdraw their labour, in furtherance of normal industrial claims (wages and conditions). But the British trade unions, in particular, have abused this privilege and have tried to turn their unions into instruments of political pressure and social change. This is an inadmissible extension of trade union functions.

(ii)   While the principle of the right to withdraw labour is not in question, there must be exceptions where public safety is involved. In general, strikes in essential services should therefore be banned: the area covered would be communications, water supplies, fuel and power and food supplies. All workers in these industries should understand that they forfeit the right to strike. It is not consistent with public safety, for instance, that food supplies should be interrupted by a dock strike; or that power supplies should be denied to hospitals.

(iii)   No public relief for strikers and their families (as in Sweden). The trade unions should be made to bear the full financial burden of their strike decision.

(iv)   The freedom to belong to a trade union should be balanced by the freedom to opt out or withdraw from one. The second of these rights was withdrawn in Britain by the Wilson government of 1974. It should be restored, and the closed shop should be declared illegal.

Finally, no security system can do without secrecy. Telephone-tapping goes to the heart of the matter. In the Soviet Union it is all-pervasive; in the USA, Britain, France and other Western countries it has been held at times to constitute an intolerable infringement of the inherent right of privacy. Yet no security system can be fully effective without it. If it is conceded that the State in open societies has the right to defend itself, then its right, subject to safeguards, to tap selected telephones and take other measures of that kind must also be admitted.

Are such measures excessively illiberal? Only, I submit, because the consequences of passivity have not been grasped hitherto. Internal subversion is a threat to all our liberties. If unchecked, it can lead only to authoritarian or totalitarian rule.

We are after all at war. That is the central theme of this book. In both world wars, as I have said, the need for some restrictions on individual liberty was instantly recognised and accepted by law-abiding citizens, who in general rightly trusted their governments to restore suspended rights after hostilities had ceased. Because the nature of internal war (or even the validity of the concept) is still so inadequately understood, the need for such restrictions in a state of internal war is not, as a rule, readily perceived. Yet an internal war can be no less damaging in its ultimate results than a war of physical destruction. Of what profit was it to the Czechoslovaks to keep their houses and buildings intact in 1948 and 1968 when they lost (then lost again) their way of life and their *de facto* sovereignty?

I repeat: the Third World War can be won, and the ideological counter-church forever defeated. But only if a

strategy of survival is adopted and implemented. I have out-
lined that strategy. It is for politicians to debate it, and
governments to apply it. The alternative is slavery.

Appendix
Revolutionary Setbacks in the Third World War

The Third World War, although marked in the main by revolutionary gains and the overall shrinkage of the Target Area, has also been punctuated by numerous revolutionary setbacks. The most important of these are briefly chronicled in this Appendix.

It is important to grasp one fundamental point, however: all the setbacks for the Marxist-Leninist or revolutionary side are *tactical* reverses and no more. The *strategic* advance goes on inexorably, and the reverses are followed by renewed action — sometimes many years later, as in the case of the abortive plot in Indonesia in 1965, seventeen years after the crushing of the Communist insurgency at Madiun.

There is a further important point: once a country has come under Communist rule it does not revert to non-Communists; at least, there has been no such instance since the Bolshevik Revolution of 1917. This does not mean that Communist governments necessarily remain at Moscow's orders, as China and Yugoslavia demonstrate. So long as the Soviet Union retains and expands its gigantic military and subversive resources, however, the possibility of Moscow's regaining control over dissident Communist regimes cannot be ruled out.

Chronology
1946. Azerbaijan reverts to Iranian control after Soviet-backed rebellion.
1948. Abortive Soviet-backed insurgencies in India (Telengana) and Indonesia (Madiun).
1949. Communist rebels crushed in Greece.

Revolutionary successes and setbacks

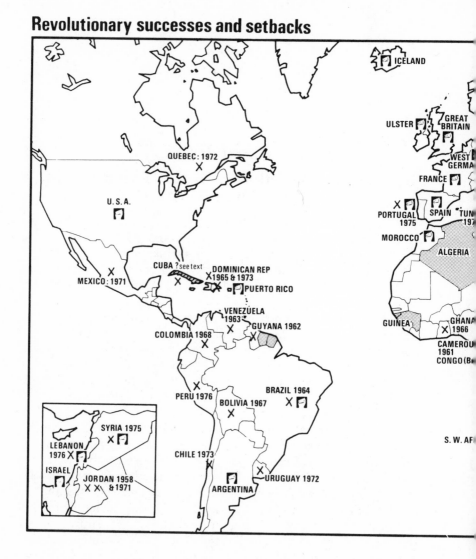

ICELAND

ULSTER

GREAT BRITAIN

WEST GERMA

FRANCE

QUEBEC: 1972
X

U.S.A.

X
PORTUGAL
1975

SPAIN TUN
197

MOROCCO

ALGERIA

CUBA ? see text
X
MEXICO: 1971

DOMINICAN REP
X 1965 & 1973

PUERTO RICO

GUINEA

GHANA
X 1966

CAMEROU
1961
CONGO (B

VENEZUELA
1963
X

GUYANA 1962

COLOMBIA 1968
X

X
PERU 1976

BRAZIL 1964
X

BOLIVIA 1967
X

SYRIA 1975
X

LEBANON
1976 X

ISRAEL

JORDAN 1958
X X & 1971

CHILE 1973

URUGUAY 1972
X

ARGENTINA

S. W. AF

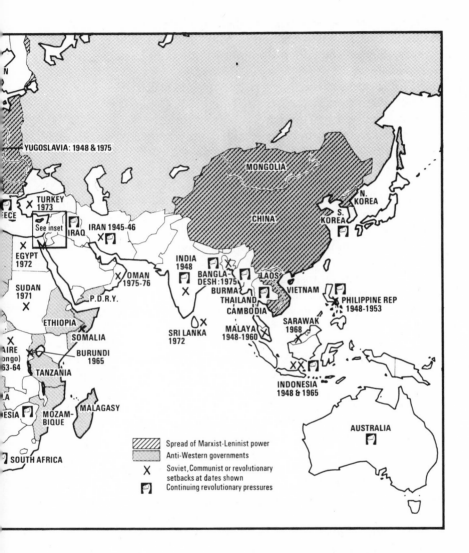

YUGOSLAVIA: 1948 & 1975

TURKEY 1973

ECE

See inset

IRAQ

IRAN 1945-46

EGYPT 1972

SUDAN 1971

OMAN 1975-76

P.D.R.Y.

ETHIOPIA

SOMALIA

AIRE
ongo)
63-64

BURUNDI 1965

TANZANIA

ESIA

MOZAM-
BIQUE

MALAGASY

SOUTH AFRICA

MONGOLIA

CHINA

N. KOREA

S. KOREA

INDIA 1948

BANGLA-
DESH:1975

BURMA

THAILAND

CAMBODIA

LAOS

VIETNAM

PHILIPPINE REP
1948-1953

SRI LANKA 1972

MALAYA
1948-1960

SARAWAK
1968

INDONESIA
1948 & 1965

AUSTRALIA

Spread of Marxist-Leninist power

Anti-Western governments

X   Soviet, Communist or revolutionary
    setbacks at dates shown

Continuing revolutionary pressures

1953.   Communist rebels crushed in Philippines.
1960.   Communist rebellion in Malaya defeated after twelve years. Soviet and other Communist missions expelled from Congo.
1961.   Peking-backed terrorists crushed in Cameroun.
1962.   Communist rebels defeated in Congo. Pro-Communists ousted in Guiana.
1963.   Iraqi Communists rounded up, many killed. Soviet and other Communist missions again expelled from Congo (later Zaïre). Communist rebels defeated in Venezuela.
1964.   Leftist government ousted in Brazil.
1965.   Chinese Communist mission expelled from Burundi. US landing in Dominican Republic foils communist coup. Indonesian Communists massacred after abortive coup.
1966.   Communist-backed Ghana regime of Nkrumah overthrown.
1967.   Guevara's insurgents defeated in Bolivia.
1968.   Terrorists defeated in Colombia. Communist terrorists defeated in Sarawak. Leftist students defeated in France and Italy.
1971.   Communist coup crushed in Sudan. Palestinian terrorists defeated in Jordan. Soviet-recruited revolutionaries crushed in Mexico. Marxist terrorists killed off in Brazil.
1972.   Marxist terrorists crushed in Uruguay. Soviet advisers expelled from Egypt. Pro-Soviet plot foiled in Tunisia. Marxist separatists crushed in Canada (Quebec). Marxist rebels crushed in Sri Lanka.
1973.   Marxist terrorists defeated in Turkey. Allende dies in Chilean forces' coup. Communist-trained guerrillas defeated in Dominican Republic.
1975.   Portuguese Communist coup foiled. Soviet-backed insurgents defeated in Oman. Pro-Moscow plot foiled in Yugoslavia. Mass arrests of Communists in Syria. Soviet-backed insurgents defeated in Oman.
1976.   Pro-Soviet government ousted in Peru. Marxists defeated in Lebanese civil war.
1977.   Soviet advisers expelled from Somalia.

Works by Brian Crozier

All Brian Crozier's previous books contain material that is relevant to *Strategy of Survival*. These are:

The Rebels: A study of post-war insurrections (London and Boston, 1960)
The Morning After: a study of independence (London and New York, 1963)
Neo-Colonialism (London and New York, 1964)
South-East Asia in Turmoil (London, 1965; 3rd edn, 1968)
The Struggle for the Third World (London and New York, 1966)
Franco: A Biographical History (London and Boston, 1967)
The Masters of Power (London and Boston, 1969)
The Future of Communist Power (London, 1970; New York, *Since Stalin*, 1970)
De Gaulle (London Vol. One, 1973, Vol. Two, 1974; New York, one volume, 1973)
A Theory of Conflict (London and New York, 1974)
The Man Who Lost China: The first full biography of Chiang Kai-shek (New York, 1976; London, 1977)

As editor or part-author:

Contr., Evan Luard (Ed.), *The Cold War* (London, 1964)
Contr., Sibnarayan Ray (Ed.), *Vietnam: Seen from East and West* (Melbourne, 1966)
Ed. and contr., '*We Will Bury You*' (London, 1970)
Contr., Alastair Buchan (Ed.), *Problems of Modern Strategy* (London, 1970)
Contr., *Our Twentieth Century World* (London, 1970)
Contr., Philip Toynbee (Ed.), *The Distant Drum* (London, 1976)

'Political Crime' in Encylopaedia Britannica *1976 Book of the Year*

The following is a selected list of the Author's pamphlets, articles or contributions relevant to this book:

Pamphlets

Soviet Pressures in the Caribbean (Institute for the Study of Conflict, *Conflict Studies* No. 35); *The Soviet Presence in Somalia* (*Conflict Studies* No. 54); *Security and the Myth of 'Peace'* (*Conflict Studies* No. 76); *Testimony on international terrorism*, Hearings, Committee on the Judiciary, US Senate, 14 May 1975.

Articles or Contributions

Introductory articles to the *Annual of Power and Conflict* (ISC) for 1971, 1972–73, 1973–74, 1974–75, 1975–76, 1976–77; *Brassey's Defence Annual* (Royal United Services Institute for Defence Studies), 1975; 'The End of the Cold War?' and 'The 25th Party Congress – Bad News' in *National Review* (New York) of 16 March 1973 and 14 May 1976 respectively; *Soviet Analyst* (London), especially Vol. 3, Nos. 1, 7, 8 and 15 (1974); Vol. 4, Nos,. 1, 10 and 12 (1975); Vol. 5, Nos. 1 and 6 (1976); and Vol. 6, No. 1 (1977); 'The Tensions of a False Détente' in *Art International/Lugano Review* (Lugano), 20 September 1974, and 'My Pilgrimage to Kent-Connecticut' (Homage to James Burnham), in *New Lugano Review*, 1976, 11–12.

Index